In Search of Adventure and Moments of Bliss:

MAIDEN VOYAGE

Lois Joy Hofmann

To: Julia

May you enjoy this first third of our world circumnavigation, from France to San Diego. And always remember to pursue your passions and live your dreams!

Lois Joy Hofmann
March 2021

First published 2010 by
PIP Productions
San Diego, CA 92109

Copyright © 2010 by Lois Joy Hofmann

All rights reserved. No part of this publication may be reproduced, stored in a retrieval system or transmitted in any form or by any means, electronic, mechanical, photocopying, recording, or otherwise, without the prior permission in writing of PIP Productions, Lois J. Hofmann.

Library of Congress Cataloging-in-Publication Data
2010940811

Hofmann, Lois.
In Search of Adventure and Moments of Bliss: Maiden Voyage / Lois Hofmann.

ISBN-13: 978-0-9845493-2-0

1. Hofmann, Lois—Travel. 2. Education. 3. Sailing. 4. Geography. I. Title.

First reader and copy editing: Rebecca Brist
Editing and development: Mel Weiser and Joni Browne-Walders
Designer: Alfred Williams, Multimedia Arts
Printer: Brittan Burns, LightSource Printing & Graphics
Cover design: Priya Garcia, LightSource Printing & Graphics
Photography: Lois Joy Hofmann, unless otherwise noted
Production Assistant: Melanie Kellogg
Messing with Boats column: Günter Hofmann

Maps courtesy of Google Earth.

AUTHOR'S NOTE
The coordinates of favorite anchorages listed in this book are shared with you only for planning purposes to show approximate locations and must not be used for navigation.

All sea miles mentioned are in nautical miles. One nautical mile equals 1.852 kilometers.
All dollars mentioned are United States dollars, unless otherwise stated.

Printed in the United States of America

ACKNOWLEDGMENTS

During the interlude between our maiden voyage and continuing our circumnavigation, I began the process toward becoming a seasoned writer and photographer.

Thanks to the many followers of my website, www.pacificbliss.com, who kept asking me—not whether, but when—my online stories and photos would be incorporated into a book (or books).

Thanks to each of you who followed our voyages throughout the eight years of our circumnavigation.

Thanks to Bob Bitchin, publisher, and Sue Morgan, editor, of Latitudes & Attitudes magazine for publishing my stories and articles. Thanks to Jack Warren who invited me to talk about my photography on internet radio and to those educational publishers who have purchased my cultural photos. This all gave me a start.

Thanks to those who helped me shape the final product: first reader and editor Rebecca Brist; editors Joni Browne-Walders and Mel Weiser, whose keen eyes, positive feedback, and energetic discussions took the manuscript to another level; web and graphic designer Alfred Williams, who kept his cool and creativity through years of website and book revisions; and to writing assistant Melanie Kellogg, who helped during the production phase.

Thanks to those who crewed on *Pacific Bliss* during her maiden voyage:
- From Canet, France: Jeanne, John, Chris, and Yana
- From Gibraltar to the Canary Islands: Christian
- Atlantic Crossing: Anne, Georg, and Maria
- France to St. Lucia: Gottfried, skipper
- St. Lucia through the Panama Canal: Phyllis and Richard
- Puerto Vallarta to Cabo San Lucas: Stu and Sharon
- Cabo to San Diego: Bix

Thanks to family and friends who supported and encouraged us in our dream of sailing around the world.

And finally, a special thanks to my husband, Günter. Without him, the voyages and the book would not have been possible.

DEDICATION

To the memory of Jack Lewis, "Captain Jack," who persuaded me to write this book.

TABLE OF CONTENTS
MAIDEN VOYAGE

PROLOGUE: Force 10!   9

CHAPTER ONE: Fromage in France   13

CHAPTER TWO: The Difficult Delivery of *Pacific Bliss*   25

CHAPTER THREE: Braving the Fearsome Med: Spain, Gibraltar, and Morocco   41

CHAPTER FOUR: Through the Pillars of Hercules, Beyond the Sea of Darkness   55

CHAPTER FIVE: Crossing the Big Pond: The Canaries & Cape Verde Islands and on to St. Lucia   61

CHAPTER SIX: The Best of Times: Voyaging through the Caribbean   83

CHAPTER SEVEN: The Worst of Times: Night of Sheer Terror Underway to the Spanish Main   105

CHAPTER EIGHT: The Surprising San Blas Islands   125

CHAPTER NINE: *Pacific Bliss* Transits the Big Ditch and Goes up the Creek   139

CHAPTER TEN: Slogging through Central America: Costa Rica and El Salvador   165

CHAPTER ELEVEN: Semana Santa in Guatemala   195

CHAPTER TWELVE: Mexico: Magic, Meltdown & Mayhem   213

CHAPTER THIRTEEN: San Diego: Re-entering and Re-evaluating Our Lives   247

EPILOGUE   251

APPENDICES   252

Pacific Bliss
Circumnavigation of the Globe
2000-2008

- 34,000 MILES
- 62 COUNTRIES
- 8 YEARS

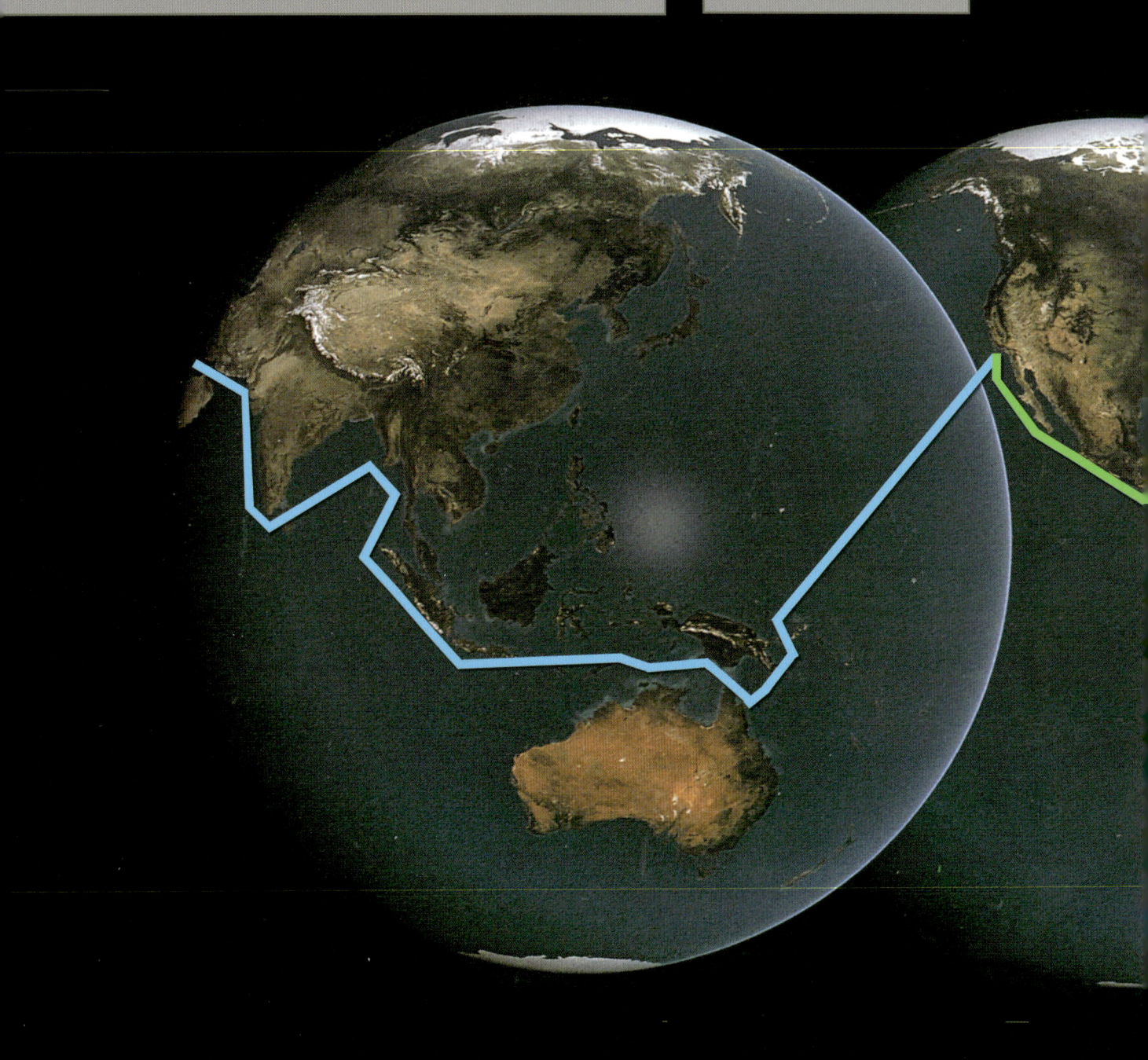

We invite you to join us as we share our stories of adventure and moments of bliss, sailing around the world on our catamaran, *Pacific Bliss*

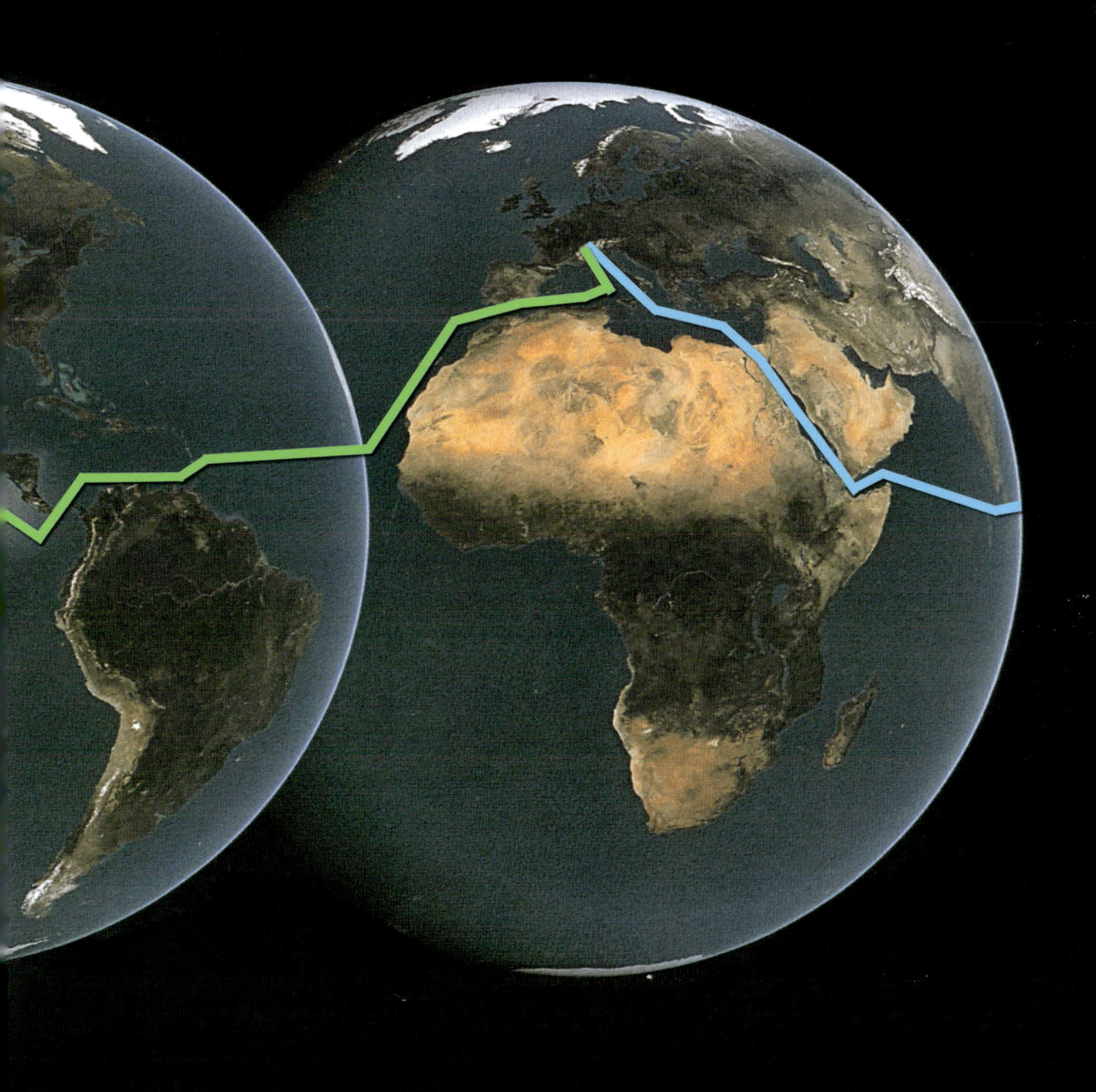

Voyage 1
From Canet, France to San Diego, United States

"LIFE IS EITHER A DARING ADVENTURE OR NOTHING AT ALL."
HELEN KELLER

Prologue

Force 10!
January 2001, off the Pirate Coast of Guajira Peninsula

Howling like a pack of ravenous wolves, the insatiable wind chases *Pacific Bliss* through the churning seas off the lawless Colombia coast. With a maddening roar, it claws through the rolled-up bimini shades surrounding the cockpit, tearing fasteners and ripping them loose. The straps flail wildly against the hardtop, adding to the pandemonium. The seat cushions come alive like demented sea monsters, flopping up and down and straining at their snaps. Stoic Richard, our crew, controls the helm, helping our autopilot maintain some semblance of control. Captain Günter, my husband, struggles to stand upright, inching forward during the pauses (if you can call them that) between each violent gust. I imagine those loosened straps gouging his eyes, the beginning of a downhill slide from chaos to catastrophe, as one problem leads into another and eventually we are short crew and into a survival situation—our own *Perfect Storm*.

Inside the salon with my friend Phyllis, Richard's wife, I stare at the display at the nav station. *Force 10!* My stomach clenches like the jaws of a shark. My tongue turns into cotton. There are only 12 wind states, Force 12 being a hurricane. A 43-foot catamaran can't survive a hurricane.

I pry open the sliding Plexiglas® door to the cockpit to see what I can do to help.

Günter takes charge, motioning me out of the way. Calm and determined, he yanks off each of the three bimini shades, then turns to me and mouths, "Come here."

Together we release the cushions one by one and throw them into the salon. I feel better doing something. Finally, we can hear each other. I point to the dagger boards that stand like sentinels midway on each hull. "You raised them so that *Pacific Bliss* can surf?"

Günter nods, grim-faced. The seas mount to frightening heights—three stories or more—with breaking crests. As we watch, a monstrous wave breaks over the top of a dagger board. "Probably forced water into the window. We'll deal with that later," Günter says, his jaw set. "More important—we need to keep the boat surfing…so that we don't flip."

The dinghy mounted at the stern bounces wildly on its davits as each monster wave rises angrily above it, then slides underneath the dual hulls. Every so often, a wave sprays its frothy venom from crest to cockpit, drenching the three of us with buckets of water that slides off my foul weather gear. I feel the tepid water running down my cheeks. I can taste the salt. Yet my tongue is sandpaper dry.

What if a rogue wave breaks into the cockpit? What would that be like?

Richard, Günter, and I slosh in and out in our rubber boots, pants tucked inside, while Phyllis manages the salon—handing out towels, wiping the floors, and keeping the inside free of salt water.

"Lois, you stay in here now," Günter directs. The salon, in the center of the boat, shrieks and grates, teak against Kevlar. I glance over at Phyllis, who winces, white-faced, at each chalk-against-blackboard screech. This salon is no place of refuge.

At the nav station, the multi-meter holds steady at F10 as the wind continues to howl. *Pacific Bliss feels out of control. I feel out of control. I've never felt so out of control in my life!* I switch the multi-meter to Boat Speed to find that we have accelerated to 25 knots. Fine for experienced catamaran racers. Not for us. We are just cruisers.

Up and down. Up and down. We ride high over colossal crests and then slide rapidly down the backsides, leaving our stomachs at the top, like a roller coaster ride that will never, ever end.

"What's going to happen?" Phyllis asks.

"I haven't a clue. If we hit the face of the next wave wrong…after coming out of the trough…I guess we could flip. I never expected that the winds here would be more dangerous than the drug-running pirates."

From deep inside, I gather strength for the long ride ahead.

A wild wave breaks between the hulls, causing the entire structure to shudder as if a bomb has exploded underneath. It feels as if the yacht will fly apart at any minute. The noise is awful. *How much more can Pacific Bliss can take? We must slow her down.*

"In an age when mass society has rendered obsolete
the qualities of courage and independent thought
the oceans of the world still remain,
vast and uncluttered, beautiful and forgiving,
awaiting those who will not submit.
Their voyages are not an escape, but a fulfillment."

The Slocum Society

Chapter One

1. Old Perpignan Centre; 2. The wooden boat dock, Canet; 3. Lois demonstrates the narrowness of the street at Hotel de la Lodge.

July 2000, France

New Catana vessels released from the factory, awaiting the commissioning process.

Chapter 1
Fromage in France

July 2000

The eastern horizon—burnt orange, fringed with gold—goes on forever, surrounding a million glowing embers, remnants of evening in the "City of Light." Paris spreads out below us in all her grandeur, awakening to the new day. As the 747 decreases its altitude, a smaller aircraft twinkles over the charcoal ribbon that is the River Seine. Freeways wind through the dark like a backlit printed circuit board.

The descent reminds me of the last time I flew into this city, dressed smartly in a black business suit and high heels, armed with a leather briefcase containing slides for an investor presentation. This time, I am wearing blue jeans, a navy-and-white tee, and topsiders. My husband Günter, reaching across from his aisle seat to grip my hand, is the one with the briefcase. The two of us are now the proud partners in a nautical venture, co-owners of a state-of-the-art sailing vessel being built for us in the south of France.

⚓

So much has happened so fast since that fateful day, nine months ago, when Günter and I made the decision that propelled us here. During intense discussions with attorneys, friends, and family after the traumatic coup that ended our business lives, we preserved our sanity by dreaming of our future. It would be a better life—one in which we could be truly independent and self-sufficient, answering to no one. We would be back in control of our own destiny. We would go to sea.

Leaving our beloved biotech company was like being forced to give up our baby—or having that baby kidnapped or killed. "Time heals all wounds," our friends back home in San Diego assured us.

"Time and distance." Günter would answer them, clenching and unclenching his fist, a habit he'd picked up during those terrible days. "I just want to get outta here."

As we took our usual walk around Sail Bay, the unmistakable call of adventure broke through the smog of our grief, invading our souls. "There is a 'whole new world' out there for us, just waiting to be explored," Günter stretched his arms to the expanse of the great Pacific beyond the bay. "Out there. Beyond the seas and over the horizon. Excitement. New people, places, and cultures—the vast unknown."

I bought into his words because I also wanted to know the unknown. Growing up on a poor Wisconsin dairy farm, I'd escaped my world of tedious chores through books that glorified adventure—macho stuff like flying airplanes through Mach 1, the speed of sound; exploring the jungles of the Belgian Congo; rafting down the Amazon. By the time I was forced to retire at 58, my concept of adventure travel had matured. I had fallen for the gushing promises of the high-end travel magazines that target execs: "Challenge your preconceptions and most cherished views…sew strands of different cultures into your own character…become more understanding in the process."

After my world collapsed, my concept of travel and adventure changed yet again. Understanding? I just wanted to *escape*. But I also wanted to get back into a world where values matter and people can be trusted. My foundation had been shaken to its very core. Yet I wanted to believe that the values of courtesy, justice,

The hulls of a catamaran dwarf Günter and Lois on the factory floor.

love, and honor still existed somewhere in the world. I was open to change. I was ready for new beginnings.

I looked across the bay fronting our condo to the tempting ocean beyond. *How would these fundamental human values translate themselves in the ports we planned to visit? How would they differ from the destructive power and greed that had turned me off to the corporate world?*

I turned to Günter for a big bear hug and snuggled into the warmth of his chest. "So let's just set ourselves a new mission, then. Of sailing around the world."

"Do you really mean it?"

"Of course. Why not?"

"Then let's just *do it*!" I could feel his body relax and let go.

⚓

Günter and I have always been goal-oriented. That's why we've never even *considered* the possibility of merely testing the waters—just putting one foot in—like most West Coast sailors. Those who even bother to leave the shore just tend to sail from marina to marina. The brave ones cruise along the California shoreline to Mexico, and the really brave ones might venture out to sea after a few years of coastal cruising.

"Why the decision to circumnavigate the world?" our friends would ask. Some of them, I'm sure, thought we'd lost our senses.

Günter would shrug and my eyes would roll. "Because it's there," one or the other of us would answer.

After the big decision, our lives fell into place like it had been planned for us all along. While still employed, we had taken many bareboat vacations, chartering both monohulls and catamarans. We had also taken the ASA (American Sailing Association) courses from *Basic Sailing* through *Coastal Cruising*. We had survived a basic training boot camp for would-be ocean cruisers: a ten-day South Pacific voyage from the Cooks through American Samoa on John Neal's *Mahina Tiara*. Post-decision, our training went into overdrive. Günter obtained his Radio Technician license and I passed my ASA navigation exam. Meanwhile, we had brokers searching for our ideal ocean going vessel.

One day in November of 1999, our San Diego broker, David Renouf of *Yacht Finders*, called Günter: "I have a Catana 431 here in San Diego for a few days, on its way to a delivery in San Francisco. Do you and Lois want to go out in the bay for a day sail?"

We jumped at the opportunity. The Catana brand is the Rolls Royce of catamarans. The lines feed through to the cockpit, eliminating the need to go forward while underway. If one of us should be disabled, the other could sail the boat. I warmed to the idea that a catamaran sails on the level and cannot sink. The only reason to abandon the boat would be in case of fire. Günter loved the strength. The hull is "sandwiched" with Taewon fiber, similar to the Kevlar® product used in some bulletproof vests. After one hour of sailing, we realized that this was the yacht for us. She sailed like a dream.

We placed our order in euros that same week.

⚓

And now, here we are, landing in Paris, en route to a city called Perpignan. From there we will visit the Catana factory in Canet en Plage, a village on the Mediterranean Sea. Like a butterfly eager to soar to new horizons, our new yacht has morphed from her cocoon, a tub of high tech fiberglass. She is fresh out of the mold. We are the proud parents, eager to see our new baby, *Pacific Bliss*, for the first time.

At the Perpignan airport, we rent a little blue Renault. "Smells like cheese," I sniff as I climb into the passenger side. We drive toward the old part of the city, near the imposing round brick Castille and the Perpignan Centre. But no matter how many times we navigate back and forth through the narrow, winding streets, we cannot find the *Hotel de la Loge*. After we pass the Castille tower for the third time, we decide to park alongside the river walk and proceed on foot,

14

1. The top deck of a catamaran; 2. Lois and Günter walk through the interior of *Pacific Bliss;* 3. The cockpit; 4. Walking the factory dock.

15

> "HOW CAN ANYONE BE EXPECTED TO GOVERN A COUNTRY THAT HAS 246 KINDS OF CHEESE?"
> *NEWSWEEK* INTERVIEW OF CHARLES DE GAULLE, 1961

rolling our luggage along the bumpy cobblestone streets. Finally, we find the street fronting the hotel. It is about the width of two adults with outstretched arms. Parking and walking is the *only* way to get there.

⚓

We awaken early in our tiny but comfortable room, electric with anticipation. Our appointment at the Catana factory in Canet is not until 11:00 a.m., but our eyes are wide, our heads spinning.

We navigate our way to Canet easily via a series of roundabouts, and once there, directions to *Zone technique du port* are clearly marked. As we enter the *Zone*, red and blue Catana signs at each turn provide directions to the factory.

Arriving early, we park and explore the Catana shipyard. The stark white factory—with its eye-catching red, white, and blue Catana logo and clean surroundings—makes a favorable impression. We walk onto the dock—about 200 feet or so from the factory building. Wow—what a feast to the eyes! New and used Catana cats line the pier—431s, 471s, and an older 401. After all the correspondence, phone calls, and contract negotiations, we are finally here—going forward with our dream!

As we enter the factory, I admire the sleek and modern reception area that carries out the red-white-and-blue Catana colors and theme, even to the finest detail—red knobs and trim on white doors contrast with blue handrails on the stairway.

Christophe, the Operations Manager, welcomes us, extending his hand. "You're *Pacific Bliss*." I recall the counsel of cruising books and articles: "You will be called by the name of your boat, not by your own name, so take that into consideration when you select a name." This is the first time we are called *Pacific Bliss*. I like the sound of it. If we are called "the Blisses," it's okay by me. I recall our intense discussions prior to settling on a name. *Bliss* means more than happiness to us. It also conveys contentment and *joie de vivre*. How apt to hear this name first spoken here in France! Many languages, like German, have no direct synonym for *Bliss*.

"I suppose you'd like to see *your* yacht first," Christophe says in careful, clipped English. Taking our grins for an answer, he leads us to the bays where the yachts are built. We follow his confident stride onto a gangway above the huge factory floor and then onto a platform leading down onto *Pacific Bliss*. We note that the hulls and first deck have been completed, with the bulkheads in place. "The workers have finished the engine compartments and storage lockers," Christophe says. "Now they are stringing the electrical cables. They will add the top last, after finishing the interior."

Christophe leads us down to the factory floor. Looking up at the row of catamaran hulls, I can imagine how the Lilliputians felt looking up at Gulliver. Since the bulk of the hulls are underwater when a catamaran is at sea, I had lacked an appreciation of the volume, the sheer immensity, of our new floating home.

Back in Christophe's office, being able to talk face-to-face proves extremely valuable. Günter makes small modifications, such as switching the location of the weather fax output with that of the battery indicator, for easier viewing without his glasses; he changes the location of the fan in the master cabin; we discover that the curve of the hardtop does not allow for the larger solar panels; now, we add four more regular-sized panels, doubling our capacity for generating solar electricity.

After a late lunch at a nearby restaurant, Günter and I return to Christophe's office to further refine the items in our contract. Günter adds a seawater pump to the locker forward of the mast, and then he adds another to the galley as well, just in case we run low on water. Then, he finalizes the design for the instrument panel at the nav (navigation) station, the brains of our ship. Because we have shipped the electronics from the U.S., interfacing them to work well with the other French components is one of the key reasons for our visit. After Günter and Christophe make a rough sketch of the equipment interface, a software engineer completes the graphic layout on his CAD (computer-aided design) system while we watch. How efficient! We approve the design the same afternoon.

We leave the clean and orderly factory after 6 p.m., congratulating ourselves. We are convinced that the visit has been quite necessary. We believe that we have visited at just the right time in the manufacturing process and are relieved to learn that *Pacific Bliss* remains on schedule. The Catana employees are helpful and courteous, and the workflow appears to be well organized. We look forward to a smooth commissioning and sea trial process within three months, sometime in October. That will allow us to sail from the Mediterranean into the Atlantic that same month, before the winter storms set in. Based on what we have seen, how could we expect otherwise?

Back at *Hotel de la Loge*, I flop onto the small bed with the smug exhaustion that follows a mission successfully accomplished. Günter wraps his taller, hefty frame around mine, his short graying beard against my cheek. After napping for an hour or so, we're awakened by a curious cacophony of sounds—the

MESSING WITH BOATS

Part I
by Günter

In addition to the goals we set, part of our circumnavigation plan is "just messing around with boats." Along this line of thinking, I was given a plaque by a dear friend Phyllis that says:

*Believe me, my young friend (said the water rat solemnly), there is nothing—absolutely nothing—half so much worth as simply messing about in boats.
Simply messing…nothing seems really to matter, that's the charm of it.
Whether you get away,
or whether you don't,
whether you arrive at your destination or whether you reach somewhere else,
or whether you never get anywhere at all, you're always busy, and you never do anything in particular.*

The Wind in the Willows

Günter walks the docks.

Specifications for
PACIFIC BLISS

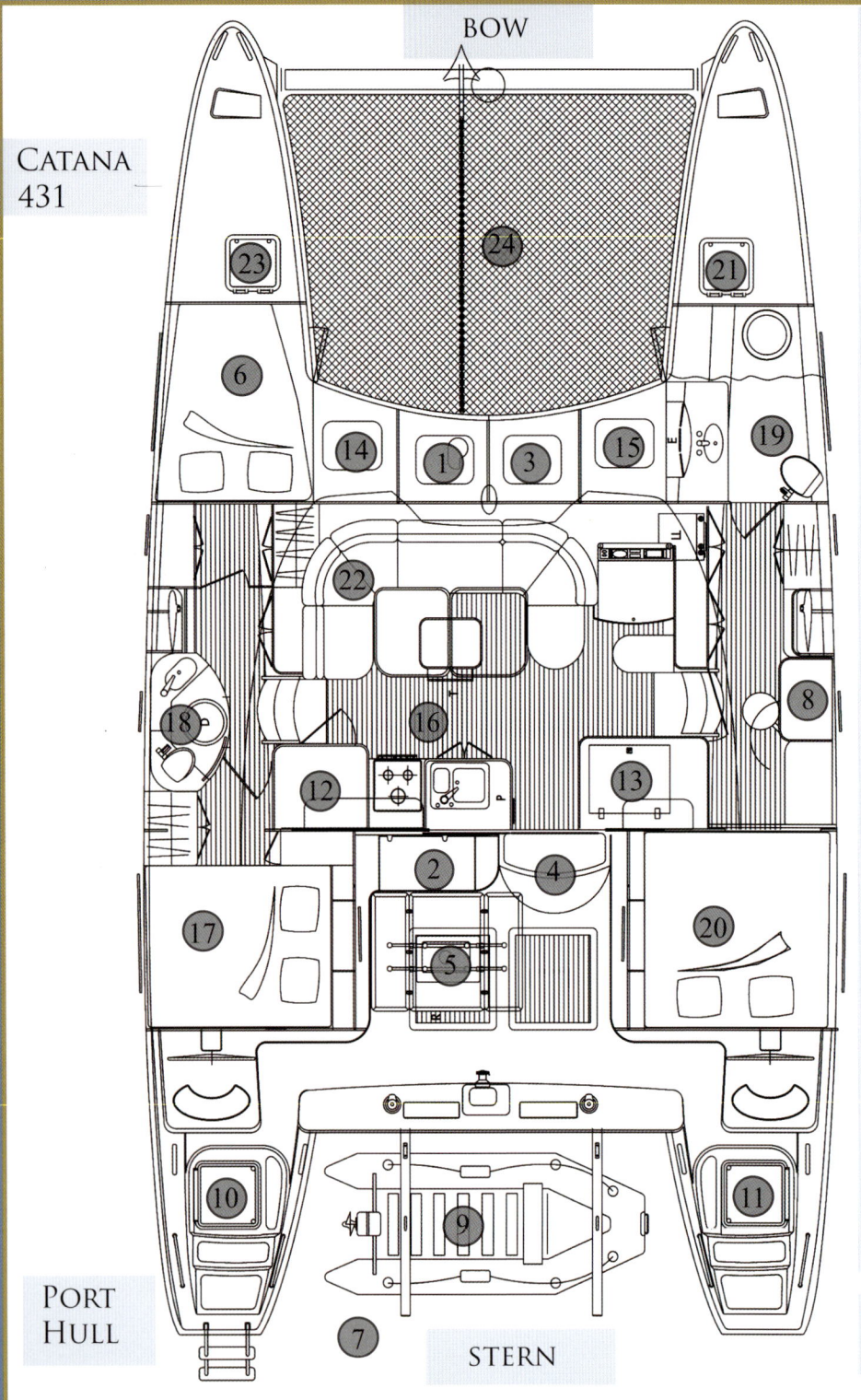

Catana 431

BOW

1. Anchor Locker
2. Bench
3. Chain Locker
4. Cockpit Locker
5. Cockpit table
6. Crew Berth
7. davit
8. desk
9. Dinghy (*Petit Bliss*)
10. Engine Room
11. Engine Room
12. Freezer
13. Fridge
14. Fuel
15. Fuel
16. Galley
17. Guest / Crew Berth
18. Head
19. head
20. Master Berth
21. Sail Locker
22. Settee
23. Storage Locker
24 Trampoline (Net)

Port Hull

Stern

Starboard Hull

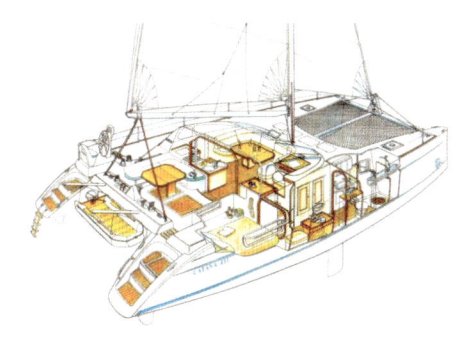

CATANA

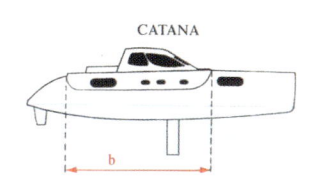

Catana Design with Daggerboard

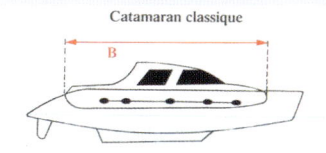

Catamaran classique

Classic Catamaran Keel

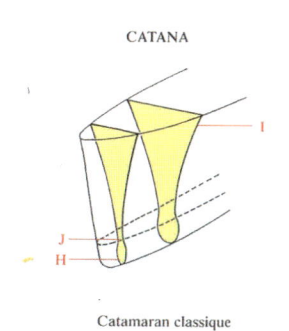

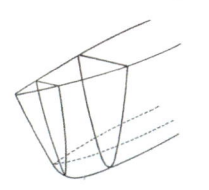

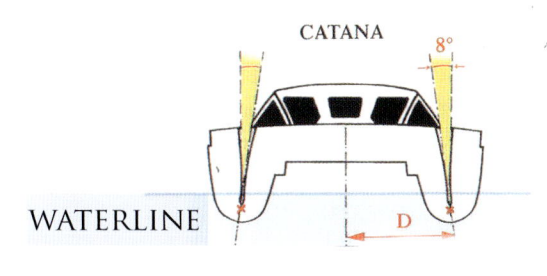

CATANA

Catamaran classique

REEFING & HALYARD CONTROL AT STERN

MAIN SAIL

JIB

CATANA

WATERLINE

Fields of lavender near Canet, France.

solicitous voices of waiters amid the crashing cymbals, horns, and drums of a Catalan band. We change clothes, go downstairs, and follow the music to the courtyard of Le Castillet (the Castle). Then, seated under the blue striped awnings of *Le Catalan*, we unwind and relax, enjoying the lively band, excellent seafood tapas, and a smooth red called *Cotes du Roussillon*.

Since we don't need to return to the factory, we have a "free day" before catching our flight out of Perpignan. We can find no place to park within three blocks of any Mediterranean beach, and this is only July. I cannot imagine what August will bring, when all of France closes up shop and heads to vacation villas here in the south.

We have no choice but to explore inland. Soon our little blue *cheese-mobile* is purring through lush vineyards in the foothills of the purple-mauve Pyrenees that straddle France and Spain. We've purchased a bottle of local wine, a couple of plastic goblets, a baguette, and, yes, a round of brie, which smells *nothing* like the interior of the Renault. Günter turns past a vineyard and drives down a dusty road leading to a sunlit field of lavender. He turns off the ruts and into the field, then stops. As I shove open the door, fragrant stocks of lavender caress the underbelly and creep into the interior of the car.

"There!" Günter leaves his door open as well. "Let's have our picnic out in this field so the *cheese-mobile* can finally air out. I think it was driven by a salesman hawking tons of blue cheese." A gentle breeze whips up the sensuous scent of lavender. We toast, then kiss, savoring each other's wine-lips. Thus begins my love-hate relationship with France and all things French.

Fabric shopping in France.

Children entertain themselves by climbing a tree along the coast near Cyprien.

CHAPTER TWO

September – November 2000, Canet, France

1. Simone, Günter's daughter; 2. The castle at Collioure; 3., 4. Our grandson Manuel at two months.

23

Pacific Bliss is launched without mast and sails.

CHAPTER 2
THE DIFFICULT DELIVERY OF *PACIFIC BLISS*

The gestation has been longer than expected, over nine months since we placed the order, but finally one fine September day in San Diego we receive a call from Canet. "Christophe here. Make your flight arrangements. *Pacific Bliss* will be ready to take delivery on September 29. Be prepared for the final payment and closing on that day."

With the continued slippage in the delivery date, we are prepared! We have already delayed the arrival of the crew by one week and shortened the sea trials from three weeks to two. In my new role as the ship's navigator and weather woman, I have been concerned about sailing into the unruly Med so late in the season. This call allays my fears.

For now—but I will soon learn how terribly justified they are.

We arrive in Canet on September 28, bursting with anticipation. The balmy sun of early autumn patterns its glow through a mass of stately evergreens as we enter the reception area of the *Clos de Pins* hotel. Ten minutes later, my stepdaughter Simone enters the lobby. Her husband follows a few steps behind, our new two-month-old grandson, Manuel, gently cradled in his arms. He is bundled in a lightweight flannel baby blanket, sound asleep.

"Simonchen!" Günter wraps his arms around her tall, lissome frame, thinner now. (She gave birth within days after we flew from Paris to Munich following our July visit to Canet.)

I greet her warmly before rushing over to the little Bundle of Joy. I spread open the baby blanket to reveal Manuel's navy-and-white nautical outfit. "Our new little sailor! We can rest this afternoon, then go to the shipyard tomorrow for your first look at *Pacific Bliss*." Simone nods her relief. "Turnabout is fair play," I continue. "Now *you* are here for the delivery of *our* baby."

That evening, the four of us stroll along the beach streets of Canet-au-Plage, pushing Manuel in the smart navy-and-white polka-dot carriage. The beach is deserted now. I prefer this September solitude to the frenzied throngs of summer vacationers, but we find that many of the cafés have already closed for the season. While waiting for the Café Madrid to open for dinner at 7:30 p.m., we commiserate with the locals who are relieved that all the noisy tourists have finally left to attend to school and careers. At dinner, I am impressed that those restaurants that *are* open never lower their standards, no matter how few customers they have. Only one other group enters the café, yet the meats and fish are superb, and the vegetables market-fresh.

Here, this is to be expected. In France, the obsession with food can be traced back to the special relationship the French have with their land. Only Italy comes close to matching the diversity and abundance of France. Even Germany, Günter's country of birth, declared the European food rivalry over long ago. *"Leben wie Gott in Frankreich!"* Günter holds up his wine glass and we all toast to "living like God in France."

Mastless in Canet

Closing Day is a big disappointment. *Pacific Bliss* has been hastily delivered from the factory to make room for other yachts on the production line. The term "delivery" merely means that our boat has been moved from the factory, launched, and placed in a slip at the factory dock. Our "baby" is quite premature. We catch our first glimpse of her as we park our rental car and walk toward the shipyard gates.

"She's a long way from becoming a cruising sailboat." Günter's face goes slack, his spirit sapped.

Lois and sister-in-law Helga at the helm of a Catana.

"I agree. For starters, she has no mast. And so, of course, she has no sails. I can't believe they asked us to take delivery today."

"Probably wanted—or needed—the money."

The interior of *Pacific Bliss* has fared no better. The fridges have yet to be installed. Much of the wiring remains to be done. Construction debris litters the boat.

"Well, we're here. Might as well stay in France." Günter walks around his *Baby Bliss*, disconsolate.

We will need to adjust our expectations substantially. We expected to conduct the closing and quality control process after the vessel left the factory, to launch within the week, and then to undergo three weeks of training and sea trials, a process the factory calls "commissioning." Günter's sister and other friends and family from Germany are scheduled to be here for the first part of those sea trials. For the final week, we have planned for a crew of two couples from the U.S. and Canada to join us. They will continue to sail with us through the Med as far as the Canary Islands, where I have scheduled another crew to replace them for the Atlantic crossing. We have also hired a German skipper—a friend of the family with Atlantic crossing experience—who is due to arrive during the second week of sea trials.

During the evening, we make the necessary calls. Our friends will come as planned because their vacations are committed; our crew will delay again for yet another week. I'm stymied.

This new venture of ours was planned to run just like a business should. What happened?

Sailing at Last

By October 4, we are finally sailing. No…not on *Pacific Bliss*, whose mast still hasn't been delivered, but on a 47-foot Catana loaned to us by the factory for the day. We have promised this sail to our guests from Germany. What a wonderful day for a sail! The wind is favorable—less than 20 knots, but steady—with a benevolent sun beaming over a gently rolling sea. As I take my turn at the helm, the wind pushes gently at my back as our boat speed settles in at 8 knots. *Delicious ecstasy! We are sure to leave this port in similar conditions, continuing all the way to Gibraltar and westward around the world, chasing the setting sun.* I am living the typical *bon voyage* wish: "May you sail with the sun, and may the wind be ever at your back."

The world doesn't end when you do what you want to do. It merely begins.

We sail to the historic village of Collioure, about 15 miles along the French coast toward Spain. Although we decide not to stop, I take note of the ancient castle and brick fortress lining the shore, resolving to visit the enticing village again on our own vessel, *Pacific Bliss*. We tack back to Canet with the wind on our nose, forcing us to don our sailing jackets. Even so, it has been one spectacular, delightful day!

This Old House

Resigned to the situation, Günter and I settle comfortably into our rented "vacation villa" at 52 Bd, Herriot, Canet. As the gray days drone on, we grow to love the mismatched French wallpaper and squares of faded linoleum, the high ceilings storing the grit of generations, and the hodgepodge of so-called art hung on the walls—ranging from portraits of children in oil to romping horses on poster board to colorful ducks in needlepoint. Our beloved books stand atop the massive dining room buffet, giving our house character and comfort, making it ours.

We have even adapted to the strange bath, which trickles ever so slowly. We simply turn on the hot water and

This Old House, our villa in Canet.

wait patiently for an hour or so, sipping *vin rouge*, while our water warms through the flow-through heater and slowly fills the big, cast iron tub.

"Life's looking up!" Günter says one night, as he beckons me to the tub filled with bubbles of French lavender. Carefully, I carry my glass of *vin rouge* with me into the tub. These are my first steps toward slowing down and understanding the French.

On weekends, we go touring in our rental car. (This one doesn't smell like cheese.) And when we're not touring, I'm busy taping my favorite photos to the walls of our *Great Room* to give the old house added life and personality. Though they are 8 x 10's, the collection is dwarfed by a huge, conference-size table at which I sit. But, even so, the pictures energize me as I write for the *Pacific Bliss* website at night.

Before retiring, we hunker over our Sony worldwide radio receiver, tuned to BBC. The news, in this long autumn of 2000, is good from Serbia and discouraging—as usual—from the Middle East; the American election campaign is in full swing; Vice President Al Gore is debating presidential contender George W. Bush. Although we have arranged to vote via absentee ballot, all of it seems irrelevant and so far away.

The Catana Winers Club

Each morning after breakfast, Günter and I leave for the boat dock outside the factory to supervise "progress" on *Pacific Bliss*. Most of the Catana managers attend an English language course from 8 to 9 a.m. (The family-owned company has big aspirations; they plan for 50 percent of their business to be from North America in future years.) By the time the English class is dismissed, we are already on board *Pacific Bliss*, checking with the workers on the production plans for the day. We make sure that the electrician, plumber, or carpenter planned for that day actually shows up and that he performs his assigned tasks. Because the 1998 work week law limits the French laborer to a 35-hour week with no overtime allowed, we strive to use each hour of a worker's time wisely when we *do* have

one assigned to us. By now, we realize that we must treat the finishing of the yacht just as one would supervise the building or remodeling of a home: Be there every day to prevent mistakes or to discover them early.

But we aren't the only prospective yacht owners who have come to that realization. Three other couples are pushing for completion of their overdue yachts as well: Brenda and Pratt of *Enduring Echoes*, Marsha and Paul of *Traveler*, and Kim and Kim of *Delphinius*. These couples are fellow American sailors and therefore our friends; at the same time, they have become competition for Catana's electricians, plumbers, and carpenters. The French managers, aiming to please and unable to say no, promise each couple the same workers on the same days—an impossible situation. So by day, we each vie for workers to complete *our* project. After hours, we all sip *vin rouge* and party together. By the second glass of wine, our complaints turn into laughter.

"No one at home in Utah is feeling sorry for us, stuck here in the South of France indefinitely," says Brenda, never at a loss for words, as she tosses her chestnut hair.

"They don't get it," answers Marsha.

"Well, it beats working," Günter says, who is mellowing after his second *vin rouge*. (Ironically, he is not so complacent during the day and has discovered that occasional swearing and temper tantrums work wonders with the French.)

After a dark and dreary October day of gray, interspersed with pounding rain, we hold our first "American Therapy" party at our villa, which we have named "This Old House." The laughter warms our souls as the four couples gradually gel into a close-knit group. The euro is 85 cents to the American dollar. The new wine being harvested at nearby vineyards sells for less than we would pay for bottled water. *Vive la France!*

By the end of this evening, we have chosen a name for our group: *The Catana Winers Club*, a word-play on *Whiners*, and we resolve to hold further "American Therapy" sessions every chance we get.

A Roller Coaster Life

On the Monday morning after our party, we arrive at the shipyard to find *Pacific Bliss* dry docked. She has been rescued and returned to the shipyard.

"She sprung a leak last night," says Pierre, the friendly "commissioning skipper," in his delightful French dialect. He has been put in charge of our boat. "Good thing some people are living 'ere on their boats. Someone 'eard the bilge pump running and notified me."

This pump, placed in the bilge underneath the floorboards, is preset to start if the water exceeds a certain level.

"Thanks for coming in, Pierre," Günter says, his face sagging.

"That's okay. Found out the electricians installed your new fridge with the polarity reversed. Caused leaking at the

Door of rock-hewn villa in Eus, France.

electrical ground at the bottom of the 'ull; the ground on your boat is a piece of metal called the *Dyna Plate*. It will 'ave to be replaced."

"So much for keeping an eye on things," Günter complains. "We face yet another setback; even worse, we *still* don't have our carbon-fiber mast." The promised delivery date for the mast has come and gone. The high-tech mast is still being manufactured, and then it has to be shipped from the French port of Marseilles.

Günter calls Frederic, the yacht surveyor we hired weeks ago. "Sorry," he explains, "we have to delay the survey because we don't even have our mast yet." A thorough survey is required before our yacht insurance coverage will be granted, and we must have that in place before we transit the Med.

Frederic is young and ambitious, driving the family business. "So what if the mast delivery is delayed?" he replies. "We can begin to survey the *interior* of the boat."

"Okay, let's do it tomorrow." We depart the shipyard, slightly relieved by Fredric's quick solution of that problem.

The next morning, we climb up a stepladder and hoist ourselves onto the deck of *Pacific Bliss*. We encounter the buzzing of electric saws and the pounding of nails; dusty workers in coveralls are crawling throughout the interior. It's bedlam. We thread our way to the forward cabin in the port hull and find it in total disarray. Entire wall panels are being removed and replaced. Apparently, a leak from the deck to the interior has been discovered and we are in the midst of damage control.

"Things are in motion, all right," Günter grumbles. "Only they seem to be going backwards."

Now we have to delay the interior survey as well. But after a few days, the "finishing" is finished, and the survey can begin.

Frederic arrives with his mother, who is also his business partner. Her dynamite reputation precedes her. She is sure to catch anything wrong with a yacht. Tall, trim, and nautical in blue jeans and a blue-and-white striped knit top, her long blonde hair swept upward into a severe bun, she boards *Pacific Bliss* with a serious, determined gait. She springs onto the teak hatch covering the engine compartment, frowning as it gives a little.

I am duly impressed.

"The quality of Catana's finishing work has certainly improved. Yours is excellent," she pronounces, while marking slight aberrations in the salon's teak flooring.

"Catana respects her judgment," Frederic says, his voice lowered, even though we have moved over to the trampoline, well out of earshot. "They 'ave never denied her request."

In my former life as an executive, I gave speeches that compared the life of an entrepreneur to a roller coaster ride: lots of ups and downs, but eventually one will get to where

MESSING WITH BOATS

Part II, by Günter

A deserted beach town, rows of houses with closed shutters…large condominium buildings without people…dog turds on the side walks calling for frequent "turd alerts…" cloudy skies turning to downpours every evening…cold nights in an empty unfamiliar house…and an unfinished catamaran without a mast…all this is our reality here in Canet. But who would feel sorry for us here in the South of France?

I have learned to savor little things to make our lives not that unpleasant: Every morning, the brief walk to the boulangerie to pick up fresh croissants and a flute or two…a nice conversation with the baker's pretty bra-less, ample-bosomed wife who guesses every morning whether I want un or deux croissants…laughing together at my French—of course there is the big disappointment if she is replaced by her dour husband—fantasizing funny games behind his back as the typical French movies suggest…meeting our fellow Americans who are also future Catana owners and exchanging the funny or horror stories of the day—quite often there is no difference…going shopping at the Supermarche and guessing what is what…going crazy at the cheese counter looking at a fromage universe I've never seen before, asking for goat cheese by making a horn on my head with two fingers—the girl laughing and saying, "Oh, chevre!"

Being refused entry into the Casino on the beach because of wearing sports shoes—my offer to enter barefoot rejected in excited French by the 200-pound bouncer…making the mistake of ordering a complete meal for lunch with wine—which takes two hours and incapacitates you completely for the rest of the afternoon, yet leaves you with a sense of completion, lack of ambition, and a deep understanding of French culture… the satisfaction of catching the last International Herald Tribune in the morning, so we can verify in print what we heard the evening before on our little Sony World Radio…and good thoughts about our friends back home; we appreciate all of you.

Some day we will have a working yacht, sail in warm waters under a blue sky, and experience what we thought the cruising life should be; until then, we are enjoying our little moments of happiness squeezed in between the frustration of dealing with numerous delays. Whatever is happening, one thing is for sure: it beats working.

Our first guests at the villa.

he is headed, *if* the mission has been well defined and the strategy is sound. Unfortunately, my roller coaster life has not ended with my becoming a cruiser. Some days in France, the highs just seem to be higher and the lows, lower.

The next time the roller coaster effect grips my gut, it doesn't come from mere finishing; it comes from confusion over the mast situation. Pierre arrives merrily on the scene and hoists his short, roly-poly frame onto the deck. "The mast has finally arrived," he announces.

"Great!" Günter says, and my mood soars.

"You have actually *seen* this mast?" Frederic asks Pierre. As the discussion continues, it becomes evident that the mast Pierre is talking about is a defective one and is already being sent back to the supplier. *Our* mast is scheduled to arrive on October 28. My mood plummets.

After his mother leaves, Frederic follows Pierre back to his office in the Catana factory. Günter and I slump onto the trampoline and lie there, dejected, staring at the dull gray sky. We may not reach the Canaries in time to begin an Atlantic crossing by November 19, when the ARC (Atlantic Rally for Cruisers) leaves. Even though we have not formally joined the rally, we had planned to cross the Atlantic at the same time, relying on the safety of numbers.

I take a shot at a back-up plan: "We could stay in the Med, leave next spring…"

"What? Winter in the Med when we're prepared for the tropics? Not a good idea."

"I don't like it either. I'm already dreaming of warmer climes."

"Like the Caribbean. And then on to the Pacific?" Günter rolls up to a sitting position.

"Yes! To experience *Moments of Bliss* in the Pacific. That's our dream; that's our mission." I bounce up from the net. "We'll *do it*…no matter what."

"*Forget* the sea trials," Günter says, throwing caution to the wind and waves. "Just because we *paid* for these three weeks of training, doesn't mean we have to *use* them."

Frederic returns with a spring back in his step.

"I have good news," he says. "They have found a way. Your mast will arrive on October 11 as planned."

I allow myself a tentative smile. "We shall see."

More "American Therapy" Sessions

On Friday, we drive into Perpignan to an Italian restaurant for our second meeting of the *Catana Winers Club*. The weather has remained cold and rainy; the local French newspaper provides the weather forecast: *le tramontane et forte, 19° C, Vent: Nord-Ouest @ 50 km* (about 30 mph).

Tramontana are north winds that rile up the Golfo de Leon, which borders this region. Already, we are wearing our fleece-lined, foul-weather, sailing jackets on land. We worry about what the weather will be when we sail out to face that Monster of the Med—the approaching winter.

Service is slow; we consume three pitchers of Chianti before the appetizers and salads arrive. The Kims plan is to remain in the Canaries for the holidays. The rest of us are still determined to complete the Atlantic crossing to St. Lucia before Christmas. Günter has already ordered our round trip tickets from St. Lucia to San Diego for the holidays. To complicate matters, we all have crew coming in. None of the timetables look promising.

But we aren't the only group in Canet concerned about timing. The Catana staff has also committed to several international boats that have come in for scheduled upgrades and repairs. In addition, they are busy commissioning their pride and joy, a new 58-foot Catana that is due to be introduced at a Paris yachting show.

The Winers are well aware that we are dealing with a severely overextended factory with no let-up in sight. The managers are committed to their customers, working long hours, but they can only do so much, limited by union workers on 35-hour workweeks. As a businesswoman, I feel for the managers. I can appreciate what Catana is experiencing as a dynamic, growing business. But as a boat owner, I am unhappy to see the company falling apart because of restrictive French work rules. Our entrepreneurial group blames French socialism for most of the problems.

American Therapy Session #3 is held at our villa, *This Old House*, on a Sunday evening. The three American couples arrive for dinner, along with David, our San Diego yacht broker, and two crew members, Ron and Stu, of *Enduring Echoes*, our sister yacht.

A wide array of potluck dishes graces the long, wooden table: hors d'oeuvres, salads, chili, stew, and assorted tarts. The wine continues to flow as we rant about our frustrations and lack of control. We are detained in Canet, prisoners of the French business system: We want to leave ASAP, but on a perfect yacht.

But this time, we extend our discussion beyond the same tired question: How can we love the French, yet hate the system? Now, we compare the personality traits that will be required for a cruising lifestyle with those that made cruising possible for us in the first place.

"Here's the paradox," explains Pratt, co-owner of *Enduring Echoes*, a slight, sinewy man, taut and coiled like a spring. "What it *will* take to lie back, enjoy life, and give up the Type A mentality is entirely different from what it took us all…to work hard, outsmart the competition, and fulfill the American dream… in order to buy a half-million-dollar yacht."

"It requires a massive change in attitude, a paradigm shift," I join in.

"But who here is capable of doing that?" he counters.

No one answers him.

After a while, his wife, Brenda, volunteers. "Not Pratt. He's competitive by nature. He's into racing cars now. Soon, he'll be into racing boats. But I'm tired of him starting businesses and me running them. We have certainly gained all that we needed of the American dream, starting with nothing at 18, without even a college education. I say, there's a time to quit working and to start enjoying."

After our guests leave, I think back on the conversation. *Perhaps we have hit on the real reason for our therapy sessions! We've all been in business and learned how to push. What we don't know is how to relax and let go. I wonder: how many of our group will be able to learn this after they sail off into the vast unknown? How many will be able to keep on cruising, relaxed and easy-going—with their marriages still intact?*

Will we?

Rigging the Mast and Raring to Go

Pacific Bliss has been re-launched and put back into her former berth at the dock. We endure another week of promises and disappointments as we continue to wait for our mast. On Tuesday evening, we toast to the delivery of a huge mast that is arriving on a long, flat-bed truck. But our celebration is premature, because on Wednesday, we arrive at the shipyard to learn that it is not even a Catana mast—let alone ours! This is the fourth delivery date that has been missed!

Finally, on Friday, it arrives, and *Pacific Bliss* begins her transition to a "real" sailboat with mast and sails. That means the testing of the vessel's seaworthiness can begin on Monday. I'm intrigued and follow each step of the process with my digital camera: First, the mast is "rigged." Everything that needs to be attached to it—spreaders, shrouds, lights, and wind vane—is connected while it lies on the ground. Then it is placed on sawhorses—all 58 feet of it. A massive crane arrives from Perpignan, and the workers wheel the mast toward the dock where it is attached to the crane, pulled high over *Pacific Bliss*, lowered into place, and fastened into a footing attached to the deck. A wiry, slight-of-build lady skipper who does all Catana's rigging climbs into the bosun's chair, ready for action. The workers crank the winch to lift her high, swaying in the wind, to unhook the top of the mast from the crane and attach it to the rigging. This delicate operation is performed flawlessly.

The rigging completed, Pierre backs *Pacific Bliss* to our slip at the Catana owner's dock.

Over the weekend, our crew finally arrives. (We had called to delay them twice.) Günter and I welcome Jeanne and John at the Perpignan airport and drive them to our villa in Canet. How I've missed Jeanne, my competent, yet audacious, friend from my former business world! Through business, we had become fast friends and she had even joined us on a Tahiti sailing charter. A svelte, sloe-eyed brunette, Jeanne is always curious, full of life, and ready

Sailmakers hard at work.

to party. She brings her partner, John, with her, and we're delighted to see him again. We know him as a serious, self-assured patent attorney, but have never sailed with him.

Later, two more members of our crew arrive from Toronto, Canada. Günter and I had met Chris during that same Tahiti charter with Jeanne; but his girlfriend Yana, a poised yoga instructor with cropped, strawberry-blonde hair, is new to us. Chris pulls hard, rolling luggage, instead of the soft-side duffels we had recommended. A short, scruffy-bearded pensioner, who once served with a North Sea merchant fleet, he's a man with his own mind and not the kind of person anyone would want to antagonize! We settle the two couples into spare rooms in *This Old House*. The only heating is a central fireplace in the Great Room. Unfortunately, the bedrooms are cold. We had purchased electric space heaters to take off the chill, but what was once a charming, summer villa is turning into cold and dreary quarters.

Gottfried arrives, looking exactly like the charter captain he is, with a long, straw-colored lion-mane, weathered red sailing jacket, and his sea-bag slung over his back. I recall the only time we met him, in the Munich home of Günter's mother, whom we both call *Mutti*. He had traveled there from Regensburg, his home town, for the interview with us. We didn't think we would need a skipper for crossing the Atlantic; however, 88-year-old *Mutti*, a strong, determined woman and the matriarch of the Hofmann family, insisted. "I believe you should go. If I were younger, I would undertake such a voyage myself," she stated emphatically. "But don't worry an old woman. You haven't crossed an ocean before on a sailboat. I know Gottfried well. He's somewhat of a rogue, but a good sailor. Hire him."

Gottfried stays for dinner to meet everyone, but declines to stay here with the crew. "I'll move onto the boat to keep an eye out…get used to her."

Let the Party Begin!

We have never had so many people on board *Pacific Bliss*. A cluster of managers from the factory (including Jean-Pierre, the founder of Catana) is standing on the trampoline at the bow, patiently waiting for the official christening. Groups of yacht owners and crews from the Catana docks have gathered on the side decks—spinning their sea yarns. At the stern, our skipper, Gottfried, is exchanging tall tales with the skippers and crews of other yachts. Our crew—Jeanne, John, Jana, and Chris—tend the cockpit, their first assigned duty on board, making sure that the guests have ample food and drinks. Ron, an enterprising crew member of *Enduring Echoes* and already sporting a rather rakish sailor's beard, roams the deck of *Pacific Bliss* with a tray of red wine, pushing drinks on the stunning French girls from the office, while he repeats the only French words he knows: "*Vin rouge? Vin rouge?*" (That phrase becomes his new nickname that we'll never let him forget.) Jana's leathery 80-year-old uncle, who lives in a village nearby, sits at the starboard helm turning the wheel like a delighted child, pretending he's a Captain underway. Jana's shriveled aunt begs him to come to sit by her, but he stays put.

A three-tiered assortment of hors d'oeuvres, cheeses, crackers, and wines covers the cockpit table. Private label Catana champagne flows as music blares from the surround-sound speakers. Inside the salon, our best dishes have been set out; the table abounds with sweets and desserts. In the three cabins, the beds are freshly made, complete with spreads and toss pillows. Guest towels are laid out in both heads (bathrooms). The teak shines; the brass and stainless steel glows. *Pacific Bliss* looks better than I ever imagined she could!

A Catana secretary hands me a corked bottle of champagne as I weave through the revelers toward the trampoline. She whispers, "It's time."

The sun has set, but someone has thought to turn on the spreader lights.

Günter joins me at the starboard bow. "Okay, now!" I position the bottle carefully over the bow, then wham it down. Tough glass slams against even tougher Kevlar—and bounces off, right on into the harbor. The secretary calmly hands me another bottle without a word. She has obviously been-here-done-this before.

"Here, *I'll* take it," says Günter, reaching for the new bottle.

"Don't you dare! A vessel is supposed to be christened by a *lady*."

"Then go to the center and hit it against the anchor," he whispers.

That's fair. After all, that *is* the middle of the vessel, since a catamaran has two bows. I raise the bottle high over my head and slam it forward hard. A million pieces of glass reflect the lights of the marina as the bottle shatters and its fragments fall into the sea. A chorus of *yeas* drowns out the music.

The partying goes on, and all is well…for now.

Ah, if only the approaching voyage can be as happy and free of danger as this wonderful evening. But I've read too many sailing adventure stories. I know that is too much to ask.

1. Hors d'oeuvres served at the christening party; 2. Günter discusses heavy weather sailing with Jean-Pierre, Catana's founder; 3. Jana's uncle at the helm; 4. Günter and Lois, proud owners of a new Cataná; 5. Local wines served at the party; 6. Gottfried with Lana's aunt; 7. More hors d'oeuvres.

34

Günter reviews a local tourist brochure. During the long commissioning process, we tour the countryside whenever there is a break in the schedule.

Vineyards abound within 20 km of Canet and Perpignan. Who could feel sorry for us waiting here?

1. Günter prays for a safe voyage; 2. Villagers surround our new boat; 3. A daysail to Collioure, our one and only sea trial; 4. Gottfried, Pierre (our commissioning skipper), Günter, and Lois.

CHAPTER THREE

Voyage One: France to San Diego

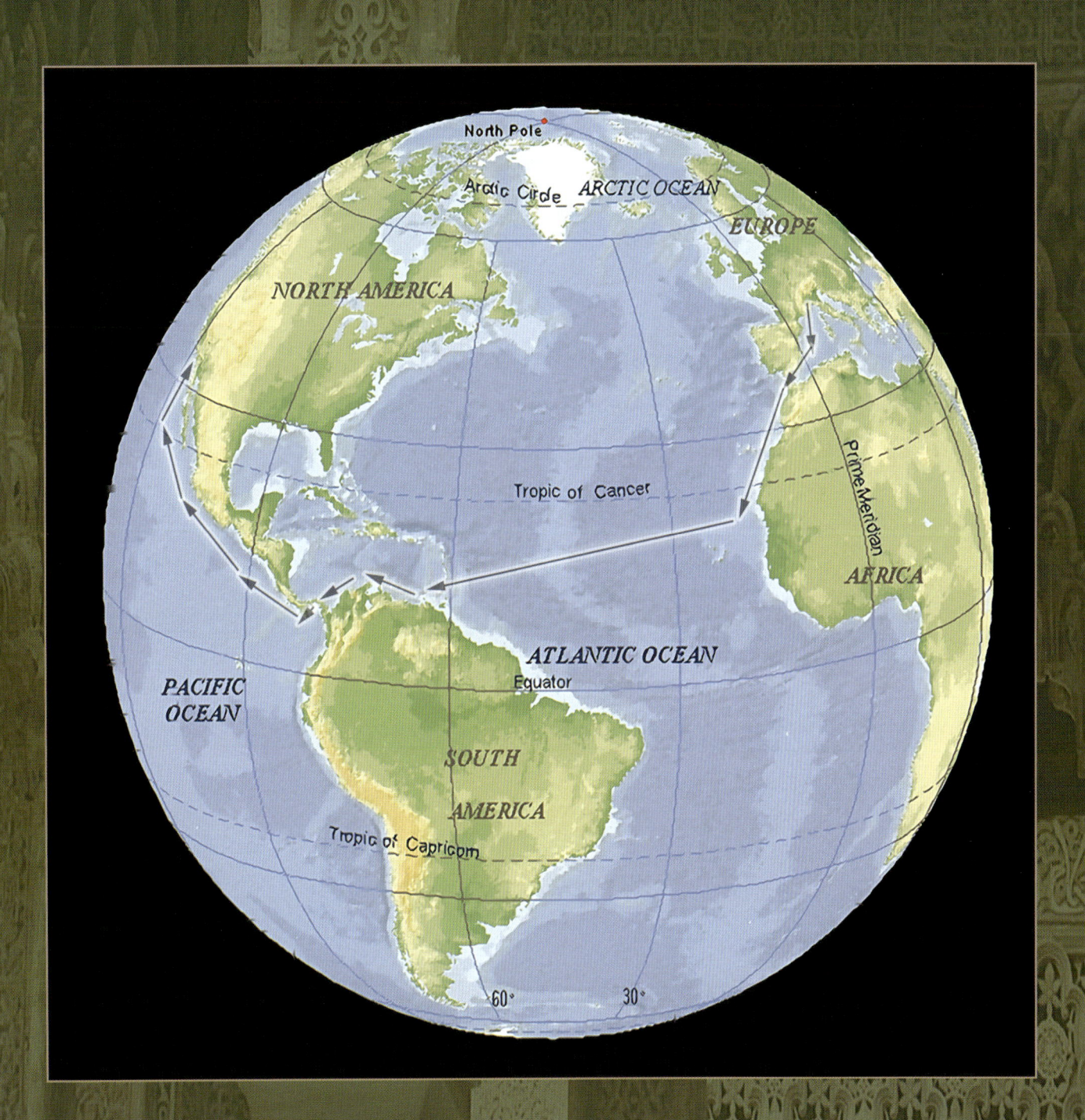

November 2000 – June 2001
9214 Nautical Miles

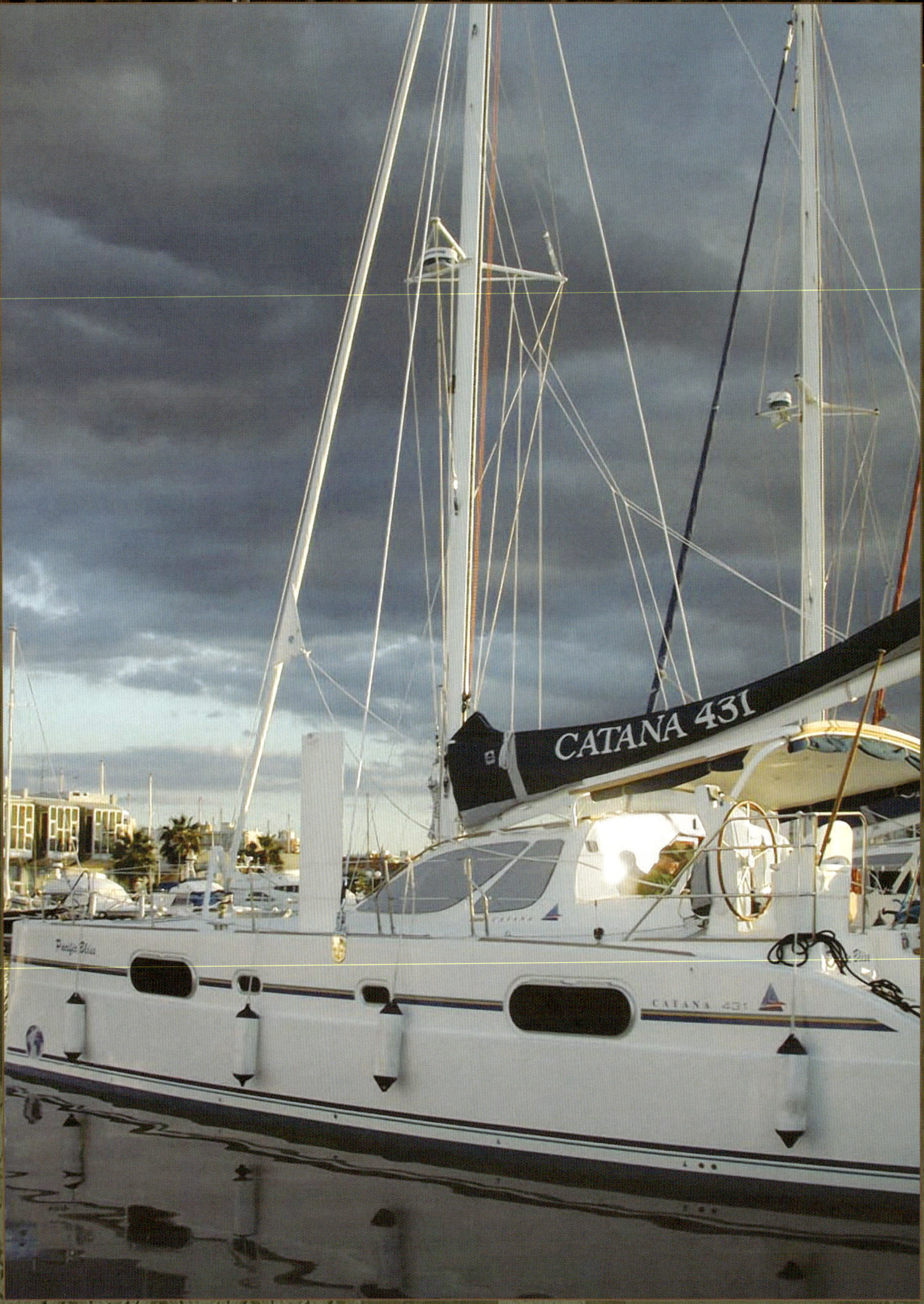
CATANA 431
CATANA 431

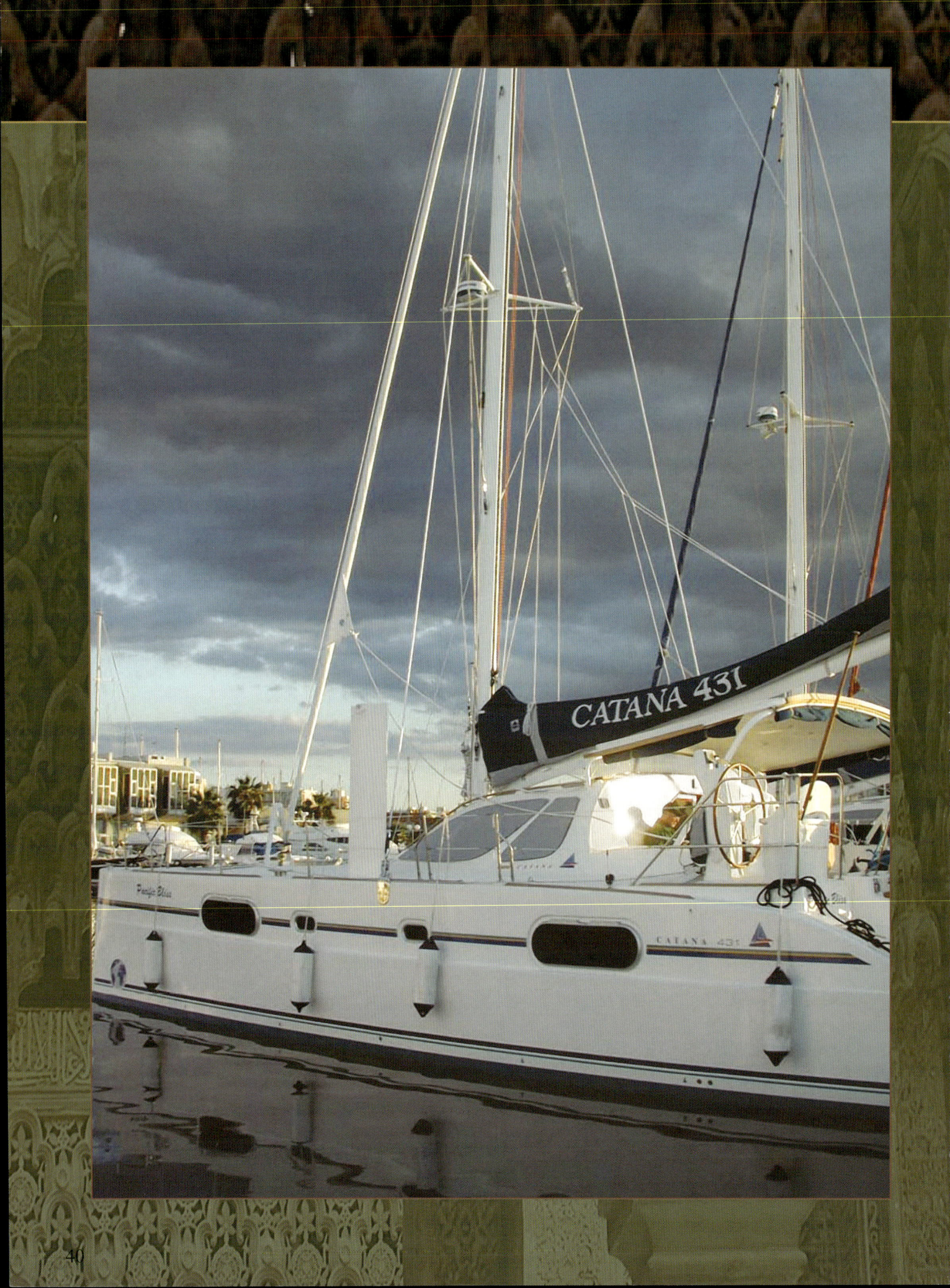

Chapter 3
Braving the Fearsome Med: Spain, Gibraltar, and Morocco

Our First and Only Sea Trial

The week following the christening, all are on board for this climactic day sail: Pierre, our commissioning skipper; Gottfried, our own skipper; the two couples who will be our crew to the Canaries; Frederic, our yacht surveyor; and Catana's U.S. National Sales Manager. We head toward Collioure, where we sailed on the Catana 471 two months earlier. The sail to this charming village provides excellent training for our crew. As we enter the harbor after an easy trip, the Catana managers invite us all for lunch at their favorite restaurant. We anchor and launch our dinghy, *Petit Bliss*, for the first time, to get the party to shore. Pierre is embarrassed to find that the new 9.9-horsepower outboard motor refuses to turn over. He gives up and we pull anchor to dock along the brick seawall opposite the fortified castle. Soon a crowd of onlookers surrounds us. Günter is beaming, proud of his baby, *Pacific Bliss*. During the two-hour, French-style lunch, the wine flows and our exuberance grows.

However, good times like this never seem to last. While sailing back to the factory, Frederic notices a crack in the mast foot, the form that holds and supports the mast, and he alerts Günter. The compression at the mast foot can be huge. To continue sailing with such a risk would be foolhardy in the extreme. The entire mast structure could fall down, including the sails, the rigging—everything.

The mood on board darkens as, one by one, the management and crew venture up to the bow to take a look. There is no easy solution. *Pacific Bliss* will need to be dry docked yet again. All cables running through the mast must be disconnected, a new mast foot installed, and the cables restrung. Their vacation time dwindling day by day, our crew wonders whether they will *ever* leave Canet by boat.

⚓

Four long days are spent in dry dock with this serious problem unresolved. Workers crawl all over the boat yet again. Günter, Gottfried, and I supervise the mess, frustrated beyond belief. I shoo the crew away. "No need for *you* to stay here in this pressure cooker... Go wine tasting...Visit the historic towns nearby... Have a *real* vacation."

The crane returns again from Perpignan; the boat is dismasted. The new mast foot is built and installed. The cables are restrung. There are minor nuisances as well: The hand pressure bulb in the dinghy had been installed backwards and had to be changed. But everything is addressed and, finally, *Pacific Bliss* is re-launched.

We turn in our rental car and say good-bye to all the friends we've made. But we are attached to Canet like jumpers on bungee cords. On November 4th, the day we plan to leave, a fierce Force 10 storm is forecast for the Mediterranean coasts of Spain and France. We delay our departure, yet again, as we wait for the storm to pass by the Golfe de Leon.

Our skipper and crew trudge the miles from the factory dock to Canet-Plage, bundled in layers of winter clothes. Stray autumn leaves catch the whirling wind along the deserted beach as the whitecaps spin from crest to crest in the violent sea beyond.

I don't even want to be out there now. I want to be...nowhere. I feel like there's a sea-wolf in front of me and a precipice of failure behind my back.

41

Leaden with gloom, my robotic legs follow the sailors into one of the few remaining restaurants that are not boarded and covered with plastic sheeting. We slump at the table, envying the other Americans' yachts that are well underway, imagining the accolades being given to the *Monster Cat* now being exhibited at the boat show in Paris and picturing Catana craftsmen working merrily inside their heated factory, manufacturing yachts to be delivered in the spring.

An Unusual Bon Voyage and a Tough Beginning
November 7, 2000

After two days of stormy weather, the forecast allows us to depart. We slip out of our berth before anyone is stirring on the dock and get underway without any fanfare at all.

Out in the Gulf, *Pacific Bliss* turns west to face the wind, whitecaps, and huge rollers left over from the storm. Even with my thick fleece shell *underneath* my heavy fleece-lined sailing jacket, I cannot get warm. With both engines laboring, *Pacific Bliss* bucks against the oncoming wind all day. By 1645 (4:45 p.m.), we pull into Port L'Estartit, across the Spanish border, with two seasick crew. We are all dead tired.

Whew. What a lousy first day of our world circumnavigation!

We walk around the quay to a small, inviting restaurant and are seated next to the fireplace. By the time our dinner arrives, the captain and some of the crew members are fast asleep in their seats.

⚓

As *Pacific Bliss* leaves Estartit the following morning, the wind is a nice-and-easy Force 4, about 12-15 knots, and we are able to sail it close-hauled, to windward. We continue on through the night under full sail; the main is full and our foresail is unfurled. But the seas are still rolly in the aftermath of the storm. During the night watch, we add layer upon layer, from long underwear to windproof jackets, including wrap-around ski hats, woolen face masks, neck warmers, and mittens over our sailing gloves. We have doubled up on two-hour watches; Jeanne is on the 2200-2400 (10 p.m. to midnight) watch with me. It is even too cold to sit at the exposed helm seat, so we are huddled under the bimini in the cockpit. Our electric autopilot steers the boat like an invisible helmsman. Jeanne takes her turn, standing on top of the sheltered cockpit bench to look out through the plastic window. As she hops down, she says, "I so wanted to show John about how much fun it was to sail a catamaran in Tahiti. Now here he is, sick in his bunk the entire time."

This is not Tahiti. This is winter in the Med.

"Never again will I sail in such cold weather," I vow to Jeanne. "I look forward to the tropics."

John, a former Navy submarine sailor not accustomed to surface weather, is seasick for the entire two-day, 111-nautical-mile passage to Tarragona, Spain. Seasickness can drain the life from the strongest man, making him fold like a rumpled deck of cards, making him crawl into his bunk, making him wish for death as a means of release. There is no escape, except for the restorative kiss of dry land.

Tarragona, Our First Cultural Tour

Finally, I am experiencing one of my real reasons to go cruising: living the culture of other lands, bonding with the locals. Günter and I are touring Tarragona, an ancient UNESCO world heritage site called Tarraco in Roman times. Walking from the port along the brick streets of the old walled city, I forget the nasty wind and the unforgiving sea. A welcoming sun shines on the golden brick remains of Cyclopean walls near the Cuartel de Pilatos, walls that are so old they are believed to pre-date the Romans. I remember something I read about Tarragona: this fortress facing the sea is part of Costa Dorada, where the sun shines almost every day of the year on fine, golden sands. This fortified wall is now an architectural wonder, but it is the wall's military role that fascinates me: It is as solid now as in the days when it was attacked by Ethiopians, Phoenicians, Romans, Goths, Saracens, Christians, and finally, the French. Imposing and majestic, it could not be breached for 30 centuries. The enemies entering the city always came from the sea. Now this wall, which could withstand arrows, catapults, bombs, mines, and cannons, opens its gates to welcome us, two peaceful visitors from a foreign land.

Wherever we are, Günter and I tend to migrate naturally toward the sea. Now, without a plan, we head toward the seaside amphitheatre. Huddled on a section of tiered seating that still remains (the rest having been used as a quarry), I imagine gladiators in Roman times, performing here to an audience of 24,000. Did they all cheer—even the women—or did some avert their eyes from the bloody spectacle below?

We locate a barber shop behind the cathedral. With a bird's-eye view of the Old City, Günter undertakes his first haircut of the circumnavigation. It's an opportunity to use our broken Spanish. "*El corte del pelo, por favor?* A haircut?" Günter asks.

"*No breve*, not too short," I add.

Somehow, we mess it up. By the time I see Günter's soft curly locks—blond when I met him, now turning silver—falling to the floor, it is too late. Too bad. I loved the look of errant locks, sneaking out of his blue cap, with its embroidered *Pacific Bliss* script.

In a courtyard restaurant nearby, we recover with a cold *vino blanco* followed by heaping bowls of steamed mussels, Catalan style (lots of garlic and more *vino blanco*). We wander back to *Pacific Bliss* where we are surprised to find Jeanne and John's luggage already packed. The message is clear: On the fourth day into our maiden voyage, we are already losing two crew members. They had originally planned to sail with us to the Canaries, but obviously ran out of patience and time. No doubt, John's seasickness also played a role in their decision.

A Perfect Day at Sea

Our second day out of Tarragona, during my 0500 to 0800 (5 p.m. to 8 p.m.) watch, I sit at the helm of *Pacific Bliss*; we push on to the hum of our steady and dependable pair of 40-horsepower Volvo engines. Myriad stars twinkle over the charcoal waters. Rounding Punta de la Bana and on through Golfo de Valencia, I fixate on the rotating lights of the 280-foot-high Benecason lighthouse atop Islas Columbretes. The lights appear to be directly ahead, on our compass course of 200 degrees, but they are actually thirteen miles away!

Things out here are not always as they seem. There is still so much to learn!

The moonset during this watch is the most dramatic I've ever seen in my life. A sphere of gold in the early morning sky, it morphs into a blood orange as it dips beyond the night lights of the Spanish coastline. This drama is followed by a slender sliver of sunrise from the east, orange at first blush, turning to another sphere of gold as the eastern sky lightens. Ever so slowly, the rocky *Islas* come into focus, with three sailboats tucked safely in her lee. I change the autopilot to +10, then +10 again to aim toward the seaward side, situating the islands between us and the shore.

A 16-knot wind comes up from the stern, strong enough to sail. With the rest of the crew sleeping, Gottfried and I hoist the main and then the genoa, the sail in front of the boat. But our huge main blocks the wind meant for the genoa. We take it down and hoist the spinnaker, our light balloon sail, at the bow, to catch the following wind. We had named our multi-colored spinnaker after Joseph's "Coat of Many Colors" in the Bible.

Jana, preparing breakfast in the galley, comes out to lend a hand. Our spinnaker snaps open as it catches the wind. What a glorious sight! *Pacific Bliss* surges forward. Soon we are sailing at 7.7 knots SOG (speed over ground) with a wind speed of only 17 knots. The sun has swelled into a full golden globe, creating a halo for *Pacific Bliss* and her beautiful spinnaker. She greets the sun by surging to 13 knots, then up to 16 as the wind increases.

The islands, spreading over an area of five square miles, with their string of dangerous rocks, are far behind

DID YOU KNOW?

SPAIN

The first circumnavigation of the world was organized by Portuguese navigator and explorer Ferdinand Magellan but financed by Spain. Born to nobility, Magellan served in Portuguese expeditions to the East Indies and Africa. Twice he asked King Manuel for a higher rank and was refused, so in 1517 he offered his services to King Charles, proposing to sail west to the Moluccas (Spice Islands) to prove that they lay in Spanish rather than Portuguese territory. He sailed from Sevilla in 1519 with five ships and 270 men.

Sailing around South America, he quelled a mutiny on the way and discovered the Strait of Magellan. With three ships remaining, Magellan crossed the "Sea of the South," which he later called the Pacific Ocean because of their calm crossing. He was killed by natives in the Philippines, but two of his ships reached the Moluccas, and one, the Victoria, commanded by Juan de Elcano (1476?–1526), continued west, rounding Africa and returning to Spain, accomplishing the first circumnavigation of the world in 1522. (Britannica.com)

Ferdinand Magellan

us. We can make out the faint glimmer of Mallorca far to the east as the Spanish coast villages to our west wake up to begin their day. Truly, this is a precious *Moment of Bliss*. I think back to when *Pacific Bliss* was merely a dream and her name just a wish. This day, for the first time, I realize what joy this cruising life can bring. *Pacific Bliss* rocks me gently, with an occasional surge as the wind fills the spinnaker and tugs her forward.

After breakfast and off-watch, I succumb to a blessed, peaceful nap. Absent is the constant hum of the engine that has been interrupting my sleep. We gather around the salon table for lunch, spreading out *jamon* (ham) from Spain and pâté with baguettes from France.

"This is as good as it gets," says Günter with a satisfied smile. Gone are the miseries of the choppy, vicious Med that has made our lives so uncomfortable. We now have a taste of better times to come. We all spend much of the afternoon reading—without the constant rolls, jerks, and yaws that have been our fate to date. At dusk, the sun sinks into the horizon as perfectly as it rose.

Glory be to God. How I love this special day. How I wish it could last!

Pacific Bliss Draws First Blood
Malaga, Spain

It is an uneventful Sunday, and all seems well with the world. The seas are quiet; a gentle Force 3 breeze blows; visibility is fair. We have been averaging 5 knots, motoring toward our next landfall, Torremolinas, Spain, a few miles past Malaga. It is 1420.

"Crew, prepare the dock lines!" Gottfried calls out from someplace on top. "Prepare the fenders." I scramble to the forward locker to retrieve the new, sausage-shaped, white bumpers with the blue trim.

"Yow!" Günter screams from the bow. He rushes into the galley, blood dripping from his left hand.

"What happened?"

"I just *happened* to have this hand in the anchor locker…I was closing it after taking out the lines… when Gottfried slipped coming down from the cabin roof."

Jana and I quickly wrap Günter's deeply cut middle finger with a makeshift bandage and secure it firmly with duct tape—not pretty, but it will hold until he has the quite necessary stitches.

After we dock at Torremolinas Marina, I hail a taxi to *Clinica Salus Benalmadena*, an emergency facility a few blocks away. We arrive at 1520, only an hour after the accident. After we fill out forms and assure the clinic that we will pay cash, a beefy nurse leads Günter into an examining room. She treats him in the composed, condescending manner that only a heartless person can.

1. Günter gets a haircut in Tarragona; 2. The barber-shop sign; 3. Jeanne, John and Günter upon arrival in Estartit.

Following her, Günter grimaces, white-faced. "She reminds me of Nurse Ratchet. You know, the one in the Jack Nicholson movie?"

"*One Flew over the Cuckoo's Nest?*"

"Yah, that's it."

There would be no small talk, no sympathy today.

"Get on here and lie down!" Nurse Ratchet points to the examining table, as a white-coated doctor enters the tiny room. She lays Günter's left hand over his stomach, frowning as she unravels my crude bandaging. The doctor, quite professional and in perfect English, asks when Günter last had a tetanus shot, and, after administering four stitches, he leads Günter to another room for the shot and x-rays. More money for the clinic on a slow Sunday! The x-rays show no breaks.

The huge wrapping around Günter's middle finger causes it to stand up in a certain disrespectful position. I muffle a laugh, waiting for Günter to crack a joke. He takes another look at dour Ms. Ratchet and wisely decides against it.

"Can I take these out myself?" Günter asks her as we leave the clinic. She waggles a finger at him, horrified.

"Absolutely no. You must come back here in five days."

"I can't," says Günter. "We're sailing. We'll be gone by then."

"Well, then, go to another hospital."

Hmm. I wonder whether our bandaging job might have caused her to believe that our crew might be incapable of further doctoring.

As we wait in the lobby for the completion of the paperwork, my eyes roam to the local paper on the table. A photo of broken boats piled up on shore dominates the front page. The lead story describes the Force 10 storm that wrought havoc up and down this coast. That storm hit Malaga the day *Pacific Bliss* departed from France! We had battled the wake of that storm most of the way up the Spanish Coast. Thank God we had the good sense to pull into shore in Estartit on Monday evening.

As night falls over the masts at the Marina, we and our crew are treated to one of those sunsets that seems to go on forever. All is well with the world again as the trauma of the day fades with the disappearing veins of purple and red.

The Alhambra Magic

There's no frame of reference for the indescribable beauty and mystique of the Alhambra, the epitome of Islamic art in Spain, the last hurrah of the Moors' 800-year reign here. Gottfried, Günter, and I rent a car, taking the Ronda Sur, Granada's ring road, to the car park in the Generalife Gardens. Then we walk through the Gate of the Pomegranates, built by Charles V,

DID YOU KNOW?

GIBRALTAR

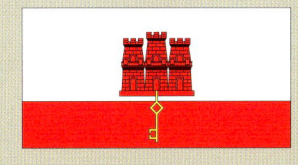

The Barbary ape is the only primate that lives in Europe. A small colony has existed at The Rock for many years, having made their way from Morocco, some say by way of a tunnel under the straits when Gibraltar and Morocco were joined many years ago.

Legend says that "The Rock" will remain in British hands only as long as these apes survive. In 1942, the ape population decreased to seven, causing British Prime Minister Winston Churchill to fire off a cable to those in command at Gibraltar, ordering that the apes were to be maintained at all costs. New recruits for the colony were hastily transported via an American military flight from Africa, so by the end of that year they numbered 20. Now this ape colony on British welfare has increased so much that they are being culled.

Barbary Ape

Looking down toward Malaga from the Alhambra ramparts.

and enter the tree-lined avenues of the Alhambra. We haven't bothered to hire a guide, so we just take it as it comes. It turns out to be a magical fairyland.

We find ourselves in a marble-floored room, with a small fountain bubbling at its center. The overflow follows a channel along the floor and runs outside to join water displays in the adjoining courtyard. The soothing music of bubbling water seems to keep time with the lineal rhythms of intricately carved walls and ceilings. Up to wainscot height, the walls are covered with geometric knots in colorful, yet subdued, tile. Then they abruptly change to soft sculpted stucco. I take a deep breath and gaze toward the ceiling, which explodes in a harmony of scrolls and script, flowers and vines, reaching its crescendo on a ceiling that is covered with stars.

My favorite space in this delightful castle is the *Patio de los Leones* (Patio of the Lions). It is a rectangular courtyard with a centrally placed white marble fountain. A huge basin rests on the backs of twelve lions that look more like panthers, all springing forward in a circle. Around the perimeter is a gallery; it is supported by dozens of marble columns with slender shafts and capitals. These are carved with a delicate floral motif, and lead to other arches of filigree stucco. As I walk around the gallery, arches and columns shift grouping and positions, sometimes standing straight and alone, at other times standing in groups of twos or threes. I stop short as I realize suddenly that this is a Moment of Bliss for me. The columns beside me and those across the way become a wonderful world of almond and alabaster, delicacy and delight, lace and lightness of being.

Later, fulfilled, we return to *Pacific Bliss,* only to learn that Chris and Jana have decided to leave us here to tour on land. Less than a week into our maiden voyage, we are down from seven sailors to three.

When the Apes Leave Gibraltar

"Watch out!" I peer into the ink ahead. "We're going to hit the dock."

"Can't be. The dock would be lit," our skipper replies.

"Well, it isn't. Stop!"

Gottfried slams into reverse just in time, about ten feet in front of the unlit mole at Queensway Quay. Günter and I fasten the dock lines, grim and silent. We have motored a full day, 55 miles, to get here. Still neophytes, we are not happy about coming into a strange marina after dark and coming so close to crushing the bows of our new boat.

Lesson learned: When we're in charge, arrival after dark is not an option.

⚓

Sunday dawns sunny and cool. The close call shoved aside, Gottfried, Günter, and I arrange for a private taxi tour of The Rock. This time, I've done some research in advance. Gibraltar is a large promontory of Jurassic limestone, 5km (3 miles) long, with the highest point at 426m (1,400ft) above sea level. An internal, self-governing, British Crown Colony on the southernmost tip of the Iberian Peninsula, Gibraltar contains 143 caves, over 48km (30 miles) of road, and miles of tunnels.

Although it is cold and windy at the overlook on top of the hill, the view from there is awesome. I strain to identify a beetle-sized *Pacific Bliss* at the marina docks far below. Spain is to the north and west; I can make out Morocco 26km (16 miles) to the south, including the jutting peninsula that is Ceuta, a tiny piece of land still under Spanish control. I'm humbled to think that this is just the beginning of what I will see and learn about this wonderful world.

We make our way through a horde of monkeys to explore St. Michael's Cave. A tailless Barbary Macaque, in a rather cheeky move, jumps onto my shoulder and stays there until I shrug him off. 1000 feet above sea level, we walk part way into a labyrinth of tunnels. The Upper Galleries, hewn by hand from The Rock in 1782, house old cannons and tableaux evoking the Great Siege (1779-1783).

When we return to *Pacific Bliss*, Gottfried

View of the old city from the Alhambra.

The reflecting pool at the Alhambra.

introduces us to raven-haired Christian, his former partner in a sailboat chartering business. A conversation ensues with Günter about the relative merits of monohulls versus catamarans. The discussion ends with a surprise: Christian decides to "jump ship," deserting the monohull he is crewing on, to make his passage to the Canary Islands on *our* catamaran. Now we are four. I'm beginning to realize how weak a sailor's commitment can be. We can't complain; this time, *we* are the beneficiaries!

In the late afternoon, we stroll down the main street casually, looking for a restaurant. All the hiking and fresh air has created an enormous appetite, but unfortunately, most of the restaurants are closed on Sunday. We select an English-style buffet that posts a set menu of Roast Beef and Yorkshire pudding. Seems harmless enough. But by the end of a meal that has no flavor and tastes like paste, I wonder why the English can't take some cooking lessons from the French.

Is there a doctor in the house?

Our sister ship, *Enduring Echoes*, is docked right next to us, and we have made plans to "buddy boat"— that's the cruiser practice of making a passage together. The two crews have decided to head for Tangier sometime during the night. But now everyone is on our boat, engaged in a lively discussion about the merits of waiting three hours or five hours after high tide to cross the Strait of Gibraltar.

Günter has been quietly coping with the clumsiness of eating and crewing with one hand while wearing a rubber dishwashing glove on the other for protection. Frankly, we have all become used to seeing him that way and have forgotten all about taking out his stitches. It is not like him to interrupt a serious nautical discussion. Perhaps it is the talk of going to Africa that causes his concern.

"I was supposed to get these stitches out in five days. Now a week has gone by. Who here of all of you wants to take out these stitches?" Almost every hand goes up. Sensing that sailors must have a weird affinity for another's discomfort, Günter rephrases the question. "Who among you is the most qualified? Any vets, for example?" A lot of hot air flies around the salon, as qualifications are exaggerated, but Günter manages to find one sailor in whom to put his trust: Stuart, an *Enduring Echoes* crewman, had been an emergency medical technician.

Stu holds forth at the end of our salon table. "The ship's medical kit," he commands, extending his hand

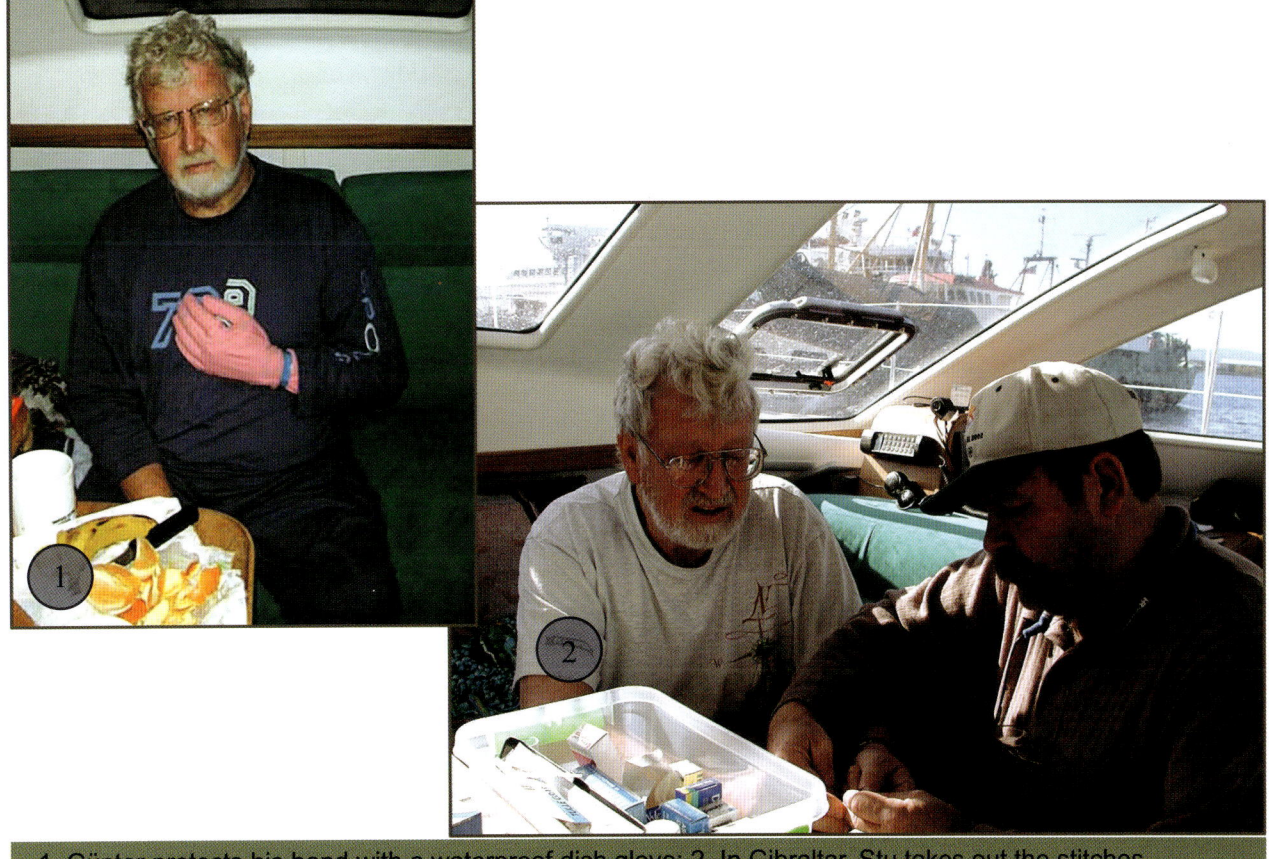

1. Günter protects his hand with a waterproof dish glove; 2. In Gibraltar, Stu takes out the stitches.

to receive it. He even *looks* like a ship's doctor, rotund and jovial. All that's missing is a pair of wire-rimmed glasses. I hand him the kit that was supplied with *Pacific Bliss,* from which he selects appropriate bandages and antiseptic. "A small scissors," he snaps. I slap one from my manicure kit, acting like a nurse in an O.R. "Perfect," he smirks.

Not satisfied with the callous lack of attention to pain control, Günter insists on taking out the last stitch himself. He gasps and looks around. "That crooked Malaga clinic…there were only four stitches…and they charged us for *five!*"

After we stop laughing, the talk returns to our plans for crossing the Strait. Tangier is only 40 nautical miles away, an ideal one-day rest stop before the long sail to the Canary Islands. Topics range from timing the tides, to crossing the shipping lanes at 90 degrees, to identifying freighter lights at night, using the West Marine cheat sheet that is posted at the nav station. Finally, departure time is set for 0100, 1 a.m. The two crews set up watch schedules and prepare to turn in for a short night.

I am not happy about traversing the Strait in the dark, but the captains have made their decision.

Agitated by the flood of data flowing through my brain, I cannot sleep.

There is a significant exchange of water through the channel. A two-knot current flows eastward through the center, except when affected by easterly winds. Below 400 feet, the heavier, colder water with a high salt content flows westward. If it weren't for the Strait, the Med would become a shrinking salt lake.

The channel is 36 miles long and 8 miles wide between Spain and Morocco. At the eastern extreme it is 14 miles wide between the classical world's Pillars of Hercules, which have been identified as the Rock of Gibraltar to the north and Ceuta to the south. The Strait is 1200 feet deep in the arc formed by the Atlas Mountains of North Africa and the high plateau of Spain.

All of that sounds innocent and safe. What bothers me is this: We'll face a geographic funnel that accelerates the wind. It's called the *Venturi Effect*. This happens when a fluid, flowing through a constricted section of a tube, undergoes a decrease in pressure; it's like a stepped-on garden hose. This means that the wind could be blowing at 5 knots at the beginning and end of the Strait, and 50 knots in the middle! As if this isn't scary enough, ship traffic will create huge turbulence in the already choppy sea. Over 80,000 vessels pass through the Strait each year, and that promises considerable difficulty.

Gottfried and Christian in a Tangier rug shop.

Taste of Tangier

Pacific Bliss slows as *Enduring Echoes* follows in her wake. The harbor where the sailboats are assigned is a sight to behold. Piled planks and scrap line the shore. A tattered Moroccan flag waves in front of a dilapidated shack. The shack is on wheels, as if it could disappear any minute. It has a weathered, wooden sign that boasts in French: YACHT CLUB DE TANGER, FONDE EN 1925, above the usual Arabic. A half-submerged wreck lies right in front, between us and the quay. Three men are waving, directing us to side-tie to a white French catamaran. Then they motion for *Enduring Echoes* to tie up alongside us. We place bumpers on each side; fortunately, we had purchased two large round fenders at the Chandlery in Gibraltar to augment the six long fenders that came with the Catana "Sail-away Package." We call the new ones our "*Fat Boys.*"

The men step from the French catamaran onto *Pacific Bliss*. We seat them around our teak cockpit table. After introductions, one bushy-browed official in a black leather jacket points to the United States flag flying from our stern. "Do you know who won your elections?"

"No," Günter answers. "Do you?"

"No. Seems they are still trying to deal with those torn chads in the state of Florida. But we think we have a solution."

"What is that?"

"Well, we Africans can help your country. We were taught by the Americans how to count ballots and run fair elections. We could go over there and supervise…" He pauses for effect. "Anyway, welcome to Morocco!"

The two Germans, Gottfried and Christian, guffaw while Günter and I exchange surprised looks. Then we chuckle as well.

The paperwork is surprisingly simple and quick. Afterwards, the officials step over our lifelines and onto the cockpit of *Enduring Echoes*.

Upon completion of the immigration process, we

The beginning of our crossing is pleasant, with a light, Force 2 northeast wind and calm seas. But right after dawn, the wind changes to south-southwest and increases to Force 6. By the time we change course to cross the busy shipping lanes, the wind is up to Force 7, about 35 knots, right on the nose. *I don't like this. This is no casual crossing.* My heart pounds as the bows lift then crash through the waves, both engines grinding at the stern. Despite all our earlier talk, it turns out there was no "right" time to make this crossing. The meeting point of the cold Atlantic and the warm Mediterranean, the Strait of Gibraltar is simply a worrisome and fickle weather zone.

⚓

As if it isn't enough to buck through heavy seas, we must watch out for ships—because they certainly aren't watching out for us. I mumble a key instruction: Always cross *behind* a freighter. Gottfried is at the helm, and I peer into the mist to figure out the course of each container ship. Finally, I'm exhausted. Günter takes over, assisting Gottfried. The bucking bounces me up and down on my bunk. This short crossing seems to take forever. Then all at once, the crashing stops. *What's wrong?* I rush topside. It's nothing—we have traversed the worst of the turbulence. The seas have suddenly calmed. Before long, we can make out still waters off the opposite shore.

Morocco, here we come!

all cross over the French cat to shore and on through the guarded gates of the marina. The touts (street peddlers) are waiting for us, begging to show us the sites of Tangier, which—so we have been told—will lead us inevitably to carpet showrooms. We walk along the dusty main street, trying to ignore a half-dozen touts, shouting for our attention.

We escape by entering a restaurant and winding our way through a crowded, smoke-filled tearoom. It is filled with men wearing *djellabas* (long, loose-fitting, hooded robes), turbans, or pillbox-type hats called *fezzes*. They are yelling and cheering at a TV hung from the ceiling, in a corner of the room. I want to stop to take it all in, but I'm dragged along by the two hungry crews headed toward the cafeteria in rear of the restaurant. Once there, we fill our plates with couscous, lamb curry, and assorted vegetables swimming in a seasoned broth; then we sit at a wooden picnic-style table to chow down. The food is different, but tasty.

Günter agrees to my request for ambiance. He orders a round of mint tea. Our group crowds around a small table in the tearoom, which stands before a bench sporting soiled and faded Moroccan pillows. This is the first time I have been on the continent of Africa, my first experience in a Muslim country. My senses are overwhelmed. The lingering tastes of lamb and unfamiliar spices mix with the refreshing mint in the tea. My eyes smart from the smoke. Could it be *kif*—tobacco mixed with hashish? I wouldn't know the difference. I'm seduced by it all, watching and listening. Tangier. A mixture of hedonism and history. The haunt of beat poets and musicians like The Rolling Stones. The haven of writers like Burroughs, Bowles, and Beckett. A mecca for speculators and gamblers. And a reputed safe house for international spies and secret agents.

When we leave the restaurant, the touts are still waiting, ready to pounce. Gottfried hires one of them to shoo the others away. He has been here before and knows the ropes. We saunter down the crooked, narrow streets of the souk, dashing in and out of shops that offer ten kinds of dates, a dozen kinds of olives, and hundreds of spices. Of course, we end up at the obligatory rug factory, lured there by our devious, master tout.

Brenda and Pratt actually purchase a huge rug, which they will load onto *Enduring Echoes* and, after they reach the Caribbean, ship to their home in Utah. I whisper to Günter, "Amazing. They plan to load that heavy thing onto their boat."

Günter breathes a sigh of relief. "Well that takes us off the hook. Now *we* don't have to buy one."

We escape to another part of the store, pretending to explore the racks of hooded *djellabas*. From there, we move to a rack of wide-sleeved *gandoras* with striking embroidery at the neck and sleeves. "I already have something similar," says Günter, who had already

DID YOU KNOW?

MOROCCO

Along with Bombay, the city of Tangier was given to Charles II as part of the dowry from Catherine of Braganza (Portugal). The English granted Tangier a charter which made it equal to English towns. This strange turn of events began when the Portuguese started their expansion in Morocco by taking Ceuta in 1415. But the city they really wanted was Tangier. They finally captured the city in 1437. Portuguese rule lasted until 1661, when they gave it away.

Tangier is an ancient Phoenician city, founded in the fifth century B.C. The name probably came from the Berber goddess Tinjis. It came under Roman rule in the first century B.C., first as a free city and then, under Augustus, as a colony. A century later, Tangier became part of the Byzantine Empire. In 702, it came under Arab control.

By the opening of the 20th century, Tangier had a diverse population of about 40,000, including 20,000 Muslims (with Berbers predominating over Arabs), 10,000 Jews, and 9,000 Europeans (mostly Spanish). Early in the century, the city was partitioned between France and Spain. Then in 1923, the city was made an international zone, jointly administered by France, Spain, and Britain, with Italy added in 1928. What a challenge! During that time, the city served as a playground for eccentric millionaires; a mecca for speculators, gamblers and crooks; and a meeting place for secret agents.

Finally in 1956, the city was reunited with the rest of Morocco as part of an independent country.

Charles II

51

Alabaster arches in the Patio de la Leones, Alhambra, Spain.

backpacked around the world and traveled extensively before I met him. "Let's look for something for *you*." We find a spectacular, shimmery gown in a lavender pastel print with gold trim at the neck and sleeves. Then we discover another in deep purple, also trimmed with gold. "Take both," says Günter. "Why not?"

Why not, indeed? I have no idea where or when I'll wear such things, but since Günter is buying…

The gowns are beautiful, but the local women do not wear such things in public. Instead, except for their eyes, they are covered head to foot in colorless sacks. Walking back along the street, past tall, white-plastered walls, I imagine them dressed in these same gowns. *Do they lead very different private lives? Do they line their eyes with the smoky kohl like that used by women in the Middle East? Do they seduce their men while wearing silken gowns trimmed with gold—with nothing underneath?*

Right in front of the gate to the harbor, a table of knick-knacks has magically appeared. Stuart, a confessed shopaholic, who loves to bargain, draws Günter to the table. They make a game of bartering over a wooden giraffe about a foot high. Günter wins (if one can call it that), meaning he spent the most.

Back on *Pacific Bliss*, I set the giraffe carefully on our knick-knack shelf. Of course, the creature will have to lie down when we go to sea. Today in Tangier I have found the first of a crazy menagerie that will travel around the world with us.

Tomorrow, we must enter that turbulent Strait again, then to the sea beyond. Only God knows what I will find out there.

Chris and Gottfried adjust the spinnaker.

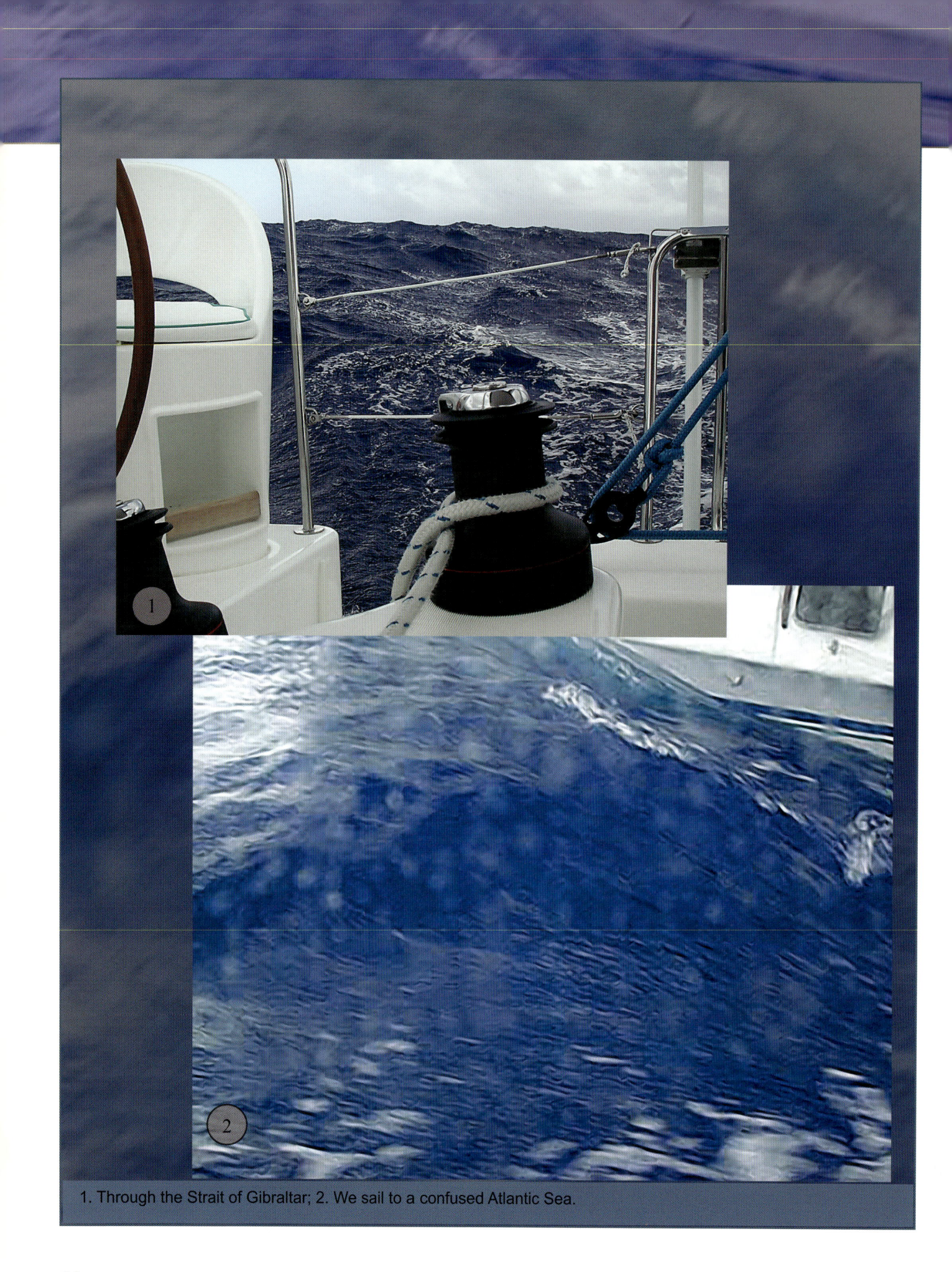

1. Through the Strait of Gibraltar; 2. We sail to a confused Atlantic Sea.

CHAPTER 4
THROUGH THE PILLARS OF HERCULES, BEYOND THE SEA OF DARKNESS

Entering the Atlantic Ocean
November 21, 2000

On both sides of the coastline where the Mediterranean meets the ocean, the great king Hercules built lighthouses of stone and bronze. Covered with inscriptions, surrounded by statues, they signal that there is no way beyond: "No ship can enter the ocean, where it begins and where it ends are both unknown, no rational beings dwell there." To the Latins during the Middle Ages, the Atlantic was the *Mare Tenebrosum;* for the Arabs, it was *Bahr al-Zulamat*. Both meant *Sea of Darkness*. Anyone who looked west from the northern coast of Portugal could see for himself the heavy cloudbanks lying across the horizon, confirming the evil omens. Later, the Greeks called this dark sea *okeanos* and the Western Islamists, *Bahr al Atlasi*, the Sea of the Atlas Mountains. Today most call it the Atlantic Ocean. Except for us cruisers, who call it simply *The Big Pond*.

As *Pacific Bliss* departs the port of Tangier at dawn, we follow in the wake of many intrepid sailors who proved Hercules wrong. We leave the turbulent straits behind and head right out into that Dark Sea, to find long, rolling waves of deep navy blue. We set our watch schedules and fall into a routine.

During my first watch, I ponder the theories of ancient philosophers and early explorers. The Babylonians, and perhaps the Sumerians before them, imagined the inhabited world as an upturned boat, a *gufa*, floating in the sea. *Gufa* is still the name used for the round-bottomed reed boats used in the marshes of southern Iraq. The Babylonians passed on the idea to the Greeks, and geographers from Herodotus on described the world as surrounded on all sides by a universal ocean. Long after Aristotle demonstrated that the world was a sphere, the old Babylonian image persisted. Writing 1400 years after Aristotle, perfectly aware of the earth's spherical shape, the historian al-Mas'udi still compared the world to an egg floating in water. Another 400 years after that, Ibn Khaldun compared the inhabited portion to a grape floating in a saucer. It was this idea, passed on to medieval Europe, that contributed to the geographical discoveries of the 15th and 16th centuries.

I go to our ship's library to look up the Hernando Columbus biography of his father Christopher. In it, he lists the classical and medieval sources that led the Admiral to think he could reach the Indies by sailing westward. Christopher was most likely swayed by this passage:

"There is much change, I mean in the stars which are overhead, and the stars seen are different, as one moves northward or southward. Indeed there are some stars seen in Egypt and in the neighborhood of Cyprus which are not seen in the northerly regions; and stars which, in the north, are never beyond the range of observation, in those regions rise and set. All of which goes to show not only that the earth is circular in shape, but also that it is a sphere of no great size; for otherwise the effect of so slight a change of place would not be so quickly apparent. Hence one should not be too sure of the incredibility of the view of those who conceive that there is continuity between the parts about the Pillars of Hercules and the parts about India, and that in this way the ocean is one."

This was the prevailing theory, which we now know to be true. The Seven Seas *are* one. Even so, there was a tremendous psychological hurdle for the early explorers to overcome: the ancient belief that *nothing*—except the Garden of the Hesperides, the lost continent of Atlantis, and the gods of darkness—lay beyond the hellish seas of the Pillars of Hercules.

After my watch, it is Christian's turn. He has become increasingly pale and peaked since crossing the strait, as *Pacific Bliss* climbs up and drops down the humongous rollers of the Atlantic. He had so looked forward to sailing on a catamaran! I feel sorry for him as he takes the helm seat. He is determined to take his watch, despite his queasiness.

Since Gottfried has raved about Christian's cooking, I have been looking forward to some relief in the galley. Such a break is not to be. In addition to my regular watches, I take on most of the galley chores.

Thanksgiving at Sea
33 ° 30.5' N, 9° 56' W

Two days pass in a blur of night and day watches, cooking, cleaning, and trying to fit some sleep in between. As I take the helm for my early morning watch at 0445, the moon is a slender silver cradle rising in the east, above the coast of Morocco. We have sailed beyond the lights of Casablanca, that city known to me only through the movie of the same name. *Casablanca*. Humphrey Bogart and Ingrid Bergman. War and adventure. Romance and passion. To think that it was released back in 1942, the year I was born. Now, Casablanca is the largest city in Morocco and the sixth largest on the African continent, an industrial port not nearly as exotic as its name implies.

Our Atlantic crossing crew was due to arrive in Tenerife yesterday, and we still have over 400 nautical miles to go! The instructions for this watch are to keep on motoring with both engines to make better time, maintaining a 235-degree course to the Canaries. The seas are too rough to raise the sails, with wind at Force 5 (20 knots), changing gradually WSW to WNW. We have felt far too much of this south wind, directly on the nose. More than we deserve. I am hoping that the wind will veer away from the south so that we can sail this Thanksgiving Day without beating against it.

So far, the "fair winds and following seas" have been but an elusive dream. My thoughts wander back over our voyage. Since leaving Canet, France, I can recall only one perfect day of sunny skies and following seas, when we flew the spinnaker along the Spanish *Costa del Sol*.

As clouds race in to snatch the sunrise, my thoughts turn toward traditional Thanksgiving celebrations with friends and family at home: a giant turkey monopolizing the table, surrounded by dressing, mashed potatoes, gravy, side dishes, with an assortment of pies on the side board. I miss the phone calls to and from our children and others who can't be with us. It feels so, so lonesome out here.

Okay. Get with it. I continue my soliloquy at the helm while the guys are fast asleep. *I need to make an attitude adjustment. First, I am thankful this day that we are safe, in good health, and in relatively good spirits. I am also thankful that we have put the unpredictable Med behind us and are well on our way to warmer climes. Things will get better.*

After a short nap following my watch, I mull over what we could have for dinner. Obviously, our plan for baking "Thanksgiving Chicken" in the oven is not going to work. It is still too "lumpy" out here, as the Brits would define these rough seas. And I don't dare to go up to the forward locker in the madly bouncing port hull bow to select fresh vegetables from the hammock strung there. The pressure cooker could be a solution… problem is, I have never used it…yet. I purchased the cooker at Great News, a kitchen and culinary store near our home, and even took a cooking class there.

"How many of you are just a little afraid of using a pressure cooker?" the chef had asked. Almost all the hands went up. That's why we were there.

I remember my Swedish mother, Sigrid, using the huge cooker in the rambling kitchen of our Wisconsin dairy farm. At the bottom, she would place a big hunk of beef (from one of the cows too old and crotchety to give milk). On top of that, she would pile potatoes, carrots, onions—or any other vegetables she could dig from our teeming, exuberant garden. If she could do it, so can I!

I retrieve the pressure cooker and its cover with the rubber seals from our pan storage underneath the galley sink; then, I fill it with chicken, along with some tired celery and greens from the fridge. I take the manual down from the recipe shelf, look up the correct amount of water, and bravely set it on the burner. The cooker hisses steadily as it reaches full pressure. Mesmerized, I think back to how, as a preschooler, I hid behind my barefooted mother's muumuu-style housedress, peeking out to watch the steam volcano, waiting for it to "blow its top," an expression my German father used all the time. Now, I wait for the valve's three red lines to appear, then watch Günter carefully lift it from the stove and into the sink.

It worked! As *Pacific Bliss* lurches through the waves, the four of us enjoy a Thanksgiving dinner in the salon. The chicken is not overcooked like my mother's beef; it is surprisingly juicy and tasty, and the vegetables are firm. Christian has recovered and regained his appetite. Günter is hungry, as usual. I'm starved. And Gottfried is amazed. "I never knew pressure cookers were so useful," he admits. "When I bought my used boat, I threw away the cover to the cooker because it wouldn't fit well in the galley shelves. I thought it took up too much space, so I used only the bottom, and then couldn't find a good top to fit tight!"

This is a *Gottcha Gottfried* moment I cannot resist: "Serves you right!"

We all break out laughing—especially Günter, who is a like-minded "minimalist." The two of them have been driving me berserk because they insisted on having as few items on the boat as possible, using the excuse that a catamaran must be kept light. I'm still smarting from a scene at the chandlery in Gibraltar, when they coerced me into trading-in the hefty hardcover *North African Pilot* I'd just purchased for the pair of round fenders we now call our *Fat Boys*. My dinner is a great success, and I glory in it.

Earlier that day, I had realized our Raytheon® instruments were telling us that *Pacific Bliss* was close to logging 1000 miles. Looking up from the nav station, I'd asked, "What can we do to celebrate?"

"We need to use up some of these leftovers to make room for provisioning in the Canaries," Günter said, always the practical one. "Don't make anything new."

I searched for other goodies in the fridge. "We still have flan from France...and whipped cream," I'd announced. My search expanded to the freezer, where I found half-full containers of vanilla and double-chocolate ice cream. "Flan ice cream sundaes for dessert!" The idea brought cheers.

Now, on Thanksgiving, after gorging, we feel just like Americans always feel after their Thanksgiving dinners: stuffed like a turkey. And I store my pressure cooker, feeling I have made a new friend.

Next, I plan to tackle a big job: reorganizing the ship's pantry. The previous night, my sleep interrupted by the vinegar, oil, and condiment bottles raising a ruckus: clank, clank, clank, as *Pacific Bliss* challenged the steep waves, then swerved back and forth to adjust her course. Now, as she continues to pitch and lurch, I brace myself to clean and reorganize. Finally, every bottle is tight against each other or against something that "gives," such as zip-lock bags full of cookie mixes. That project completed, and slightly queasy from working down in the hull, I take my watch topside, followed by another nap, pleased that this day has turned into another special Thanksgiving after all.

Go South until the Butter Melts

Two more days pass. I've been watching the container of butter, sitting on a shelf, wedged between our night watch snacks—Nescafé, hot chocolate, and Ovaltine—along with our morning jams and tea. The butter has been getting a little softer every day, but today is the special day we've all been waiting for.

I now know that our experiment has succeeded. The butter has melted!

Günter and I had visited Barcelona on a side tour from Canet while *Pacific Bliss* was being built. In the city's impressive Nautical Museum, we gravitated to the display showing Columbus' voyages. On his first voyage, Columbus left the Canaries and sailed due west. On each of his three subsequent voyages, he headed farther south before turning west. Now, thousands of modern vessels follow his path south to the Tropic of Cancer, then farther south, almost to the Cape Verde islands, and *then* turn west. It's an Old Salt recipe: "*Go south until the butter melts; then turn west into the sunset.*"

Even though we plan to stop at Cape Verde, "South until the butter melts" has become our mantra. Stashed underneath our bunk is a summer clothing duffel labeled "Till the butter melts." We will replace all the cold weather gear taking up space in our cubbies and lockers "when the butter melts."

Today, during my pre-dawn watch, the metamorphosis begins. I remove my polar fleece gloves and red West Marine cap, the kind that comes down over the ears and attaches underneath one's chin. I unzip my trustworthy *Pacific Bliss* jacket (fleece inside and waterproof outside). I have already decided not to wear my navy polar fleece socks. Still remaining are my fleece top, long underwear, and foul weather pants, which I shed after my watch. In the afternoon when the sun comes out, we all change from pants to shorts for the first time.

For lunch today, our last day before arriving at port, we decide to go all out. Christian has completely recovered from his bout of seasickness; he is finally in the mood for cooking. We prepare pasta using frozen meatballs purchased at Gallerie Lafayette, lots of fresh garlic, green peppers, tomatoes, adding *herbes de Provence* to the usual Italian spices. For the first time since leaving Tangier, we dare to enjoy wine with our meal while underway. "Live like Gods in France," nods Gottfried.

"*Leben wie Gott in Frankreich*," adds Günter.

"To the tropics," says Christian.

"When the butter melts." I clink my glass against the others, looking my crewmates straight in the eyes, and grinning broadly.

It may have been the wine, but during my afternoon and evening watches, I wax lyrical:

1600: *Come on in, my Pacific Bliss. Do you read me?*

I hereby take back every bad word I said the last three days, when you were chuggin' it out, barely making progress against a 20-knot headwind. My body still feels bruised and battered from the ordeal, but you tried your best. Today, however, was your day to shine! Proudly flying your Spinnaker of Many Colors, making 8-10 knots in a 15-18 knot breeze on a beam reach, you showed us what a splendid Cruisin' Cat can do. With the long, rolling waves of the Atlantic sweeping under the wind-generated wavelets and whitecaps, you rocked and rolled us into bliss. As the sun emerged from a cloud-laden firmament to greet you in all your splendor, your adoring crew rejoiced and lolled on your trampoline, captivated by your charm. You are cookin' right along to the Islas de Canaries, and your instruments say that we just may make it by Sunday morning. Bless me with more days like this, and I will sail with you across the Big Pond just fine!

2300: *Night fell upon us. We reluctantly took down your spinnaker. We reined you in for the safety of your Night Riders. Yet you continued to gallop onward, your 60-foot high main and genoa stretching to reach the stars. Now, as the wind pushes you on from your right rear flank, it flattens your whitened wings, trimmed for racing to the Canaries. You are a winged stallion, galloping through the night, flying between the sea and the heavens, touching them both, but belonging to neither. Will you stay on the planet or will you rise up into the stars as another Orion? Please, please stay with us. We like you now.*

Over and out.

Sleepwalking in Tenerife

Out of the purple dawn, a charcoal mountain rises from the rolling navy sea. We have reached the island of Tenerife in the Canary Islands. Methodically, I navigate us into the harbor and the visitor dock of Marina Atlántico. My duties done, the guys tend to the lines, while I crash into my berth below, exhausted.

"Lois…Lois," Günter's pleading voice breaks through the dense fog of my deep sleep. I try to respond but my dreams pull me back, rising and falling like the ocean waves of the past six days. Gentle tugs pull my leaden legs, nudging me off the master bunk. "You don't need to change, just come as you are. Here, hold my hand."

A waitress breaks through the fog. "And what would *you* like?" Günter pokes me in the ribs. I come to with a start. A long rectangular table set in a tropical décor gradually comes into focus. A late afternoon sun beams through paned and curtained windows. Günter is staring at me, concern clouding his face. Gottfried and Christian are seated to my left. At the other end of the table is our Atlantic crossing crew: Anne, Georg, and Maria. They are staring a hole into me as big as a cannonball. Gradually, they come into focus: Georg with his broad shoulders and rounded face, Anne with her pixie face and punk haircut, and Maria with her shoulder-length mane of golden blonde.

I lower my head to see a folded menu with a bird of paradise on the cover, unopened on the center of my plate. "I'll have what *he* ordered." I point to Günter.

Where am I? I sense an embarrassed flush rising from my neck toward my cheeks as the two crews return to animated conversation. *The last thing I remember is leaving my bunk on Pacific Bliss, holding Günter's hand. I must have sleepwalked to this place, which has to be at least a mile from the docks of Marina Atlántico, up the hill to the streets of Santa Cruz. This has never happened to me before. It feels weird and scary. I never want it to happen again.*

Everyone is still talking, so I retreat back into my thoughts. *Could this be the result of sleep deprivation these past days? Here, in Tenerife, with this new crew, something's gotta give. I need to change my ways, and I realize that I cannot do it all. I need to delegate.*

Beginning NOW.

A rainbow appears in the horizon, approaching Tenerife.

Old ship dock in Mindelo, Sao Vincente, Cape Verde.

Chapter 5

Crossing the Big Pond: The Canary and Cape Verde Islands and on to St. Lucia

A Quick Turnaround in Tenerife

The next morning, I'm ready to delegate. As I clear the breakfast dishes from the cockpit table, our Atlantic crossing crew appears at the dock with their duffels, eager to settle in. Günter and Gottfried are already busy at the nav station solving numerous mechanical and electrical problems.

"You take care of all the provisioning." Günter looks up from the multi-meter. "Just maybe we can turn around this bucket in two days, since our crew has already been here for a while, cooling their heels."

My sleepwalking "wake-up call" has taught me well. After the crew exchange is complete, I seat everyone in the salon for their orders. This time, I will fall back on the management skills developed through a 35-year business career. Mission: to cross the Atlantic. Strategy: to provision for three weeks, even though the crossing should be accomplished in two. Tactics: Appoint one crew member responsible for each task. Delegate, delegate, delegate!

"Who volunteers to be the master chef?"

Georg confidently raises his thick hand.

"Okay. You will make out a shopping list of food to last three weeks. Then, as head chef, you will be in charge of all the meal planning. When you cook, I want you to appoint a sous chef to help you. And if you don't want to cook, you appoint someone else to take your place."

"I'll be your number one back-up, Georg," volunteers Maria, tossing her flaxen hair as she turns toward him.

I nod my approval, maintaining control of the meeting.

"Who wants to be in charge of the money?" I continue. I take a plastic box down from behind the microwave. "This small, red box will henceforth be called *the kitty*." No one volunteers, so I appoint one. "Anne, you're the Controller. Okay?"

She agrees.

"Whoever cooks, doesn't clean up. This is the rule. We'll have our safety briefing before we leave port. When that is will depend on how fast our captain and skipper can troubleshoot and repair. That's all."

Georg makes out the list and everyone takes off in different directions, to the fresh foods market, the grocery store, and the butcher. "And where will you go?" Maria asks as she turns to leave.

"I intend to de-compress, then work on the watch schedules for our passage."

Underway to the Cape Verdes

The boat becomes a madhouse. There is no time left for touring Tenerife. But after two days of frenzied provisioning, packing, and repairs, we are underway. With the captain, skipper, three crew members, and me, plus organization galore, this passage will be easy, with plenty of time to sleep between watches.

I discover there is also time to read. So, I continue to fuel my fascination with ancient navigators. These days, we have the benefit of navigating with both paper and electronic charts. But for those intrepid mariners, no charts existed for "The All-Encompassing Sea." If they were to lose sight of the coast, they would be hard put to return to it. Many a family waved good-bye to husbands, fathers, and sons—never to see them again.

"The surface of this sea is also covered with

The crew provisions and packs for the next leg of the journey.

mist, which prevents ships from making their way… therefore it is difficult to lay a course for the Eternal Isles and find out more about them." Shortly after Ibn Khaldun wrote this passage, and largely as a result of the discovery of the Canary Islands, the Portuguese and Spanish sailors learned how to use the current and wind patterns of the Atlantic to reach destinations across open seas. The Ottoman naval officer Piri Reis, a practical sailor himself, quickly realized the significance of these findings and was one of the first to describe the wind systems of the Atlantic. The technique was called the *volta da mar*, "sea turn," and went against reason, for it meant sailing well to the northwest of the Canaries in order to pick up the easterlies and return home. This discovery made Atlantic navigation, far out of sight of land, possible.

As navigator of *Pacific Bliss*, I find historical information like this particularly intriguing, and I realize that cruising is an ongoing education.

Trade Winds and Tropics
Catch a falling star and put it in your pocket,
Save it for a rainy day.
Catch a falling star and put it in your pocket,
Never let it fade away…

During my early morning watch of December 2, I follow two falling stars, humming this song by Cat Stevens. I won't make a wish, though; I'll just hold it in my memory. Because, heading out of the Strait, on the way to the Canaries, I saw *three* falling stars, and I wished very hard for fair winds—anywhere but on the nose—and those wishes were scrupulously ignored. Now, ironically, 400-plus miles south of the Canaries, what I wanted then is finally granted.

The fair winds began gradually two days ago, a light Force 2-3, varying from 5-10 knots, from the ENE. Wispy, fragile-looking fragments had appeared on the southern horizon as the sun set. "These little wimpy clouds forecast the trade winds?" I asked.

"Yes," said Gottfried, who had crossed the Atlantic before. "That is what they look like. By tomorrow, we'll be in the trades."

Sure enough. The dawn begins almost imperceptibly. The brushed steel of the rolling sea is only slightly darker than the sky. Millions of stars fade until only the brightest persist. In the east, a twinge of lighter gray appears. And, later, streaks of pale orange. Feeble wisps float in the break between the light gray and orange.

Pacific Bliss rolls gently with the Atlantic swell, but the sea has turned choppy now, in a nice sort of way. Scattered whitecaps break into gray-white foam, melting like the topping on a cup of hot cappuccino.

We continue sailing wing-on-wing (one sail on each side), under a full main and genoa, pushed along by a breeze increasing to Force 5. The damp sea air brushes against my neck and cheek as I sit at the helm, allowing the autopilot—our invisible helmsman—to do all the work. I smack my lips, tasting the warm salt air. Yes, the trade winds have finally arrived.

Since when have I watched such a special sunrise that lasts this long? Certainly never on land!

The show begins at 0630. By 0730, the entire dome surrounding our self-contained world has turned from black to bluish-gray. At 0745, while a low gray haze rims the eastern horizon, the western horizon rolls up a curtain of pale fuchsia—the opening act. Ten minutes later, the sun takes a tentative, teasing peek at her audience. Then suddenly, she flames out of the sea in robes of splendor, enveloping Anne, who is now at the helm, in her golden glow.

At 0900, a school of dolphins joins the performance. One dolphin couple commandeers the port hull; another takes the starboard; their children weave back and forth in between. They turn to take a look at us, then continue to dance, jump, and dive. Suddenly, as if following a secret command, they all disappear in unison, darting off across the Big Pond.

The trades, the sunrise, the dolphins…this is surely another Moment of Bliss. Later this day, we cross the Tropic of Cancer, located 23.5° (about 1400 nautical miles) north of the equator. On June 21, which is the summer solstice in the Northern Hemisphere, the noon sun will be directly overhead at this latitude. At no other place north of where we are will this occur.

"Let's toast to the tropics!" Maria says.

Günter acquiesces and opens a bottle of red wine.

The crew decides to treat Poseidon to a splash, just for good measure.

"As long as it's just a teaser," says Günter. "When we cross the equator during our Voyage Two next year, there we'll sacrifice some Champagne, as custom demands."

"To the tropics," we all toast.

Cruiser Nets
During this passage to Cape Verde, I become familiar and comfortable with the radio. We have designated a specific SSB (single side-band) radio frequency and specific times for communication with our fellow Catana cruisers, *Enduring Echoes* and *Traveler*. This is called a Cruisers' Net. Such Nets are typically given a name. Intense discussions ensue about calling our net *The Catana Whiners Net*. But with everyone on all three ships having such a great time sailing, whining is not in order. We decide to name our Net after Ron, the sailor who endeared himself to the French women by offering the red wine, during our christening party. So the *Vin Rouge Net* it is. Before long, other vessels

1. Flying fish on the net; 2. Lois makes an offering of Vin Rouge to King Neptune upon entering the Tropics.

64

crossing the Atlantic listen in and ask to join our Net.

We give our positions every morning and evening and brag about how many miles and how fast we have sailed. At one point, the *Pacific Bliss* logbook entry says: "15.6 knots with spinnaker flying." With that log at 2334 total miles since France, our "Trip Miles" readout shows that we have sailed 851 miles from the Canaries. Happily for us, the trades have made fast work of the first leg of our Atlantic crossing.

Mindelo: Our Introduction to the Cape Verdes
December 6

Sao Vicente looms mysteriously out of the sea like a dark, drab, newly formed island, where flora has yet to take hold. We anchor in Porto Grande, the large harbor of the capital city, Mindelo. Then we all pile into *Petit Bliss* to head for shore. Compared to the Canaries, this is like entering another world. Although the harbor hosts an occasional cruise ship, it has clearly known more prosperous times. Old ships lie rusted at the foot of two extinct volcanoes; signs of decay are everywhere. These ten volcanic islands (and five islets), 350 miles off the coast of West Africa, were uninhabited until the Portuguese discovered them in 1456. Then African slaves were brought here to work on plantations. Finally in 1975, the country gained its independence from Portugal.

As we walk into the city, I can see why my guidebook flaunts Mindelo as the cultural center of the archipelago. The streets are lively, with plenty of cafés and restaurants to choose from. We stop to admire a series of raised relief murals of musicians, guitars in hand, decorating a stucco wall leading to the main square. I talk with an artist at a gallery, which has a remarkable display of contemporary oils of people at work and play. We shop for souvenirs, finding that most of them come from Senegal and Dakar. Günter selects a wild shirt with streaks and flames and the word UPRISING in bold letters across the front.

We amble past buildings with a Moorish flair, their walls covered with frayed election posters blowing in the arid wind. I recall what we've learned about Cape Verde's turbulent past: The transition back to democracy has been complicated by a civil war and the military's predilection for meddling in government affairs, crippling the economy. In 1994, a full 20 years after the country fought for independence from Portugal, the first elections were finally held. Just two years ago, in 1998, an army uprising triggered the Guinea-Bissau Civil War, which created hundreds of thousands of displaced persons. The President was ousted by a military junta on May 7, 1999. An interim government turned over power in February this year when opposition leader Kumba Ialá took office following two rounds of free and fair presidential elections. The press is free and the State now respects the rule of law. In fact, Freedom House

City Hall, Mindelo, Cape Verde.

acknowledged this by granting Cape Verde a perfect score in its annual *Freedom in the World* report—the only African country to receive such an honor.

The primary task of the evening is to choose a restaurant. We settle on the one recommended by the marina. Even in English, it is difficult to identify the local food, with names like hominy and samp, catchupa, xerem, kuskus, and carne gizado.

Cape Verde's cooking traditions have been shaped by the combination of a dry, tropical island environment and Portugal's 15th century colonization. African slaves who worked the sugar cane fields brought knowledge of growing and cooking tropical crops. The Portuguese brought livestock. They used Cape Verde for feeding the crews of their sailing ships and as an experimental station for growing foods from the Americas, such as corn, hot peppers, pumpkins, and cassava. In addition, they transplanted sugar, bananas, mangos, papayas, and other tropical crops from Asia. That made for quite a varied cuisine. The Cape Verdeans use a lot of dried corn, either whole kernels (hominy/samp) or ground to various degrees of fineness. *Catchupa* is the national dish, sort of a stew of hominy and beans cooked with fish or meat. *Xerem* is dried corn pounded with a mortar into the fineness of rice. *Kuskus* is ground finer still and steamed in a distinctive ceramic pot called a *binde*. A special treat is kuskus served hot with butter and milk (*kuskus ku leite*) or molasses (*kuskus ku mel*).

During dinner, I propose an idea: Since Sao Vicente has turned out to be so arid, I really want to see the lush Santo Antao. I am met with 100% opposition by captain and crew.

"But we could leave here early in the morning, have the day to tour, stay overnight there, and take off the next morning. Just one day! Wouldn't you all want to see some sweeping mountain landscapes and lush green meadows before tackling all that blue?"

"We'll make above-average time on the crossing anyway, with the good weather forecast," adds Captain Günter, wisely deciding to taking my side.

Eventually, I manage to convince the crew.

We find our own Shangri-La
Porto Novo, Santo Antao, Cape Verde
17° N, 25° W

The shrillness of the alarm knifes the predawn stillness this December 7, Pearl Harbor Day. It will now be remembered in our own personal history as the day we discovered Shangri-la.

Our tea kettle whistles insistently, meaning Günter has already turned on the propane and is now ready to plunge the French Press. The pungent aroma of coffee propels us out of our berths. Once on deck, our crew moves silently, as if we are *sneaking* out of port. We loosen the thick, black, dock lines from our berth alongside Brossman's steel hulk, the mother ship where we safely spent the evening. Then, we slide out of the Porto Grande harbor as the first rays of the sun rise over Mindelo's Moorish-looking municipal building. In the early morning light, the scene is dramatically different from the strange new harbor we piloted with such difficulty during our arrival at twilight.

As we pass the channel's lighthouse, I plot the compass course for Anne, who is hand-steering at the helm. The three men spend the eight-mile passage redoing the anchor chain, which had become tangled in the anchor locker.

Entropy. The same scientific principle that tangles Christmas tree lights.

We three women (Anne, Maria, and I) are navigating and steering for a change. Anne has become quite comfortable with our high-tech catamaran, a far cry from the basic monohull she sailed when cruising the Caribbean in the '70s. Maria had sailed many charters with Gottfried, but had blindly followed his commands without understanding the process. Now she is learning sailing on her own.

We make our way across the channel, looking back occasionally to enjoy the sun rising over Porto Grande. Later, as we pull into the little harbor of Porto Novo, 30 to 40 islanders are standing on the mole, watching us.

We'll be besieged by vendors as in Tangier. My concerns prove unwarranted. Yes, taxi drivers and guides are looking for business. But the rest of the onlookers are just curious. Many of them are waiting for the ferry to Porto Grande; most likely, they work in Mindelo. The mole, a high concrete structure designed to shelter the tiny harbor from strong, north winds, is rudimentary with cracks and chips in the concrete, but looks strong. Most of the space in the harbor is reserved for the ferry to stop and turn, and there's little room to navigate, but we manage to squeeze carefully in front of a small fishing boat. This gets us against the high mole, where we arrange dock and spring lines and position our fenders against a row of black tires.

One of the guides who has been watching us approaches our boat. Kyky is a small, dark, and handsome Cape Verdean who speaks four languages: English, German, French, and Portuguese, in addition to the local Creole. He negotiates a six-hour tour of the island with us. We wonder: Should we hire a watchman for the boat? The *policio*, who clears us through in less than half an hour, tells us, "Kyky is a good choice. He is a licensed Cape Verdean guide." Then he explains that hiring a watchman is not an option; it is required.

Günter hires Kyky's cousin to stand watch. We

DID YOU KNOW?

CANARY ISLANDS

The cities of Santa Cruz de Tenerife and Las Palmas de Gran Canaria share the status as the capital city. The rivalry between the elites of the two cities led to the division of the archipelago into two provinces in 1927. This has not laid to rest the rivalry between the two cities, which continues to this day. The seat of the Presidency of the government alternates between the two capitals according to parliamentary session. The third city of the Canary Islands is San Cristóbal de La Laguna, a world heritage site, on the island of Tenerife. These islands, 100 miles west of Africa, have been part of Spain since 1479. As such, they are also part of the EU but are outside of the European VAT (Value Added Tax) area.

Nelson gave his right arm to be on Tenerife. In July 1797, the English naval hero, Rear Admiral Horatio Nelson, attacked the harbor at Tenerife's capital, Santa Cruz, in an attempt to capture the island from Spain. During the ensuing skirmish, Nelson took some shrapnel in his right elbow and had to quit the battlefield to have the limb amputated. This was Nelson's only defeat in battle and, grateful for the humane treatment his men received following their surrender, he dispatched a barrel of English ale and cheese to the victorious General Gűtiérrez. In return, Gűtiérrez sent Nelson a barrel of Malmsey wine, at that time considered to be the finest wine in the world.

Nelson's most famous victory was also his undoing: At Trafalgar he was mortally wounded on the deck of his ship HMS Victory. Because of the distance from Trafalgar to England, Nelson's body was placed in a cask of brandy to preserve it for the trip.

Admiral Nelson

Very few cruisers visit the Cape Verdes in their haste to cross the Big Pond. What a pity! In their eagerness to join the ARC (the Atlantic Rally for Cruisers) to cross the Atlantic, they miss out on a great opportunity to take an invigorating stop along the way and to enjoy a friendly and unique culture.

The mystical mountain peaks and dramatic valleys of Santo Antao—with their forests of pine, eucalyptus, and cypress, provide a verdant feast for the eyes before a return to the azure color palette of the seas.

Our Atlantic crossing crew in Ribiera Grand, Santo Antao, Günter, George, Maria, Gottfried, and Anne, with our guide Kyky.

lock all the doors, windows, exterior storage areas, and then invite our watchman into the cockpit, to the envy of the other villagers looking on. We leave him there for this important job with a Coke and two liters of water. Taking care of the new visitors and their catamaran becomes a town event. The villagers are friendly but not pushy. As in Mindelo, every Cape Verdean we meet greets us with a wide, happy smile.

The villagers wave and grin as we bump along through the cobblestone streets, six of us seated on the two wooden benches in the back of Kyky's red Toyota truck—touring style, complete with roll bars on top. Our interest is to move through this port town quickly—since, according to the Cape Verde *Bradt Travel Guide*, there is not much to see here—then up the mountain road north and across the pass to Vila de Ribeira Grande on the north shore.

As the cobblestone road pulls away from Porto Novo, we bounce on past the depressing outskirts of the town where the inhabitants endure savage, sand-laden winds from the Sahara. The road rises through a brown, barren landscape where houses are few and far between. What painstaking patience these road-builders must have had! Each stone has been laid by hand. Here, even the sides are built up with cobblestones. The land itself begins to take on a desolate appearance reminding me of the Badlands in South Dakota.

A distinct chill tinges the air as we continue to climb. Small bushes line the road; before long, the pale yellow blossoms of acacia trees come into view. Rows of rock and stone, in perfect order, terrace the slopes. Every section shows the caring touch of a human hand—even in this difficult terrain. Sheep, imported during centuries past, grazed off the slopes, causing topsoil to vanish. But terracing now in place contains rainwater and prevents further erosion.

Just when I begin to think, *This is as beautiful as I expected; this is Santo Antao,* the road climbs higher, and the view becomes even more spectacular. Forest plantations of sugar cane begin to fill the higher valleys. We pass charming villages and old, deserted stone dwellings. Then we realize that all this is only the foothills. The mountain peaks in the clouds are still to come!

On and up we go, the Toyota lurching around hairpin turns, until we reach the clouds. We are surrounded by pine, cypress, and eucalyptus trees. I pound on the cab of the truck, as Kyky told me to do when I want to stop. I can't resist taking another photo of the incredible vistas expanding above and below. That done, we continue along the cobblestone road. It skates the ridges near the top, and suddenly comes to a Y. Kyky turns off the engine, pops out of the truck, and strides back.

"You walk down this dirt road," he says. "Then I come pick you up. We go down mountain the other way."

We all get out of the truck, happy to stretch our legs, and stroll down the road. It is a charming walk in the mountain forests, with new sights and sheer rock drops at every bend.

Then we arrive at the spot I'm sure Kyky meant for us to see: a huge plain, squared with agriculture plots of yellow and green, like a patchwork quilt dropped into the middle of the mountains, its corners climbing the sides. We are looking down into Cova Crater, so our guidebook says. But we have already re-named it Shangri-La.

We follow the winding road down and down into the crater, awestruck by the sheer cliffs on one side and the peaceful agrarian scene below. Cows, goats, and mules graze the lush grass. Workers till the fields using hand tools, farming in the ways of centuries past. I understand: It would probably have been impossible to transport farm equipment up these steep mountain slopes. As I kneel down to take a photo, I fall into a bed of fragile, dainty white flowers with the aroma of mint. I sit there, my senses saturated. It is another Moment of Bliss.

I continue to walk among colors. They range from forest green to silvery blue. The mountain breeze brushes my face with the sharp, fragrant smells and tastes of pine and eucalyptus. Still in sensory overload, I am enjoying every minute in the here and now. I will *never* forget how it feels to inhale this special place into every fiber of my being.

Suddenly a torrent of noise shatters the serenity. Kyky races his truck in a cloud of dust along the dirt road and screeches to a halt. "We have even more vistas in store," he tells us. "We have not yet reached Pica da Cruz, the top of the mountain."

Bouncing along in the back of the truck again, we fly around hairpin turns. Sheer drops on both sides. Plunging waterfalls. Rushing brooks in the valleys. More sharp bends that take my breath away. Pinnacles and spires of rock. Small villages clinging precariously to the mountainsides. The view keeps racing by. I am enthralled with the majesty of this place. At the top, rounded and domed mountain peaks in the mist, falling to verdant valleys below, transport me into the Orient—reminding me of the enigmatic art of China and Japan. But hours have flown swiftly and we must leave this Shangri-La behind. It is time to return to reality.

We descend the winding road at breakneck speed. Far below, the Atlantic stretches before us, this time to the north of the island, since we are now driving down the other side of the mountain. Before long, we see the thatched stone houses that make up the town of Ribeira Grande. We skirt around myriad dwellings, and drop—down, down, down into the town.

Kyky parks the truck. We stroll along the dusty

Torn election posters at city hall.

main street, intent on locating the local Post Office to mail a final batch of postcards, our last chance before sailing across the Atlantic. Our duty done, we hike alongside the muddy *ribeira* for which the town is named, until it lazily sloshes into the sea. We find the beach disappointing—black-and-dirty volcanic sand. The vegetable and fruit market we discover on the way back proves interesting, however, now that we know about the crops grown here. But the lowlands are hot and we are grateful to cool off with beers in the local bar. Meanwhile, Kyky arranges for a family style meal of typical island dishes to be made especially for our group. After we are seated at the lone table, we try a little of each. One hot dish, called *jag*, is a staple of the island and easy to make: One needs only rice, beans, and onions. The cook throws it into a pot and lets it stew for three hours. The result tastes delicious.

The conversation roams from food to art and music. "Do you know the songs of Cesaria Evora?" Kyky asks me.

"No, should I?"

"Absolutely! She is a famous singer, known throughout the world. Especially in Africa. She is loved by all Cape Verdeans. She, who came from here."

Kyky goes on to talk about the life of Cesaria and her haunting *mornos*, mournful songs. The singer was born in Mindelo and lived most of her first 50 years on the island of São Vicente. In 1985, a Cape Verdean women's organization asked her to record two songs for a compilation CD. She went to Paris to record and, while there, presented some concerts. Her success in Europe was nothing short of phenomenal. She packed houses in Paris in which other African divas could only dream of playing. After hearing her story, I am determined to buy one of her albums. "We don't have any here to sell," says Kyky. "Please understand, we don't see tourists so very much."

The drive back is long, breathtaking, and nerve-wracking—as Kyky guns his truck and races up the mountain and over the top. *Best to close one's eyes and pretend to sleep rather than watch.* The truck barrels down the Porto Novo side of the mountain as dusk descends.

"There's *Pacific Bliss*!" Günter cries out. She still dominates the small square harbor. She sits there safe as can be, surrounded by the locals. Our original fears about her being damaged or stolen were unfounded.

> "Let the words of my mouth, and the meditation of my heart, be acceptable in thy sight, O LORD, my strength, and my redeemer."
> Psalm 19:14
>
> "Meditation and water are melded forever."
> Herman Melville

The Meditation of My Heart
December 11
They say that sailing is 90% boredom and 10%

> "The heavens declare the glory of God and the firmament showeth his handiwork."
> Psalm 19:1

sheer terror. Perhaps I had been too busy to reach that boredom part before. Now with a full crew, only one three-hour watch at night, sufficient sleep, and endless days of rolling seas ahead, I begin to relax and let go.

They also say that the first time a sailor crosses a large ocean, his or her entire life flashes by in slow motion. It's the same phenomenon many experience when skydiving, falling from a tall building, or dying. My third night at sea, crossing the Atlantic, it happens to me…

I have intentionally assigned myself to the sunrise watch for our sail across the Atlantic. The sun peeks through the cloud cover, its rays spread wide like a gigantic fan palm, reminding me of my Sunday School days as a child. I remember opening the workbook to my favorite graphic, the creation sunrise, with the caption underneath: "The heavens declare the glory of God."

As the sky turns to bright blue and the gray clouds lighten to puffs of white cotton, I search for animals I might find there. Again, I am thrown back to my childhood, this time to the pasture of our family farm in Wisconsin. I loiter along the way as I fetch the cows in for milking. Pal, our German shepherd, points at my heels, eager to begin the roundup. I feel guilty about sneaking time for such pleasure, yet I lie down under the spreading oak with my head on a flat stone. Soon I am daydreaming about the fluffy lambs and puppies living up there in Heaven.

Occasionally, my daydreams under the azure Atlantic sky turn to other times, not so pleasant: a 20-something mother, struggling to raise and support two pre-school children who would never see their father again; a career woman, juggling stressful management positions, with teenagers in a newly combined family. Oh, the pressure! There were never enough hours in the day.

But it is the flashbacks during the night dreams that bring on the panic, the sensation of falling, of dying…

I am easily lulled to sleep, rolling to the long Atlantic waves in the bosom of my berth. After a few hours, I bolt upright. My heart is pounding again, just like during that fateful Board of Directors meeting when Günter and I were ousted from the biotech company we had built. My chest hurts with that same stabbing pain. For weeks after the coup, I had suffered these symptoms of a pierced and breaking heart. I thought that period was over. Wrong. Now it is flashing back. Stabbing and jabbing for three nights in a row.

I think back to what we could have done differently. We could have stayed and sued. In fact, we did consult with an attorney right after we were told to leave. Our attorney won some minor concessions, such as two days to clear out our offices (versus immediately) and adjustments to our stock option plans. However, reversing the coup promised to be a long, hard struggle. We could have pushed for the return of at least some of our patents. I had one granted and two pending, and Günter had over one hundred granted and dozens pending, all signed over to the company prior to raising venture capital and taking it public. But instead of digging in and fighting, we had opted to escape. *Was this the right decision? Or are we just wimps? What about those cancer patients now in clinical trials? Will the new management maintain our commitment to extend their lives and their quality of life?*

The next night I have another of these nightmares. This time little pins are pricking me, all over my body. I wake up feeling as if I'd been sleeping on a bed of nails.

During the afternoon, Günter and I retreat to the trampoline, away from the crew. We sit there silently, watching the sun reflect the spinnaker's rainbow hues onto the solar panels. I feel particularly close to him, so I divulge my nightmares.

He confides that he hasn't gotten over it either. "Those pricks? They were the points of sharp knives, of course. *Et tu, Brute…*" he pauses for effect. "Yes, the bankers and the Board got greedy and power hungry, but it wouldn't have happened without a traitor inside the palace gates. We both trusted our veep. And he turned on us."

"Do you think we did the right thing—leaving?"

"Of course. I don't ever want to see their faces again."

"That reminds me. Remember when we went for our first round of venture capital?

You explained how our technology was a breakthrough in treating cancer and other diseases at the cellular level? How you were pioneering something that had never been done before?"

"I know where you're going…I remember it well… One V.C. told us rather sarcastically, 'Pioneers are the ones who get arrows in their back.'"

"But he invested anyway."

"Lot of good it did. I wonder what will happen to the company now."

I reach for Günter's hand and squeeze it tight. "I care more about what will happen to *us*."

Moon Shadow, Moon Shadow
15° N, 38° W, the Mid-Atlantic

I enjoy the most glorious moonrise on my 2000-2300 evening watch. The moon appears early in the evening, a few hours after sunset, rising out of the eastern horizon to my stern—a full, ripe, golden orange. As clouds sweep up from the horizon, the moon peeks out gradually, turning the surrounding clouds to amber

DID YOU KNOW?

CAPE VERDE

The population represents varying degrees of African and Portuguese heritage. They are extremely proud of their country, which has the highest degree of democracy of all of Africa.

The unit of currency is the Cape Verde escudo (CVE), divided into 100 centavos. It's not a hard currency, but it's stable; in January 2002, it was pegged to the euro.

A thriving cricket team exists in Mindelo, a legacy of British influence in the 19th Century. Cape Verde played a major role in the slave trade because of its unique position, which is midway between Europe, Africa, and America and faces the Slave Coast of Africa. It is one of the crossroads in transatlantic navigation and the triangular trade that developed at the time of its discovery in the 15th century. It soon became an entrepôt that was used for some four centuries.

Life has never been easy in these islands. For centuries, isolation and cyclical drought resulted in famine. Generations of Cape Verdeans have been forced to emigrate, leaving those at home wracked by sodade, the deep longing that fills the music of singer and national heroine, Cesária Évora. Half of Cape Verdeans live far from this beautiful archipelago their ancestors once called home. Their remittances home make up a big part of the island's income.

While hunger is no longer a threat, you need only glance at the terraced hillsides baking in the sun to understand that every bean, every grain of corn, is precious.

Cesária Évora

Our halfway masquerade party. Lois as the Queen, Günter as the King of Garbage, Chef Georg, Maria as Amphitrite, Anne, the fisher, and Gottfried as Poseidon.

brown, then hides again. This hide-and-seek game continues as I sit, fascinated, in my favorite perch at the starboard helm. Orion's bright belt twinkles at me from the southeastern sky. (By now, I know that Orion will continue racing toward the northwest throughout the night, escaping from the sharp stings of Scorpion.)

Finally freed of the clouds, the moon casts its spell over *Pacific Bliss* and her crew. It lights a long, wide path down from the horizon directly to our stern, right into the open doors of the salon. The crests of waves sparkle in the moonglow. The swish-swish of the water in our wake and the sighing of the east wind become the serenade of the sea. *Pacific Bliss* is an ethereal ghost ship, pulled by her moonlit spinnaker.

As if bored with all of this, the East Wind begins to play, gusting to Force 6, filling the spinnaker, pushing the boat forward, then slacking off again. I ride high on nature's rollercoaster as she picks up speed, sometimes up to 13 knots, surfing down the long swells of the Atlantic.

Anne comes up to take over the watch. I leave the cockpit humming another tune by Cat Stevens, *Moon Shadow*: *I'm being followed by a moon shadow. Moon shadow. Moon shadow...I won't have to cry no more.*

Normally, I would have gone to bed after my watch, but I am so overwhelmed with the awesome power of God's creation that I want to learn more. I stay awake reading *Show Me God: What the Message from Space Is Telling Us about God,* by Fred Heeren.

"According to the findings of 20th century physics, matter and anti-matter must have been produced in equal amounts in any conversion of energy into mass associated with the creation event. But this forces physicists to acknowledge yet another finely tuned parameter to bring about our habitable universe. Particles of matter must have slightly outnumbered particles of antimatter by an extremely critical amount…a precise selection was made."

To think that our universe is so precariously balanced between expansion and collapse that the most minute deviation on either side after the Big Bang would have consigned it into oblivion! There had to be an expansion force that prohibited the universe from crashing back into itself early in the expansion, yet enough gravitational force so that matter could be collected into galaxies rather than dispersed into gases.

Shivers run up my spine as I continue to read. In the words of Princeton physicist Freeman Dyson: "The more I examine the universe and the details of its architecture, the more evidence I find that the universe… must have known we were coming."

And NASA astronomer John O'Keefe echoes the thought: "It is my view that these circumstances indicate that the Universe was created for man to live in."

Even our own San Diegan Nobel Laureate, Francis Crick, known for cracking the genetic code, well respected in that biotech world that had consumed Günter and me, once wrote: "An honest man, armed with all the knowledge available to us now, could only state that in some sense, the origin of life appears at the moment to be almost a miracle, so many are the conditions which would have been satisfied to get it going."

All that preparation—for *us!*

I look up from my book and back toward the salon doors. The moon shadow still follows us. Just think about all the purposeful choices that were made to bring about this wonderful creation of ours! Yes, a day is as a thousand years to God, and a thousand years are like a day. Yet the Old Testament prophesies that "the heavens will wear out like a garment."

Amazing! The farther we look into space, the further we look backward into time. And the more *I* look into space, the more I realize how insignificant, yet significant, I am. In this night of sailing beneath the stars, I come to realize that all of the eternity past has been anticipating these few moments in time that I am now experiencing.

There is a real purpose for my being on this planet. Maybe it wasn't to help bring a new medical technology to market. Maybe it wasn't to help those cancer patients. Maybe it is something else that I need to find out. Or could it be that I have already achieved my purpose? Whatever. My life, being here in the middle of the Atlantic right now, is an incredibly rare gift.

This night, I have no nightmares.

We're Halfway There! The Madness Masquerade
December 14
15° 14.5'N, 45° W

We promised our crew a halfway party to break up the crossing of the Atlantic. We've told them only that the theme will be "Madness Masquerade." It will consist of a ceremony, followed by a cocktail party. The crew will have to devise their own original costumes. I've been watching Georg caress the fruits every day, deciding which spoiled ones to toss overboard. He has taken his Master Chef assignment seriously. During the past two night watches, with never another ship in sight, he has been agonizing over what delicious hors d'oeuvres he can make for our party. I've set some treats aside in the Queen's Bilge, a compartment underneath the floorboards on the master (starboard) side. We had set the time for 3:00 p.m.

This, according to our ship's log, will be the day!

Gottfried has requested that we make this a special ceremony—like the one that would usually occur when crossing the equator. Now, he is Poseidon—god of the sea, the storms, and protector of fishermen—dressed in

Each of us puts our right foot up on the table and makes a statement, as the ancient navigators did after they'd crossed an ocean.

a drape of regal blue (or is that one of our guest bed sheets?). He stands at the mast of *Pacific Bliss,* braced with an unusual staff (our boat hook), which has a cardboard fish speared lengthwise on top. Amphitrite, Poseidon's wife, looking like an angel with her long golden hair, stands faithfully by his side, near the saltwater pump, draped in paler blue (aha, another bed sheet!).

"You will come to the middle of the net one-by-one," Poseidon commands. "The captain will be first."

Günter dutifully sits in front of Poseidon, his head bowed. The deity dumps a bucket of salt water over his head. Next, he takes a white brush (of dubious origin), dips it the remaining salt water, and sprinkles it on Günter's soaked locks. "I hereby christen you *Captain Günter of Pacific Bliss,*" he pronounces.

Next, I am called to the middle of the net. I plead with Poseidon not to give the bucket-on-the-head treatment. My pleas are honored. I receive only the half-body splash, while Gottfried says, "I hereby christen you *Lois, Ocean Navigator of Pacific Bliss."*

Next, Georg, who gets the full-bucket-on-the-head treatment, is christened "*Master Chef of Pacific Bliss.*"

Anne receives the half-body treatment, but her christening is special because Poseidon says, "I hereby christen you *Anne the Fisher.*" Then, handing her the cardboard fish, he intones, "We have not caught any fish thus far. You must change our luck."

After the ceremony, the crew has 20 minutes to re-assemble in costume. Anne created a hat from her Christmas decorations, soon to be put to other uses in our two Advent observances. Captain Günter appears, wrapped in a big plastic trash bag and looking like Darth Vader, but now claiming to be *King of the Garbage*. Georg has donned a chef's apron over his bare chest, along with a tinfoil hat. Gottfried and Maria are still swathed in the sheets.

I, *The Queen of Boabdil*, of Alhambra fame, revived from my sleep and still reminiscing about the 9th century, arrive from my chambers in the starboard hull wearing my Moroccan caftan and carrying a pillow inscribed: "IT'S GOOD TO BE QUEEN." I inform my subjects that the Queen's Stores hold more food—including tuna and Fruits de la Mer—just in case the power of Anne the Fisher fails to provide those elusive fish.

Georg had promised a meal of "just a few special tapas" to go with the champagne—brought all the way from France, thanks to Jeanne and John. Our chef has labored all day to prepare these Spanish appetizers. He admits even to dreaming about tapas all last night, as well as the night before. We devour the contents of two appetizer trays containing *jamon* and cheese from Spain and olives from France. Then he surprises us with a veritable feast! Georg sets out a tray of cucumbers and tomatoes, *and* two bowls of chilled garlic-and-oil mashed potato salad, *and* two kinds of fruit cocktail (one with blue cheese) and, *finally*, warm toast squares brushed with olive oil.

Here, in the mid-Atlantic, we are having a rollicking halfway party. We brag about how fortunate we have been to experience such an easy crossing, with never another boat in sight! But, suddenly, "Look! Over there!" Günter points. (Günter had just left the table as the clean-up began.)

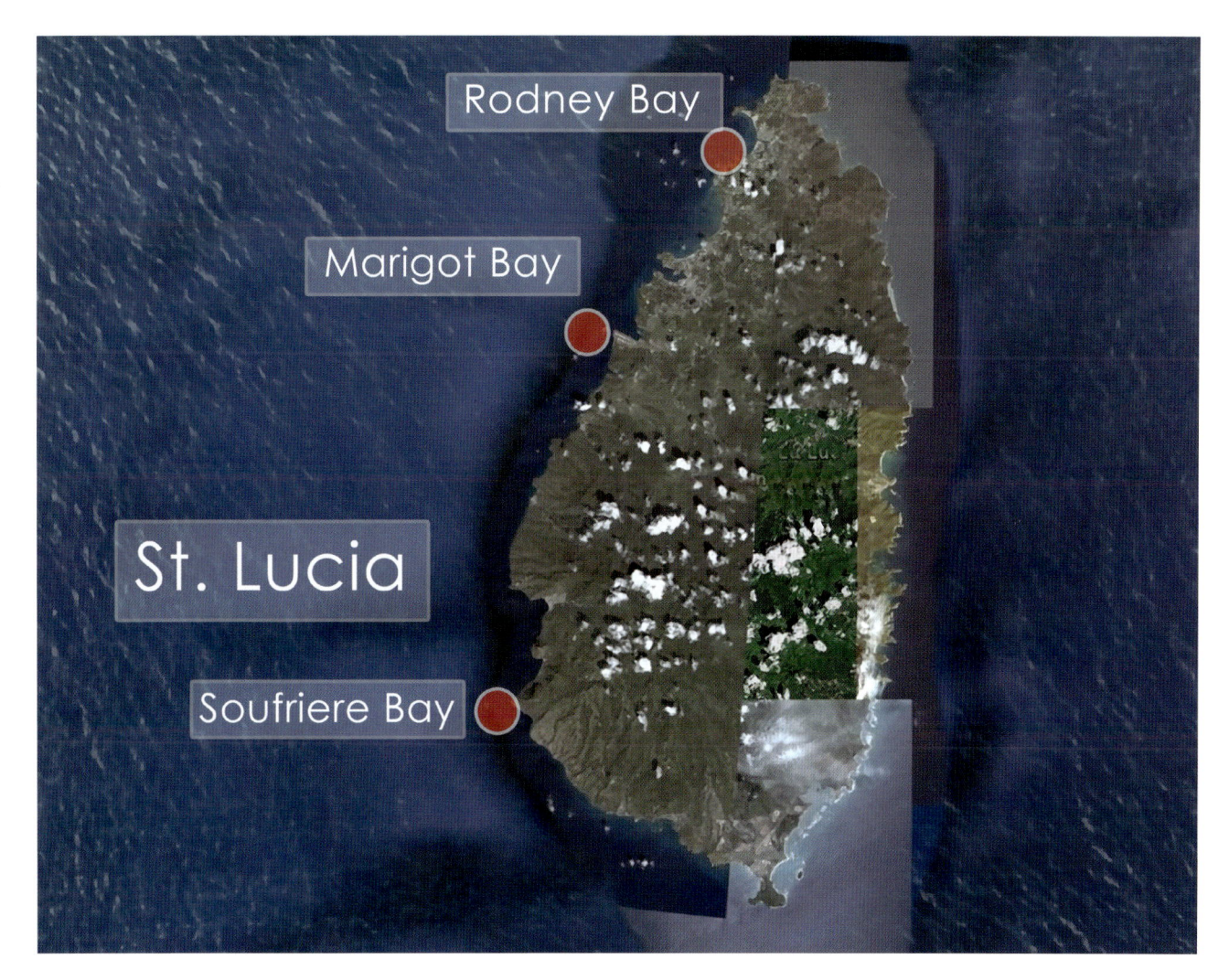

"I can't believe it," says Gottfried. "There's a big ship to our stern!" He grabs the binoculars. "I think it's a freighter."

Squinting into the sun, we can all see the ship approaching.

"He's coming on fast," Gottfried gasps.

Günter and I exchange looks, shaking our heads, feeling the shock. How could we have missed it? But of course, we were partying, and for the first time, no one was on watch.

"Gottfried, do we need to change course?" Günter asks.

"No, we're okay. Looks like he's angling from our stern to our starboard. He'll cross our wake diagonally."

The ship passes so close we can see the people waving to us.

We all breathe a sigh of relief and calm down. Maria brings us back to our partying. "What about the madness part of the theme?"

"That was just it," Günter grumbles. "The madness was not having someone on watch."

Gottfried has returned to the cockpit after returning the binoculars to their rack in the salon. "Actually, I know a true sea tale about madness," he says. "A crewman had been seasick during the entire Atlantic crossing and, with quite a distance to go, the yacht was still experiencing bad weather. The crewman had gone out of his mind, intent on suicide, wanting to open the hatches, to take the ship off its course, and he kept trying to jump overboard."

"So what did they do with this guy?" Maria asks, her eyes wide.

"The crew deflated their dinghy, wrapped up the mad crew member in it, and tied him to the mast, during the day, releasing him only at night to get him into his bed. And they kept doing this until they got him safely home."

Günter has recovered his composure. "Well *your* captain is grateful that we have such an easy-going crew, I won't have to tie anybody to a mast. It's been a great crossing. So far."

Race to the Finish

After our Madness Masquerade, we enjoy a few quiet days with calmer seas. But because of the gentler wind, the nav station instruments estimate our time of arrival later than the ticket Anne holds for her return home before Christmas. That causes some consternation on board. With the wind directly from the east at our

MESSING WITH BOATS

Part 3
by Günter

December 6, 2000: The problems had been piling up all along the Med and the Atlantic. Here in Tenerife, it was time to fix them all before we cross the Big Pond. The most nagging one was the replacement circuit board for the master bath shower, which was damaged through a saltwater leak from the starboard helm station. The factory was to have sent it to Malaga, Spain, then to Gibraltar, but somehow DHL can't catch up to us, even though we've been underway now for a month. We are expecting it here.

The antenna for the VHF broke off and fell down from the mast onto the deck in Gibraltar. Fortunately, no one was standing there. This was Gottfried's first trip up the mast in the bosun's chair, where he had a great bird's-eye view of our deck.

The big problem is our electrical system. Too bad the electrical genius of Germany could not be integrated with the catamaran design capability of France. Gottfried and I have our heads into the bird's nest of wires behind our electrical panel for two days now. Other problems have been solved along the way, such as the master head mechanism becoming clogged with foam particles from the building process. Since we had the bad experience with the cracked mast foot early in, we notice each new crack, photograph it, and e-mail the photographs back to the factory. So far, all have been surface stress cracks—just cosmetic in nature.

1. Gottfried climbs the mast to fix the broken VHF antenna; 2. Gottfried troubleshoots the electrical system.

stern, we fly the spinnaker day and night to get Anne back home on time. Then things change. *Pacific Bliss* becomes part of the team. As if she understands our predicament, she begins to pick up the pace: 178 nautical miles in the first 24-hour period the Sunday following our party, then 169, followed by 183. Her spinnaker flying, her hulls surging through the wave crests, she has begun to *race* to the finish. At 24 miles from St. Lucia, we predict arrival with over 12 hours to spare for Anne to catch her flight.

After three days of this wild ride, I'm seated at the starboard helm, entranced with the flickering phosphorescence that jumps from the waters and surges past the two aft hulls. *There is so much life in the sea.*

But *Pacific Bliss* interrupts my reverie. She surges to gain my attention, as if the wind cannot push her fast enough. 9 knots, no, 10 knots, then 12 knots, how about 16 knots? We are racing through the night! Controlling her at the helm, I feel the wind on my cheeks, I sense its power against the sails, I hear the vibration in the rigging and the rumble of the water slipping by the hulls, the whole complexity of forces and stresses that make up the trim of the ship. We race on. I connect with *Bliss* as I never have before. I am joined to her as if physically connected. I am part of her; she is part of me. I am the brain, attached to her body. I can read her condition to the minutest detail.

However, all good times must end. When the wind gusts to Force 7, I follow captain's orders, and wake Gottfried. We talk about reining in *Pacific Bliss* by taking down her spinnaker. Oh, I hate to do that! The ride is so exhilarating. Rain showers come and go. But these are only showers, not dangerous squalls, so together we decide to let her race on. Barefoot, wearing shorts and my light foul weather jacket, I keep an eye on the spinnaker, but I let *Pacific Bliss* run and run through the night, while her sleeping passengers bounce serenely on their foam mattresses.

⚓

The daylight brings a series of showers and squalls. Poseidon wants to teach us a few lessons before we escape him for land again. Until now, we have experienced a charmed crossing, but Poseidon whips the ocean into a frenzy and asks for the help of Zeus, who releases a torrent from the skies. Up goes the spinnaker, down goes the spinnaker; on with the gear, off with the gear, until we are all in swimsuits, dripping wet. But it's only a wonderful, tropical rain, which washes the salt from our bodies and the decks of *Pacific Bliss*. We are coming home. And guess what—we sight land.

We have crossed the Atlantic Ocean!

Celebrating Our Arrival in St. Lucia
December 19

I make my final entries into the logbook: The crossing from Santo Antao to St. Lucia, 2,080 nautical miles, has taken us only 12 days, 1 hour, and 20 minutes. Our average speed: 173 miles per day.

As we pull into Rodney Bay Marina, we are delighted to see Ron and Stu, the crew of *Enduring Echoes,* our sister ship, motioning us from the dock to an available slip. Their beards are long, and they've taken on a rather scruffy appearance. After we are secured, we invite them, along with Brenda and Pratt, on board to celebrate. We had kept in touch during the entire crossing but, having skipped Santo Antao, *Enduring Echoes* arrived one day earlier than we. I set out snacks, and we all squeeze around our cockpit table.

"From what I heard on the Net, you've been having far too much fun," Brenda begins. She looks tired and gaunt, a shadow of the exuberant Utah entrepreneur I'd met in Canet, where she was never at a loss for words during our American Therapy sessions. "Our autopilot broke," she continues, "and we had to hand-steer most of the way across the Pond. We arrived exhausted…lots of squalls…hit one with a 50-knot wind…spent the first day here catching up on sleep…I'm still tired."

I am flying higher than an eagle, but I try not to brag. "Yes, we did have a charmed Atlantic passage. Even the rainstorms at the end were not all that bad. I am so, so grateful."

Günter hands Pratt one of the bottles of the champagne from France. "For you," he says, "from *Pacific Bliss*." He takes the other bottle from the fridge. The two men pop the corks. And we all toast to successful crossings. Then each of us puts his or her right foot up on the table and makes a statement, a ritual that ancient navigators followed after they'd crossed an ocean.

When it is Günter's turn, a smile of satisfaction lights his face. His pride has been restored. "At least," he says," they can't take *this* away from me."

Only I know what he means.

Storms in the background as land is sighted.

"It was the best of times, it was the worst of times, it was the age of wisdom, it was the age of foolishness, it was the epoch of belief, it was the epoch of incredulity, it was the season of Light, it was the season of Darkness, it was the spring of hope, it was the winter of despair, we had everything before us, we had nothing before us…"
Charles Dickens

Chapter 6
The Best of Times: Voyaging Through the Caribbean

Jump-up in St. Lucia
January 12, 2001

The thumping base of Caribbean rhythm blares from *mobile discos,* the giant boom boxes that line the dusty streets of Gros Islet. Rastafarians, hawking cheap souvenirs and silver jewelry—their dreadlocks swinging under knit caps of red, gold, green, and black—hail us as we saunter by. The greasy-but-good aroma of grilled chicken legs competes with the sharp scent of salted flying fish, the same kind that landed on our net during our crossing of the Big Pond. We try some of each, along with a side of grilled corn-on-a-stick.

Our friends, Phyllis and Richard, arrived a few days ago from Yucca Valley, California. After provisioning for our passage through the Grenadines, we are "so ready" for our reward: partying at the weekly, Friday night Jump-Up. Phyllis' holiday exuberance is contagious.

I needed this. It is about time I have some fun with good friends.

Pert and petite in her colorful island outfit, her gray-blonde hair pulled back into a ponytail and ready for action, Phyllis becomes the life of the party. Though Richard is his usual, mellow self, the sparkle in his eyes and his wide-open smile say it all. The four of us take a leisurely walk along a village back street. A full moon beams at us between swaying palm fronds. We hear another boom box blasting out spirituals, and we sing along softly. But the insistent reggae beat of Bob Marley draws us back to the center of the action, where one Rastafarian is doing handstands while others swirl and dip, like wildly spinning tops.

"Come on. Let's get out there!" Phyllis drags us to the dusty square. After our second rum punch, Phyllis and I dance like frisky colts, without a care in the world. *I'll feel this tomorrow.* The guys laugh and try to keep up, but they stumble around like drunken sailors.

The difference in their appearances is striking. Both are wearing shorts, sandals, and tropical shirts, but there the resemblance ends. I note how Richard's high forehead, buzzed hair, and smooth-shaven face contrasts with Günter's scraggly mustache, unruly beard, and wild, curly locks. My husband has acquired the island cruiser look. And after the next six weeks with us, there's no telling what will happen to Richard.

Finally, exhausted from dancing, we sit at a bar just *limin',* which is local slang for listening to lively music. We are ready for a cold and refreshing *Piton* beer, brewed right here in St. Lucia.

I will always remember this festive night, made all the sweeter by partying with old, familiar friends.

The next morning, the familiar *Banana Boat Man* arrives, paddling his canoe up to our cat as he makes his daily rounds. Since we will sail away soon, we deplete his stores of papayas, avocadoes, and bananas.

Günter strings a bunch of green bananas underneath the bimini. "Now we look like a bona fide cruising boat." He is always happy when we are well provisioned.

The Pitons
13° 51' N, 61° W

Our first day's sail will be only a few hours long, just enough time to train our new crew. This is our first sail without a skipper, but I have full trust in Günter as captain. In fact, I prefer it this way. It is finally time for us to be in charge of our own boat! We have been

1. St. Lucia bay; 2. St. Lucia waterfall; 3. Soufriere and the Pitons; 4. Our new crew Richard and Phyllis.

84

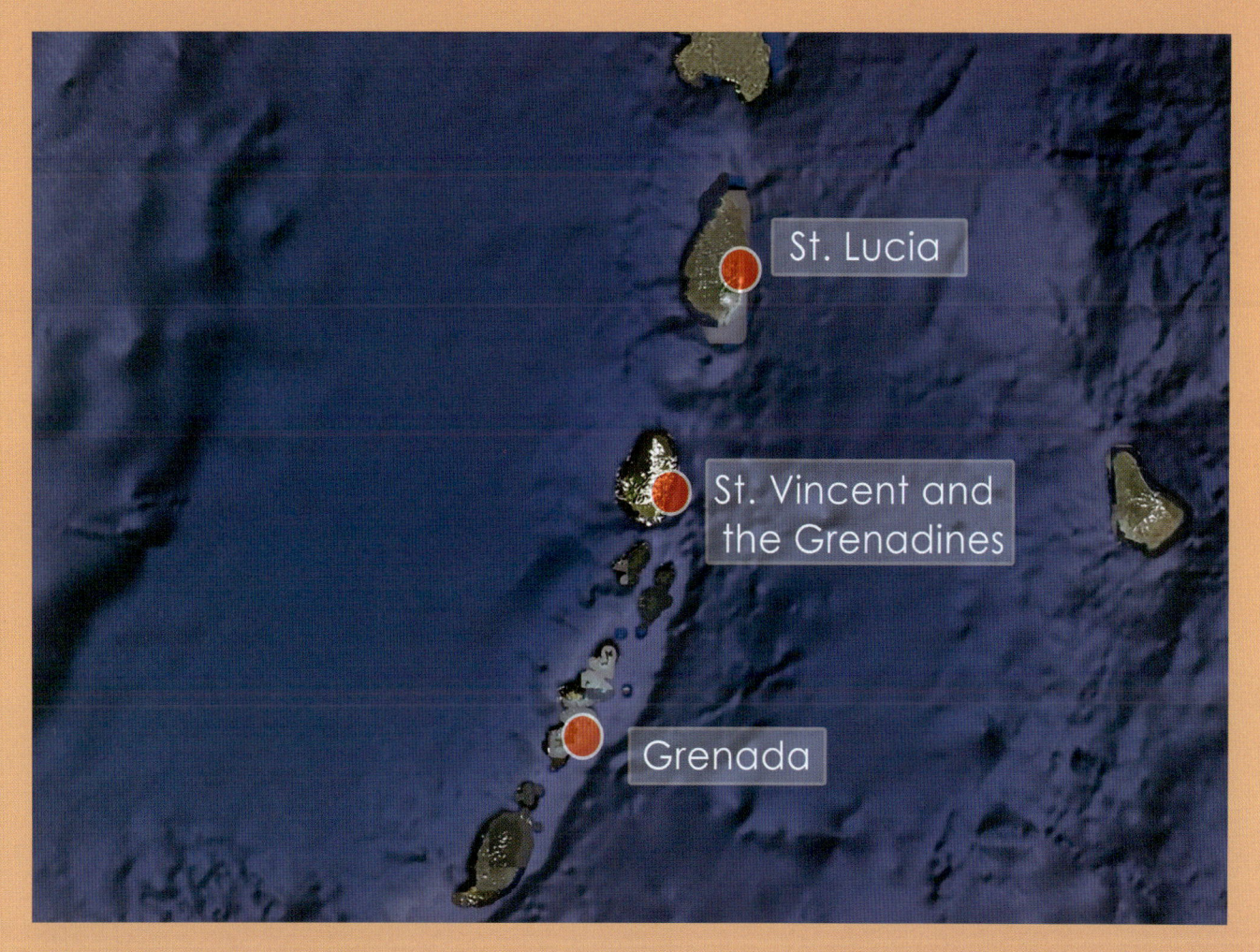

in port for over three weeks. As we leave our berth in Rodney Bay Marina, we undertake a new ritual: We play the *Amazing Grace* CD we had purchased on an earlier Caribbean *Windjammer* cruise. During that vacation, many years ago, tears had clouded my eyes every time the crew raised the ship's square sails to that song. Now it resounds through the *Pacific Bliss* cockpit speakers, first as a chorus with the words, "Amazing Grace, how sweet the sound…", then as bagpipes, and later with horns. We unfasten the dock lines to the music. Then, we all stand in a circle holding hands as I lead the prayer: "Dear God, please keep us safe though these coming weeks…"

Later, we drop the hook in the inner cove of gorgeous Marigot Bay. It has been a wonderful and uneventful sail. I spot a magnificent white egret standing proudly in its mangrove habitat. The entire environment looks inviting. We launch *Petit Bliss* and dinghy over to the sandbar for a closer look and a satisfying swim. After two hours of unrestrained fun, we return to the boat for happy hour and the enjoyment of Richard's newest rum concoction, with just the right amount of freshly grated nutmeg. Later, we eat dinner at *The Shack*, a seafood place perched on wooden piles extending out into the protected bay. The service is slow, even by St. Lucian standards, but the *Indian Hot Pot*—a traditional Caribbean spicy fish stew—makes up for it.

The next day, we motor to the Pitons and anchor between a pair of towering cones. Richard improves on his rum punch by adding mashed ripe bananas. And we become almost addicted.

Good friends, good conversation, and a nature light show as the sun sets. Life doesn't get any better than this!

The following morning, we leave the Pitons behind, brooding in the early morning haze. Wind tunnels through the peaks, wreaking havoc, confusing the seas. With the four of us in the cockpit, we all discuss whether to shorten canvas or not, to maintain control. An important safety aspect of sailing is to adjust the amount of sail to suit the wind conditions; i.e., as the wind speed increases, the crew should progressively reduce the amount of sail. On a boat with only a mainsail and jib (or genoa) such as ours, this is done by partially lowering the mainsail and partly furling in the jib, a process of reducing sail called *reefing*. Our sail plan allows for three reefs. The condition of the sea is also a factor; one can maintain control at a faster speed if the seas are relatively smooth, as they were during most of our Atlantic crossing.

Günter settles the question, turning toward Richard. "I've often heard this advice from Old Salts: *If you're even thinking of reefing, you go ahead and just do it.*"

Fun and buns in Bequia.

86

Slumming in Grenada at the yacht services dock.

Günter shows Richard how to put in one reef in the mainsail before we sail the channel to St. Vincent. "Reefing is easy on a Catana," he explains, "The mainsail is hoisted up the mast and attached to the bottom by a swinging boom. The sail is shortened by hauling on a series of lines that pull the sail in three stages. These are known as reefs. All the control lines, called 'sheets,' for some reason I never understood, are led through a pulley-and-tackle system back to the cockpit. You can then pull in the sheets, using the stern center winch if necessary, to reduce the canvas, while *you* remain safe here in the cockpit."

The next lesson for our crew is how to reef the jib. Being eager students, they learn the process quickly.

In time, the sea settles down, the men shake out the reefs, and we enjoy a fine crossing to Admiralty Bay, with speeds up to 10 knots. Phyllis and Richard are beginning to admire *Pacific Bliss* as much as we do. During our second day's passage, we make 61 nautical miles in one day.

As we enter the turquoise bay, a dark, sun-bronzed Carib Indian motors over in his boat taxi. He grabs the rail at our stern swim ladder and hands us up a line, helping us with the mooring process.

I could get used to this Caribbean service.

But not everything goes so smoothly. Richard lowers the dinghy without first wrapping the line around the center cockpit winch. The weight causes the line to slip through his fingers, stripping the skin. Learning on the go always exacts its price. Günter learned that in Malaga, Spain, submitting to the ministrations of Nurse Rachett!

St. Vincent and the Grenadines
13° N, 61° W
Admiralty Bay, Bequia

Pacific Bliss swings gently on her mooring. We hum along with Jimmy Buffet as he croons through the cockpit speakers:

But there's this one particular harbour
So far but yet so near
Where I see the days as they fade away
And finally disappear.
But now I think about the good times
Down in the Caribbean sunshine…

Günter sits at the helm, looking for all the world like a Tongan king. He wears a yellow-and-black sarong around his waist. He is voyeuring into nearby cockpits, finding another use for those boat binoculars. Richard lounges on the cockpit bench reading a paperback. I'm

87

A view of St. Georges, Grenada from the deck of Pacific Bliss.

on the other bench in the cockpit, writing in my journal. I look up just as the sun casts its final rays through the steep, verdant entrance to Admiralty Bay. Phyllis captures this newest Moment of Bliss on her drawing pad with dramatic sweeps of vivid color.

Günter and I had visited Bequia years earlier when we chartered a catamaran. Phyllis and Richard were here 27 years ago. Now, they want to revisit the hotel on Friendship Bay where they stayed. So the next day we take a taxi to check it out. The two-story hotel is still here. The old dining room amazes me with its décor of Swedish lace, combined with masks, island art, and tables decorated with hemp, cleverly knotted into napkin rings and centerpieces. The view of Friendship Bay from both stories is magnificent, just as Phyllis and Richard remembered.

During the day, the hotel is deserted. We head for the action, which seems to be outside at the beach bar. We find a lively crew there, three couples from Portland, who have chartered a cat to sail the Grenadines and are having a little too much fun. The guys are lined up, bare chests against the bar, wearing nothing but leopard-print string bikinis and dark sunglasses. They remind me of the postcards sold back in San Diego at the Pacific Beach pier: *Buns. Wish you were here*.

"They agreed to do this for us," one of the wives says. "Just for one day."

"How accommodating of them," I joke with her. "They must have lost a bet on board."

"Yep. They did, for sure."

I never did find out what that bet was. We taxi back to our own waterfront to walk the promenade again. Perky, white-and-yellow daisies overflow from the freshly painted center island. Flowering vines line the road rounding the bay, reminding me of "Heavenly," a pale blue variety of morning glory that I used to plant when I lived in Minnesota.

We stop for a sundowner at The Gingerbread, a two-story restaurant painted a cheery yellow to contrast with its white fretwork. From the second floor balcony, overlooking the promenade, we gaze down at a curious blend of yachties, fishermen, and tourists—all milling about. Sunk into the comfortable tropical-print bar chairs, I don't want to leave. But the beat of the steel drums beckons us to the *Frangipani* for dinner, where we find great ambience combined with marginal food.

After this uninspiring dinner, we walk through the gigantic whalebone arch at the end of the promenade, and I consider Bequia's past. This island has been a whaling mecca, from centuries past right up to the present time. Its background is eloquently described in the *Cruising Guide to the Caribbean:*

"High up on Mount Pleasant, impatient boys and philosophical old men scan the seas to windward for signs of the migrating humpback whale. Great excitement follows a sighting. The small boys pelt down the hill in the village of Friendship or Paget Farm, where the 18-foot, six-oared whaleboats are drawn up on the beach. Once at sea, the whaleboats are guided to the right spot by old men on the hill, who flash signals by mirror. Should a humpback be sighted to leeward, there is no way that, if killed, its huge bulk can be towed back against the trade winds. Even so, some of the more determined whaleboats refuse to give up the chase, even when well downward in heavy seas."

Heading back to our dinghy on the bay, I pass some men whom I imagine to be those old, weathered schooner salts. They are gathered beneath the shade of flame trees, watching with experienced eyes all that goes on in the harbor: shipwrights still at work, building schooners for local use; fishermen laying out their nets to dry on the sand; young boys repairing their fish traps for the next catch. Almost everyone on this island is still tied, in some way, to the sea.

Grenada's Strangest Harbor
12º 32' N, 61º 31' W
Hillsborough Bay, Carriacou

Carriacou is the first port we sail to in the Grenadines that is under Grenada's jurisdiction. Apparently, the political strife that troubled Grenada in the past did not affect this island. Little has changed here in decades. It is the strangest place.

Günter walks the dusty roads in the heat of the day to three different customs offices, spread throughout the length of the town. When he comes back to *Pacific Bliss,* nearly felled by the heat, he is not a happy camper. We spend the rest of the afternoon recovering, waiting for the heat to ebb.

Later, Phyllis, Richard, Günter, and I walk the main street of the little village, four abreast. The townspeople stare at us or turn away, as if we are invisible—or they want us to be. Hillsborough is obviously not a tourist or beach town; the main street heads inland, instead of following the waterfront. We cannot find one bar or restaurant on the beach side until we encounter *Callaloo,* at the end of the line. *Callaloo* is the name of a green leafy plant, thicker than spinach; in salads here, the callaloo brings it all together. A derivative meaning is "a gathering place." Ironically, we are the *only* customers gathered here in the little bar/dining room that overlooks the bay. We sip strong-and-sweet rum punches that do not even begin to rival Richard's concoctions. Turned off by the desultory atmosphere and menu selections, we decide we would rather cook dinner on board *Pacific Bliss.* We take a lackadaisical stroll back toward the rickety dinghy dock and tackle

DID YOU KNOW?

ST. LUCIA

Rastafarians believe that Haile Selassie, a former Ethiopian leader and descendant of King Solomon, was the returned Messiah, Jesus Christ. They follow the dietary restrictions of the Old Testament and therefore are almost exclusively vegetarian. Most grow dreadlocks in accordance with the Old Testament (Leviticus 21:5). They regard Cannabis (marijuana) as a sacrament and smoke it, hoping to clean the body and soul and bring one to a higher level of consciousness and closer to Jah (God). The movement has been popularized by reggae music, particularly that of Bob Marley. An orthodox Rastafarian views cutting his dreadlocks as sinful. Long, flowing locks symbolize values of respect, power, freedom, and defiance.

The heart and soul of St. Lucian culture is a blend of the culture, languages, and religions of the island's French and British colonizers combined with that of the Africans they brought with them. Although the population of 158,000 is predominantly of African origin, some 90 percent of St. Lucians are Roman Catholic, with the remainder made up of Protestants, Anglicans, and a small number of Rastafarians. Every Sunday, Christian hymns are sung lustily enough to raise the church roofs. On the other hand, African traditions of magic and spiritualism survive. Carnival is the best example of this fusion of Christianity and ancient belief: One of the stock characters of costume parades is the moko jumbie, a wildly attired and tattooed paranormal figure walking on stilts.

Though African languages were suppressed as soon as slaves arrived on the island, French planters still needed to communicate with their workers, and gradually, the common language of St. Lucian Creole—also called Patois—evolved, heavily laced with French, African, and English grammar and vocabulary. St. Lucia's official language is English, but Creole is spoken widely throughout the island. The Bible has been translated into Creole as well.

Haile Selassie

And God said, "Let the water teem with living creatures, and let birds fly above the earth across the expanse of the sky." So God created the great creatures of the sea and every living and moving thing with which the water teems, according to their kinds, and every winged bird according to its kind. And God saw that it was good." Genesis 1:20,21

Marine life in Los Roques, Venezuela.

Decor of a rental unit in El Grande Roque.

Another rental unit in El Grande Roque.

dinner on board.

The next morning, we try again, having noticed an interesting restaurant and hotel called Granny's. Her sign advertises great breakfast turnovers. Besides, the building has an interesting façade that Phyllis and I want to photograph in the morning light. Lethargic without our morning coffee, we all climb down to the dinghy, motor back to the rickety dock, and force our leaden legs to take us down Main Street once again.

Granny's is indeed a memorable experience, but not the kind one wants to repeat. There are no turnovers. The freshly brewed coffee we'd expected turns out to be Nescafé served in paper cups. I had looked forward to meeting the Granny of my imagination—cheery and bespectacled, her hair pulled back into an old-fashioned bun, wearing a flowery dress covered by a white, flour-dusted apron. Perhaps she'd even let me take a portrait of her! When we enter the restaurant, an unkempt, sullen (and probably hung-over) young man methodically takes the chairs down from their overnight perch on the plastic tables. Then, ignoring us, he returns back to his mop and bucket, washing the painted cement floor. The unspoken message is *Help Yourself*. The showcase is meager, with a few little salted swordfish, along with a limited selection of buns and raisin rolls. The sluggish lady at the showcase refuses to look me in the eye as I select my meal.

"I get the feeling that Granny has departed," I whisper to Phyllis as we walk out after our disappointing breakfast. We begin to photograph the building façade from across the street. A group of young men glare, then walk toward us.

"*Este mi casa*," one says. This is my house.

I take the photo anyway.

When we reach our dinghy, a boy we never saw before demands 10 ECs (Eastern Caribbean dollars) for our use of the "private dock." We all ignore him and walk on past. He shuffles away, brooding.

"Wow! I'm happy to leave this place," Günter says as we motor back to *Pacific Bliss*. "When they are not deliberately catering to tourists, the Caribs can be a hostile and resentful lot. Think of the difference in attitude, compared to the Cape Verdeans we met in Santo Antao. They were not used to tourists either, but remember how friendly they were?"

"*Si*," I agree. "*Vamanos*! Let's go."

The *Insight Guide to the Caribbean* calls Carriacou "a haven for those who want to get away from it all."

Perhaps the writer knows something that we do not…

Slummin' in Grenada

St. George's Bay, Grenada
January 19

We arrive in Grenada mid-afternoon, following a fast sail here under Force 6 winds, to find that no dock space is available in the Grenada Yacht Club. We end up slumming it here, at Yacht Services, tied to a rickety, wooden dock. Nails stick up all over, and the pier is sorely in need of "services" itself! This stop is necessary, though. We must do our laundry and provision for our passage to the Los Roques islands. And I need additional pages added to my passport.

"You should be thankful to find a space at all," says the service manager. (Following the regulations for "yachts in distress," *Pacific Bliss* is allowed a "free" 24-hour stay-over.) We drop off our laundry at Yacht Services and taxi into St. Georges, the capital, to provision. After shopping, loaded down with bags and boxes, we return to check on the progress of our laundry.

The services manager points, "Your wash lady, over there."

Phyllis and I go inside a shack that holds two rusty washtubs. All of our laundry—including the sheets—is being done by hand. A dark-haired little girl is playing on the concrete floor.

Men from the Venezuelan Coast Guard help us free the trapped anchor.

"Not dry yet," says the lady, pointing to the first batch of clothes blowing in the wind on the line behind the wash shack. Fortunately, the wind is still strong; the laundry should dry in time for our morning departure.

When we tune into the Caribbean Net, we learn that over eighty yachts are anchored in the Tobago Cays. We don't want to be crowded, so we make a group decision to venture to seas less traveled. Despite the agreement, anticipatory tension builds on board for two reasons. First, we will be sailing into lawless Venezuelan and later, Colombian, territory. Second, this will be the first overnight sail, ever, for Phyllis and Richard. We conduct a training session to brief them on what to expect when sailing at night. Then it is up to me to establish our watch schedules for the two-day sail.

Pan-pan in Los Roques
11° 50' N, 66° 41' W
El Gran Roque, Los Roques Islands, Venezuela
January 22

After a fast, exhilarating sail, pushed west by the trades for two days and nights, we arrive at an island called El Gran Roque. This is the point of entry for a Venezuelan national marine park called Islas Los Roques, about 90 miles from the mainland. We are delighted to be in this special corner of God's world, described by Columbus as "heaven on earth." The refuge consists of some 60 low-lying sandy cays (only 25 of which are named), spread over 350 square miles. Most of these cays are mangrove-studded wetlands, less than 30 feet high, and teeming with migrating birds and marine life. They are surrounded by bright-white dunes and iridescent beaches, all protected by virgin, coral reefs.

We wade through a complex immigration-and-customs process and saunter down the main street of Puerto El Roque, a quaint fishing village. After purchasing a few provisions, we dinghy back to *Pacific Bliss* and anchor overnight in the bay. The next day, we race through breakfast, barely listening to the requisite Davy Jones weather forecast on the Caribbean Net. We are eager to depart for Pirate's Cove because we have heard that snorkeling there is fantastic. Besides, we can purchase fresh fish and lobster from local fishermen. We pull anchor and motor across the bay, facing a 20-knot ESE wind right on the nose.

Anchoring at the little cove proves difficult in the wind and swells, and—as if that is not enough—there are reefs on either side of the designated anchorage. I drop the hook and Günter reverses the engine, pulling back to set the anchor. It refuses to hold. Using both engines to maintain control through the swells, we drag the anchor back away from the island into deeper waters, staying clear of the dangerous reefs. Now the anchor is hanging straight down. Günter cuts the engines. I use the windlass control to hoist it. Up and down…up and down, I continue to press the control buttons. But the windlass skips every time. It simply cannot lift the anchor. It feels like the anchor is hooked onto something, perhaps to an underground cable. Our chart does not show a cable, but that is not surprising. Much of Los Roques is not charted at all.

All of a sudden, *Pacific Bliss* begins to move of her own accord. We begin to drift towards the main island of El Roque, with the anchor hanging straight down.

"Okay. Discard the cable idea," says Günter. "There must be a very heavy weight attached to the anchor. Maybe a huge rock. Or a hunk of loose coral." He begins to take us through the options: "We could cut the anchor chain and attach it to a float. Drop the assembly into the sea for possible recovery later…"

"The wind is pushing us toward those reefs!" I interrupt. "We've got to get outta here. Quick!"

"How about making a pan-pan call to the Coast Guard?" says Richard. "They seemed friendly enough when we met them during check-in."

(Pan-pan is a mariner's distress call; it is used when there is no danger of losing lives or the boat; in desperate cases, one would put through a mayday call.)

"Good idea," Günter says. "We can still see their office, way across the bay. Help could come soon. Lois, get them on the VHF."

I head for the nav station. "Pan-pan. Pan-pan. This is *Pacific Bliss*. Over."

The coast guard responds quickly and, within ten minutes, an inflatable arrives with half a dozen young men in tight tees and swim trunks, some of them carrying diving gear. Three board *Pacific Bliss* and head for the anchor at the bow. The others joggle the anchor line from their inflatable. After a whole lot of shaking, the heavy object—whatever it is—dislodges itself and sets the anchor free. What a relief. *Thank You, God!*

But there is more to come. The anchor is free but still I cannot hoist it. Günter discovers that one of the young men has accidentally dislodged the anchor chain from the windlass. Now the chain has dropped all the way down to the *bitter end*, a section of rope that is fortunately fastened to the windlass. What a heavy mess! All 280 feet of chain and rope into the sea.

Meanwhile, the boat has been drifting to deeper waters. *Pacific Bliss* is solidly anchored again, but at

DID YOU KNOW?

ST. VINCENT AND THE GRENADINES

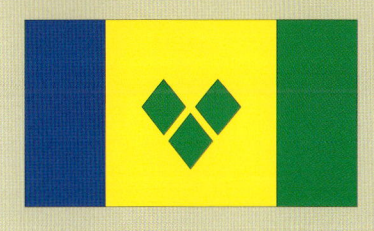

The Caribs, arriving in St. Vincent perhaps no more than 100 years before the Europeans, conquered the peaceful Arawaks, who had migrated there from Venezuela. The warlike Caribs were extremely efficient at keeping unwanted settlers from their shores and prevented St. Vincent from being colonized long after most other Caribbean islands had well-established European settlements.

GRENADA

You might know Grenada only because this small country made international news during the U.S. led invasion of 1983. But did you know that the country is still a constitutional monarchy with Queen Elizabeth II as the titular head?

The nutmeg on the nation's flag represents the premier economic crop of Grenada; this country is the world's second largest producer of nutmeg (after Indonesia), providing 20 percent of the world supply. Called The Spice Isle, Grenada is a leading producer of several other spices, including cinnamon, cloves, ginger, mace, allspice, and orange/citrus peels.

Nutmeg

After selling us two huge lobsters, Ezequiel invites us to his fish camp.

120 feet, according to the depth meter. How can we free the anchor from the ocean floor? That's a long way to dive. Fortunately, our new Venezuelan friends are real pros. One diver works his way all the way down. He lifts the heavy chain, hand over hand, to his team in the dinghy who, in turn, bring it up to those on the bow. Strenuous work. But the Venezuelans are young, strong, and fit. With anchor and chain lying in lengths along the port bow now, I wind the chain around the windlass using the electronic control. Because the last 25-foot section, the *bitter end,* must be wound by hand, I ask for help again.

A few of the Coast Guard men ride back with us on *Pacific Bliss* while the others take the inflatable back to Puerto El Roque. We anchor near the Coast Guard Station, at the outskirts of town. We thank our rescuers and offer them a well-deserved tip.

"No thanks," says their leader.

"Can we take you back to shore in our dinghy?" Günter asks.

"No thanks," says their leader again.

I admire them as one after the other dives into the water and swims toward the beach with powerful breast strokes, muscles rippling.

The four of us reconnoiter over lunch in the cockpit. Forget the lobsters! We decide that we won't be returning to Pirates Cove. Ever. Instead, we set sail to another island called Carenero. It is a painstaking passage. We zigzag through channels with waves breaking over reefs, following the three waypoints provided on our chart. Ideally, a sailor should navigate through this type of passage with the mid-day sun directly overhead, watching carefully through polarized sunglasses for coral heads. But now, the late afternoon sun is disarmingly low. We push on through shallow channels, grateful for four pairs of eyes: Phyllis and Richard are squinting from the bows; Günter watches from the starboard helm, while I maintain a sharp lookout from the port.

Finally, we reach Carenero. The bay is pristine. No boats. Not one human in sight. "Eden. Straight ahead," Günter points.

We drop anchor, this time with no problems. Günter brings out four cold Heinekens. We take them to the trampoline facing the beach, and we toast our safe arrival.

But when cruising, it is never over 'til it's over. During our celebration, one empty can manages to fall into the anchor locker, lodging itself deep down into the area housing the rollers for the control lines. We cannot leave this untended, because we dare not risk jamming the sheets. Each one of us, in turn, attempts to retrieve the can. I have small enough hands to get down in there, but hanging upside down, I'm too short to reach the can.

DID YOU KNOW?

VENEZUELA

Venezuela's population in 2001 was approximately 22 million. There are 31 indigenous tribes in Venezuela. Some of these tribes are said to have been living in what is now known as Venezuela since 14,000 B.C. At the time of the land's discovery by Christopher Columbus, the population was estimated at over 500,000.

Venezuela's national park system was established in the early 20th century. In 1935, the mountainous land along the northern coast was used to found Venezuela's first national park, the Parque Nacional Henri Pittier (named in honor of a Swiss biologist and ecosystem champion). Today, Venezuela has 43 national parks.

The archipelago of Los Roques is probably the best known of Venezuela's Caribbean islands and is Venezuela's largest marine park. Declared a national park in 1972, these islands and the seas surrounding them are perhaps the most pristine and unscathed of all in the Caribbean.

Henri Pittier

1. All part of the food chain, a lobster boils in a pot; 2. Driftwood on the shore; 3. Phyllis with "ears," or antenna.; 4. Richard, Phyllis, Ezequiel and Lois.

98

Harbour Village Marina, Krandendijk, Bonaire.

Phyllis tries next. She doesn't mind the blood rushing to her head. But she is also too short. Then Günter, feeling obligated as Captain, tries and fails as well.

"Well, I'm a little claustrophobic, but it's my can that did the damage," Richard announces, gathering his courage. He dives headfirst deep down into the locker, all the way to his belly, while we hold onto his legs. After multiple attempts, he retrieves the can.

"All's well that ends well," says Phyllis as we enjoy our dinner on the top deck. No lobster this night; canned tuna with pasta will have to do.

As the sun turns the beach into glittering amber and the wind ruffles the bay, it's feeding time. A magnificent frigate bird swoops down to pluck his dinner out of a swirling school of silvery baitfish that are frantically escaping a larger predator. A white heron snaps a snail into his beak. The brown boobies in the saw grass on shore croak cheerfully, while their mates reply with a strange sound, like a whistler with asthma. I'm reminded of the verse in Genesis where God saw all that he made, "and it was very good."

Yes, Your creation is exceptionally good.

Run Venezuela
11°52'N, 66° 56' W
Carenero, Los Roques

We begin the next day shortly after dawn, sitting on the helm seat watching the pelicans fishing for their breakfast. Smaller birds swoop in gracefully, landing in trees on the pristine shore. Fish snake through the crystal clear water. A powerboat, which arrived overnight, pulls anchor and soon disappears around the bend.

"Come, follow me," Günter says as he dives into the sea naked for our morning "shower swim" around *Pacific Bliss*. This time, he heads out for the shore. I follow. We walk along the beach, hand-in-hand, the only humans on the island, like Adam and Eve in the Garden of Eden.

Egrets roost in virgin mangroves. The beach is brimming with life. Before every bare footprint we make in the sand, sea creatures scurry away, taking their shells with them. The mollusks remind me of Günter and me, taking our own protective shell, *Pacific Bliss*, with us wherever we go. I realize how independent she allows us to be. The boat becomes its own municipality and we're in charge. We make our own water from the sea through our little desalination plant, the Spectra® watermaker located in the port engine room. The sun on the solar panels goes into the battery bank, our on-board electrical generation facility. We dump our fresh waste into the sea to be recycled by nature, saving our cans and plastic on board for land disposal later,

99

A collection of small boats at Harbour Village Marina.

implementing our own recycling process. We receive news of the weather conditions through our weather fax and over our SSB (single side-band) radio, then analyze the potential effects of the ridges of high and low pressure, becoming our own weather station.

My gaze wanders from the beach to *Pacific Bliss*, which is swinging gently at anchor. Being one's own municipality can also be achieved on a powerboat or trawler. But there's a compelling simplicity about making headway under sail: no moving parts, no need for fuel, no noise—just the wind in the sails in harmony with nature.

We swim back to *Pacific Bliss*, relishing the coolness of the sea against our nakedness.

As the four of us enjoy breakfast in the cockpit, a fisherman arrives in a bright orange skiff. "Do I see lobster in the bottom of that boat?" Phyllis asks, grinning with glee.

Soon we are all at the port swim ladder, intent on making a deal with the balding, coppery, middle-aged man below.

"My name is Ezekiel," he says.

We buy two huge lobsters from him and ask him about exploring and snorkeling.

"Come, see my camp. I come here from the mainland this time of year."

Later in the day, we pile into *Petit Bliss* and urge her across the bay. We land at the fishing camp. Ezekiel asks us why we are here with such a boat. We tell him about our plans to sail around the world and some of our experiences thus far. This establishes a wonderful rapport.

"Come. Follow me to my house," he says.

We trudge through the snow-white sand to a dilapidated, gray wooden shack.

"This is where I live during the season." The fisherman points to a single cot with a light blanket and two chairs. Cans of food line the wooden shelves next to a simple propane stove. He is happy to have company.

Phyllis points to a small, framed photo on the rough-hewn table. "Is this your family?"

"Yes, wife and children on the mainland. I come here by myself during the season."

"You must get lonesome here all alone," she says.

"Sometimes. But it is necessary. Too difficult for them to live here; I must fish to support them for the rest of the year."

Ezekiel shows off his heart-shaped coat of arms at the entryway as we leave. *Rancho de Amor*, it says. I'm intrigued. I wonder whether the "love" relates to his family or to his shack.

We then move toward the sea and Ezekiel points toward his private snorkeling spot nestled in a pristine cove. "Much to see there."

I will remember this snorkel forever. I am not a strong swimmer, but here, I can swim from the shores of a shallow lagoon and snorkel, without fear, to the reefs surrounding it, protected from the rolling waves of the sea. The set-up is ideal. I float over fish more colorful than our spinnaker: iridescent in bright shades of blue, teal, green, yellow, amber, orange, and red. After taking off my fins, I wade through the

DID YOU KNOW?

BONAIRE

Together with Aruba and Curaçao, Bonaire forms a group referred to as the ABC islands of the Leeward Antilles. As part of the Netherlands Antilles, Bonaire is accordingly a part of the Kingdom of the Netherlands. Complicated? Talks about changing the structure are forever ongoing.

The island's first inhabitants were the Arawak, the same group who migrated to St. Vincent from Venezuela. Beginning in 1623, ships of the West India Company called on Bonaire to obtain meat, water, and wood.

During the German occupation of the Netherlands during World War II, Bonaire was a protectorate of Britain and the United States. After Germany invaded the Netherlands in 1940, many Dutch and German citizens were interned in a camp on Bonaire for the duration of war. In 1944, Queen Juliana of the Netherlands and Eleanor Roosevelt visited allied troops stationed on Bonaire. After the war, the airport was converted to civilian use, and the internment camp became Bonaire's first hotel.

Although Bonaire's future revolves around its remarkable coastal reefs, the island's past is tied to an altogether different set of resources: the production of salt. For over three centuries, the island's culture and prosperity were dependent upon this most important of the world's spices. Salt is still produced on Bonaire. The stunning salt beds of Pekelmeer are also home to one of the hemisphere's great populations of flamingoes.

Bonaire Salt

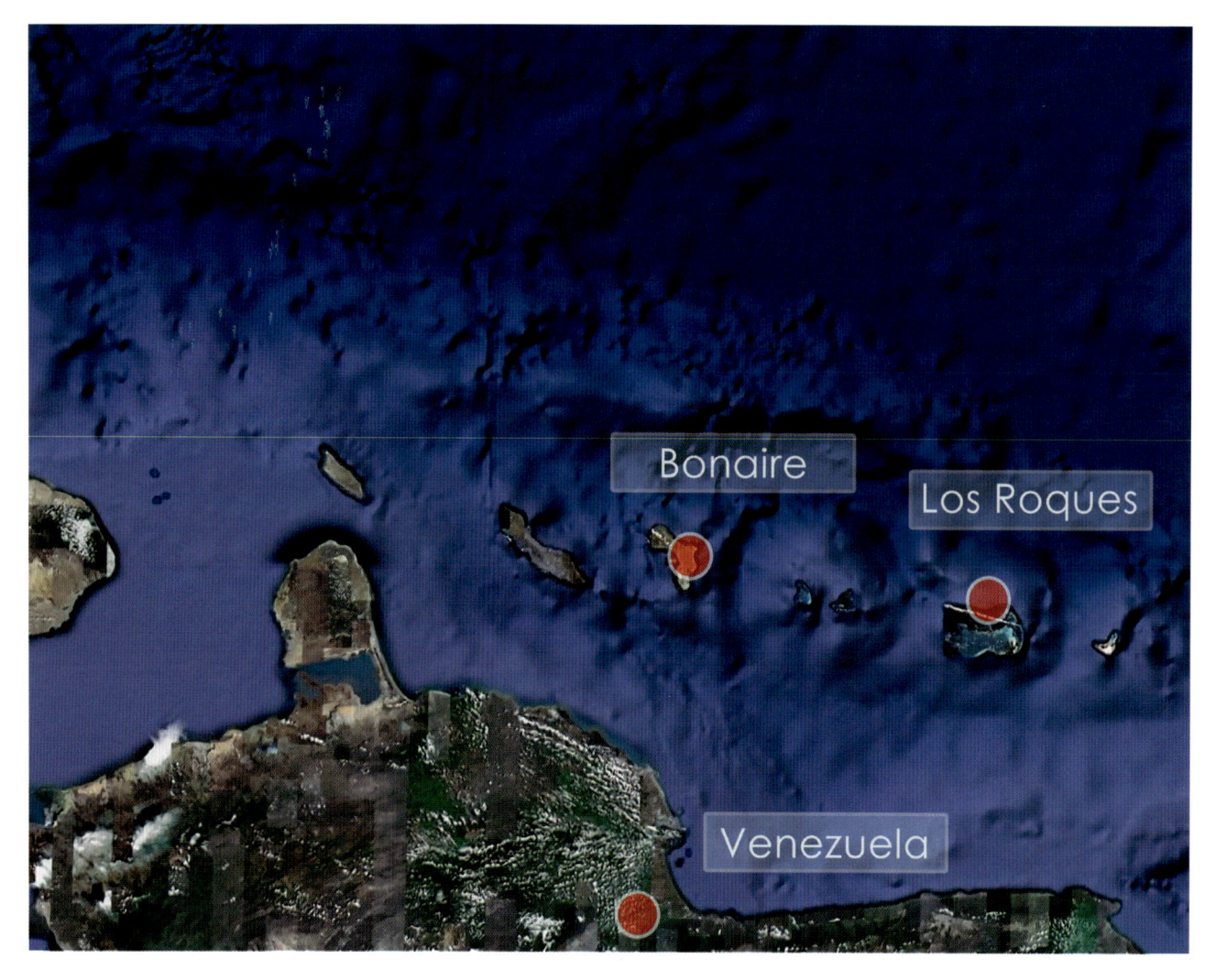

calm tide pools, photographing snails, crabs, and distinctive mollusks and crustaceans I've never seen before.

Afterwards, I sit in the pure white sand, fine as sugar, alone with my thoughts. *God must have had a blast designing all of these colorful creatures of the sea! I would like to get closer to the mind of such a Creator during our circumnavigation. But how?*

By sundown, we are all standing in the salon of *Pacific Bliss*. The lobster we bought from Ezekiel is now boiling in the pot. The table is set. And Richard has just fixed a pitcher full of his perfected rum punch. Phyllis and I are barefoot, as usual, wearing nothing but our Tahitian pareus as we sway and swoop to the voice of Harry Belafonte crooning through our stereo speakers.

She took my $500, had to sell my cap and horse,
We join unison: *Matilda, Matilda, Matilda, she take me money and run Venezuela.*
Don't you know she took me money and run Venezuela? Harry continues.
Matilda, Matilda, Matilda, she take me money and run Venezuela, we respond, louder now.
Well the money was to buy me house and land but she had an insidious plan… Matilda, Matilda, Matilda, she take me money and run Venezuela. Richard and Günter have joined the dancing.

*Just the ladies…*a whisper through the speakers. *Matilda…women over 40…Matilda…all the ladies now… Matilda, she take my money and run Venezuela.* Phyllis and I belt out the soprano, even though I never could carry a tune.

Just the men now…Matilda…Uga Lugu Uga… Matilda…Uga Lugu Uga… Matilda…Uga Lugu Uga… she take my money and run Venezuela. Richard and Günter sing out in deep bass, dressed in lap-laps and banging on their bare chests.

Just whisper now…Matilda, Shish, Matilda, Shish, Matilda, she take my money and run Venezuela.

*Now just think about it…*we stop to take a sip of Richard's rum punch, fueling for the Grand Finale. *Everybody now…Matilda, Matilda, Matilda, she take me money and run Venezuela.*

Just the last part…Run Venezuela…the very last part… Run Venezuela…here's your last chance…Run Venezuela! DAIO!! It's a primal scream out to the darkness of our secluded anchorage. We are all alone in Paradise. And we have the freedom to do just as we wish.

Before retiring, I re-create the memorable day in my mind: *This day is what I imagined during the years we dreamed about owning our own boat and going cruising. It has been a gift from God, one that I will never forget.*

"If you ain't Dutch, you ain't much."
The Netherlands Antilles
Kranlendijk, Bonaire
January 26

We spend a few more idyllic days in the Los Roques islands, followed by a perfect sail to the ABCs, the three islands of Aruba, Bonaire, and Curaçao. We have chosen the marina in Kranlendijk, Bonaire (the middle island), as our destination for a brief rest-and-provisiong stop on our way to Cartagena. After our crew docks and we settle in, the lady in the monohull that is next to us waves me over for a glass of wine.

I board her cozy, green-and-white monohull called *Bon Vibrasons*. "I'm Patricia," announces the matronly woman, her thick, graying hair pulled back by a clip. As we sip our wine, Patricia tells me about the Dutch. "First, you need to know and understand this saying: 'If you ain't Dutch, you ain't much.' All proud Dutch repeat this like a mantra." She tells me that this tradition goes back to hardy adventurers, whose commercial sailing vessels plied the Dutch East Indies.

Plucky Patricia decided that the death of her husband wasn't the end of her life; it was just the beginning. This determined widow vowed to spend the rest of her years traveling and enjoying life. And she reckoned that sailing would be the ideal way to achieve her goal. I spread some more Dutch cheese onto a biscuit, glancing over her head to all the yachts crowded into the Harbour Village Marina. "Were you and your husband cruisers?"

"No. But that didn't stop me. I sold my home in California, bought this boat and began to live on board. I took some sailing lessons while berthed in San Diego, hired a skipper, and took off."

Voila! Here she is, all the way to Bonaire, a veteran of many adventures and numerous crew changes. Right now, she is writing a book about the women of the Dutch Caribbean.

How I wish I could stay here longer with her to capture the spirit of these islands! But we have a schedule to make if we want to have Richard and Phyllis with us all the way through the Panama Canal. I excuse myself and return to *Pacific Bliss*.

We cram our provisioning into the next day, Saturday, so that we can have a "free day" on Super Bowl Sunday, January 28. This is one game that Americans don't like to miss, if they can help it. We watch the game on a TV hung over a waterfront bar, while gorging on American-style hamburgers and fries. Baltimore defeats the New York Giants, 34-7, but no one here seems to care who won. They are just having a good time.

After the game, Günter initiates a conversation with a crusty Old Salt. The old sailor sits alone and wears a faded baseball cap, sipping a cold beer. Phyllis, Richard, and I gather around.

"One famous character who is still here on the island is Captain Don Stewart," he says. "You probably know that Bonaire has a long history of preserving the marine environment. Throughout the years, we islanders have taken on many causes. We protect turtles. We stopped spear fishing. We don't allow the removal of coral, dead or alive."

The man turns toward me. "It was the flamboyant Captain Don who turned Bonaire into a world-renowned diving mecca. Do you know that we celebrated the 30th anniversary of his arrival right here?"

I shake my head no.

"Back in 1992," the old man continues, "this town re-enacted his arrival. I was there and saw this for myself: Captain Don actually cried when he spoke to the crowd!"

"Amazing!" I answer.

"Yes, he told us that when he anchored here in 1962, he was nothing but a boat bum who possessed only 63 cents and a 70-foot, topsail schooner."

The Old Salt has aroused my curiosity. Later, I research this slice of Bonaire history at the local internet facility. Captain Don was almost 36 when he and Bonaire found each other, and already he had become a colorful character. A fifth grade dropout, he joined the Navy at 17 during World War II. After the war, he patented a method to fit screens into sliding glass doors, he floated down the Mississippi on a raft, and he tried to become a Hollywood actor. Realizing he was never going to be another Errol Flynn (whom he resembled), and bored silly by instant—albeit marginal—success, Captain Don sold his thriving screen company and set sail for the Caribbean. He sailed around for almost two years before happening on Bonaire. That landing began his love affair with Bonaire and its people.

At the time, Bonaire was just a dry, windy island consisting of a few thousand people and a lot of goats and cacti. It took Captain Don to realize that this desert island is surrounded by an oasis of magnificent reefs located an easy swim from shore.

The rest, say the people of Bonaire, is history. This little island, only twenty miles long and three-to-seven miles wide, is located right in an upwelling of the Atlantic Ocean. Here, cool water rises from the deep to the surface. This water is rich with plankton and other nutrients. It feeds the reefs near Bonaire, growing them into some of the most spectacular in the world.

Captain Don started the dive resorts and established moorings along the coast. Then he became a conservationist and lobbied for funding. The Bonaire Marine Park he founded has now evolved into the well-respected and loved National Park of the Netherlands Antilles.

On Monday, I pay a visit to the Ship's Chandlery where I learn that our next proposed landfall is very popular with cruisers. Cartagena, a city on the romantic Spanish Main, will be an intermediate stop on our way to the San Blas Islands and the Panama Canal. "Cartagena? That's one of the most attractive harbors you'll find," the clerk confirms.

Our crew had planned for just a quick rest stop there. However, based on the feedback here, I plan to propose some sightseeing as well. Before we depart, I purchase a detailed chart of the Bay of Cartagena. Then I check on the weather. There are no lows and no storms in the five-day forecast.

So why do I feel uneasy?

Storm clouds roll over the western Caribbean.

Chapter 7

The Worst of Times: Night of Sheer Terror Underway to the Spanish Main

Living on the Edge
January 29, 2001
I check and re-check the weather forecast for our 600-mile passage to Cartagena, Colombia. It does call for "reinforced trades," beefed-up winds of 20-30 miles per hour.

That's about what we had during our fast Atlantic crossing. It should be a good, fast sail. So far, the uneasiness I feel in my gut seems misplaced.

"Every day and every week has been about the same…this is normal here for this time of year," an experienced cruiser docked nearby assures me. "The Colombia Coast Guard might stop you, though. Maybe even want to board. Drug-runners are the biggest danger along the mainland. Before you turn south to go to Cartagena, that is."

Richard and I plot the waypoints recommended in the "cruisers' bible" for planning passages, Jimmy Cornell's *World Cruising Routes*. It recommends heading north of Curaçao and Aruba, continuing 28 miles north of Point Gallinas, only then heading back southwest toward Colombia to our next waypoint off Barranquilla.

We set sail from beautiful Bonaire at 0915 under fair skies and calm seas. With a full main and jib, we sail all day under Force 4-6 winds, enjoying the ride over 10-foot westerly swells.

Shortly after sunset, I'm at the helm when we experience our first scare. There's nothing like a pair of blinding white lights appearing suddenly—with no red or green visible—to tie a sailor's stomach into a knot bigger than a monkey-fist. "White lights!" Phyllis shouts. "Behind us!" There is no time now to turn on the radar to know for sure whether the ship is headed directly for us, but that is what white lights mean. I make a sharp turn to get out of the way and end up "in irons" (directly into the wind, having lost all headway). Now *Pacific Bliss* is a sitting duck, wings flapping, just waiting for the explosion.

Günter rushes to start both engines and gain control. I head down to the nav station to turn on the radar, which takes forever to warm up. When it does, I pick up the VHF. "Vessel ahead of us, come on in." The captain calls out his latitude and longitude, then asks nonchalantly, "Where are you?"

"Right behind you now. You nearly ran us over as you passed by! And, you have no red and green running lights on."

The captain mumbles something I cannot understand and then breaks the connection.

Captain Günter calls us together to announce new rules for night sailing: "The radar will be on stand-by from now on. And always track each new light you identify."

Phyllis is not comfortable standing night watches alone, so she continues to take the 1800-2100 (6-9 p.m.) watch while at least one other crew member is awake. Günter is scheduled for 2100-2400, and Richard has the dogwatch from 0000-0300. I bring in the dawn at 0300-0600. Usually, I stay up with Phyllis in the early evening. We have tidied up the galley after an early dinner. The guys are resting below in their berths. We sit at the helm seat side by side, old friends baring their souls.

105

Phyllis at the mast of *Pacific Bliss*.

Our conversation evolves to the subject of taking risks. "I never had to stretch in any way when I grew up in the '50s," Phyllis begins, "so taking this voyage is a big deal to me. I was a coddled teenager, cheerleader, life of the party, and all that." She looks at the sea, deep in thought, then continues. "My parents sent me to a fine Eastern college, where I earned my psychology degree. Then I got married and raised two kids—we were the typical suburban family. I didn't want my sons to grow up as protected as I was. So when they were young, Richard and I sent them to *Outward Bound…*" She pauses again but I don't want to interrupt. "We wanted them to learn risk-taking, danger, and teamwork. And Richard—he has stretched himself with his businesses and walking in marathons."

"And you?"

"Nothing, so far…before this voyage."

"That's so different from my life. I had to work my way through college; my scholarships covered only the first year. Then I supported my kids all by myself. I struggled up the corporate ladder and through six entrepreneurial ventures. Finally, I ended up as CEO of a publicly-traded company. That last part you know."

"Yes, I know you were struggling many times for your very survival. Yet you seem to *thrive*, living on the edge. How did you learn to do that?"

"It isn't something I learned intentionally. After all, my first memory is being thrown out of our burning farmhouse to safety when I was only three years old. The house burned to the ground. My mom was burned over most of her body trying to find my younger sister… who didn't make it."

Phyllis edges closer to me on the two-person helm seat. "I remember you saying something about this before, but not the details."

"Yes, I lived with my grandparents while Mom spent the next two years in a hospital and a mental institution. She made up for losing that child by having more children—there were ten of us. I'm the oldest. I didn't really have a childhood, taking care of the others, and we were dirt poor. I guess that explains it."

"Well, that explains learning how to survive and take charge. But risk-taking behavior, I'm not so sure."

"Maybe not. You're the psychologist! I guess learning to survive *could* have made me cautious. Instead, it turned me into a fighter—like the fiery bantam rooster ruffling his feathers back on the farm."

"Did you have any role models?" Phyllis prods. Her curiosity is contagious.

I scan the horizon and the dark sea below. Nothing out here but the stars. "No role models for risk-taking…" I pause to search my memory banks. "But somehow I always knew that I could do anything I wanted if I set a goal and then worked at it hard enough. There were writers…for example, I admired Helen Keller. She said, 'Life is either a daring adventure…or nothing at all.' This is my favorite quote and I've used it effectively many times."

"How?" Phyllis is still curious.

"As a divorcee, I would ask a new suitor this question—right out—on the first date: 'What do you think of these words by Helen Keller?' If my date didn't snap it up, he was not for me."

"And, of course, Günter liked the quote?"

"Right on! He agreed immediately. Günter is even more adventurous than me. He'd backpacked around the world in the '70s, you know. From Papua New Guinea to the Celebes, through Indonesia, Malaysia, Nepal, Tibet…you name it. When we married, he promised to show me the world. But he didn't say how."

"But Lois, traveling around the world by sea is something else again. It is a different level of adventure. You're deliberately ratcheting risk."

"Hmm. I never thought of it this way."

For the rest of the watch, we lapse into a contemplative silence, each thinking her own thoughts.

Later, trying to sleep after the girl-talk, I forget the conversation and drift into a troubling uneasiness.

These are clearly not the long benign rollers of the Atlantic. I don't know what it is, but there's something about this sea that just doesn't feel right.

"It's a little lumpy out here."
430 miles into our passage through the Colombian Basin
11° N, 73° 49' W

We named our ship's autopilot and computer system "Ray" (short for Raytheon® the brand name) because he is on watch more than we; he is our faithful, fifth crew member. Now, Ray informs us that he has managed *Pacific Bliss* over 6000 nautical miles without so much as a hiccup. True, he has lost his GPS "fix" occasionally, but that, he assures us, is due to the satellites up there, not him!

"Yea, Ray!" our crew cheers. None of us has any macho desire to hand-steer, taking the helm in these boisterous, rolling Colombian seas! Ray does just fine, swerving around the humongous rollers, controlling the rudder, and steadily moving *Pacific Bliss* back on her course. We have given Ray plenty of leeway, allowing our invisible helmsman a 30-degree variance. Ray talks to *Pacific Bliss*, who talks with us. Would I expect anything less of a highly technical yacht, one that we depend on for our very lives?

The old salts of England
Used to say
In their understated way
It's a little lumpy today.

I invent this little ditty and write it into the ship's log to calm my nerves. Our stomachs are reflecting those lumps right now. No one has been interested in cooking or eating for the last few days. We seldom talk. We have withdrawn into our shells—a sea creature's survival mechanism.

The trade winds have been in the 20-30 knot range as forecasted, pushing *Pacific Bliss* along at an average boat speed of 7.53 knots since we left Bonaire. But the Force 7 gusts push her to 10-13 knots, with a trip maximum so far recorded by Ray at *17.7 knots.* We are sailing these waters with a double-reefed main, prepared for anything that might come our way.

And what might come our way in these waters? The weather here is influenced by the landmass of the South American continent. The season of the strongest winds is from December through April, when the trades blow NE to E. (The wind we have experienced so far has been directly East or ESE.) "Don't leave Bonaire with winds over 30 knots," we were told. We followed that advice. For pleasure, most would choose to cruise this area from June to September, when the winds are lighter and more variable. But we are not just casually cruising; we are *passage making*, with some leisurely interludes thrown in.

I'm having misgivings, not only about this current leg, but about the long voyage coming up. Günter and I plan to reach Costa Rica by mid-February and then slog up the coastline, back to San Diego for repairs that must be completed within the first year under our warranty. We will sail mostly against the wind. After pounding through the square waves of the Med, we are confident of our vessel's structural integrity. We know *Pacific Bliss* can take it. But can we?

The fast ride so far has not presented a problem; however, the 8-12 foot swells do cause uncomfortable rolling and yawing. The continuous Slap! Slap! of the waves against the hulls keeps us awake all night.

Eventually, our stomachs acclimate to the rough ride and our dispositions improve. Landfall is only two days away. Our talk is again spirited, vibrant with plans: Perhaps we will hire a guide to take the four of us on an historic city tour…perhaps we will take a carriage ride along the bay…or perhaps we will just hang out.

The Build-up

Early during my 0300 to 0600 watch, our third day at sea, I am in the cockpit as the new cradle moon feathers its way to the horizon. The dark sky flickers with stars. It is not what's above that's threatening; it's what is happening below. The wind whips against the port beam of *Pacific Bliss*. An occasional giant wave crashes into the port side of the cockpit, spewing salt water over the white side cushions and the teak table. *This is not a pleasant place to be. If this is living on the edge, I want to be someplace else.*

The sea behind the stern is coal black and menacing. A few waves are starting to build and break. Ashen spumes froth over foam crests. I've never seen this before. What does it mean? I search my memory to recall the page on "Beaufort Sea States" (see Appendix B) provided in the ship's library weather book. Then it comes to me. *Oh no. The beginning of spindrift, a sign of gale-force winds. The wind must be gusting to a Force 7 or even Force 8.* I return to the salon to don my life vest, then "cat walk" into the dangerous cockpit, keeping my center of gravity low and using every handhold I can. I fasten my harness to the stanchion at the stern behind the helm seat. The wind is from the aft port, not in my face. For three long hours, I endure this onslaught. By the time my watch is over, I'm exhausted.

I report the conditions to Richard, who is next on watch. I stumble to my berth and fall into a deep sleep, awakening three hours later to a monochromatic world. By midday there is still no sun. Everything is different shades of gray: The sky is overcast and smoky gray, the sea is dark and charcoal gray, and the foam on top of the waves is more gray than white. Poseidon is furious, continuing to whip up whitecaps. The height of the tumultuous rollers has been steadily building, building…

We had plotted a wide swing around the peninsula of Guajira, a lawless piece of land between Venezuela and Colombia, overrun with drug trafficking. The last thing we need—on top of this miserable wind—is to encounter drug cartel pirates. We are now approaching that crucial waypoint. It is time to change direction to make that swing. It will not be easy.

With everyone awake, Günter gives the order: "All on deck. We're going to take in another reef before we jibe." Günter and Richard fight the mighty force of the wind upon the sail, to pull in the third reef. Günter winds the main sheet around the electric winch roller while Richard tails, pulling on the sheet hard, struggling for every foot, then clamping the sheet down with the breaker. A large section of main canvas whips and screeches as it reluctantly folds into the sail bag. When the sheets are yanked tight, only a small canvas remains. This is as far as we can reef without taking the entire canvas down. Then the men furl in the protesting jib until only a handkerchief remains to stabilize the boat.

"Okay, team, good job," Günter says. "I'm proud of you. Now, prepare to jibe."

Thank God we have a sail system that allows us to make a controlled jibe without a dangerous, swinging boom! Soon we are on course, heading for our waypoint four: 11° 34' N, 74° 25.2' W. Gallinas Point, the *northernmost* cape in South America. This cape is the north version of perilous Cape Horn, the *southernmost* cape on the continent.

Force 10! Night of Sheer Terror

We tackled the cape for the rest of the day. It was a major accomplishment to skirt this lawless peninsula of Guajira. By evening, we are approaching the Magdalena River. This is a major path for the flow of shipments to and from inland Colombia. The fertile Magdalena River basin extends from the South American Andes through the Magdalena river valley. Then it crosses into the Caribbean region, a very rich ecosystem for fauna and flora, as well as a fertile ground for agriculture and raising livestock. The port city of Barranquilla, known as Colombia's Golden Gate, is strategically located on the delta by the river's mouth, where it flows into the Caribbean sea.

At 1900, 7 p.m., I receive a VHF call transmitted by a Colombian Coast Guard vessel. The officer, William, warns me that we might encounter fishing vessels with nets within twelve miles from the breakwater. When I clarify our destination as Cartagena, he reminds us that a notification is required whenever a ship sails within 12 miles of the shoreline. After hanging up, I immediately plot our position. I'm surprised to discover that *Pacific Bliss* has been pushed by the strong winds to within 22 miles of the coast. I re-plot our course to route us 60 miles offshore.

During the next two hours, the sea conditions worsen. The menacing rollers behind us are the largest I've ever seen—probably 20 feet! The wind maintains a steady Force 7, gusting to Force 8. We are all uncomfortable and uneasy. The sky turns pitch black, heightening our fears.

Since I now know that their ship is in our vicinity, I decide to contact the Coast Guard for an up-to-date forecast.

"It will continue like this," William answers. "You can expect about 30-35 knot winds with high waves as you round that tricky point coming up."

What! We thought that we had rounded the most dangerous point. Now, we learn that point is Baranquilla, a jutting cape past the outflow of the Magdalena River, coming right up!

"Sir?" I ask. "We intend to go about 60 miles out when we round the point."

"That should be fine."

But it is not fine. The erratic motion of *Pacific Bliss* this night requires more care than the usual "cat walk." Inside the salon, our ride turns wilder than a bucking bronco. Phyllis and I remove anything that can fly off the counters. We put the thermos filled with hot water into the sink, grabbing onto handholds as we work. The towels, hung on the drawer pulls, dance frenetically. Cans clang against the locked pantry doors. The instruments at the nav station display a steady Force 8. Those mere Force 7 gusts are history now.

At 2100, 9 p.m., the wind increases from Force 8 to Force 9. Our boat speed varies from 9-13 knots—and that's with the jib furled, in addition to the triple-reefed main! *Pacific Bliss* is racing hard before the waves and the wind. The wind wails and howls like a pack of wolves, tearing through the rigging. Phyllis and I cannot hear each other talk. I force the sliding salon door to the cockpit shut against the rushing wind. We suit up in foul weather gear.

Günter has the 2100-2400 watch. He and Richard are in the cockpit facing the brunt of the blow. They struggle to take down the handkerchief of a main all the way, but the wind proves too strong.

So far, Ray has managed to hang in there. *But what if he conks out on us? He has always been so dependable; I trust him.* I cannot imagine us hand-steering in these conditions. We have little practice, and virtually none in heavy weather. I had hand steered for a while crossing the Atlantic, but those rollers were benign. These have become ominous.

Around 2300, an hour before midnight, all hell breaks loose. With nothing more to do in the salon, I'm out on the cockpit bench, huddled next to the innermost bulwark. The multimeter above the salon door has been set to wind speed. The wind had been approaching Force 9, but now it is a *consistent* Force 9 with lengthy gusts of Force 10, a true wind speed of 50-plus knots. Seeing that F10 sends shivers down my spine. My stomach knots.

Force 8 equals gale, I recall from studying the Beaufort wind scales (see Appendix B). Force 9 equals *strong* gale. In 9, the crests of the waves begin to topple, tumble, and roll over. Dense streaks of foam are blown along in the direction of the wind. I can't see this foam in the dark, but I can imagine it hissing along the surface of the waves. And Force 10… my mouth is so dry I can barely swallow. Force 10…very high waves with overhanging crests. Great patches of foam streak along in the direction of the wind. The sea becomes white.

The wind howls through the bimini shades surrounding the cockpit. It attacks the bimini fasteners, ripping them loose. The loosened straps flop wildly against the bimini hardtop like a crazed bungee cord. Richard is now at the helm, helping Ray maintain control. Günter is managing the cockpit. Watching the straps slap uncontrollably, I'm afraid they might hit Günter, taking out his eyes. *This could go from chaos to catastrophe.*

Günter takes command of the situation. He motions me off the seat and out of the way. Then calmly—but determinedly—he rips each of the three shades off the bimini. Meanwhile, the seat cushions have come alive, flopping up and down like demented sea monsters, straining at their snaps. Together, Günter and I pull them

The storm builds in the western Caribbean.

cleats. Exhausted after what seems like forever, he slumps onto the cockpit bench to catch his breath. His immense effort decreases the boat speed by only 2-3 knots. We are still flying at over 20 knots, fine perhaps for catamaran racers. But we are only cruisers! We didn't sign up for this!

Finally, our reliable, dependable Ray just can't handle the strain any longer. He reacts too slowly to overcome a roller and can't make it back. We broach, turning sideways into the wind. *Pacific Bliss* goes into a jibe that back winds the sail. The boat is drifting out of control.

Without the speed and the rushing wind, we are lulled into a strange and eerie silence. Time slows down. The four of us gather in the cockpit near Richard, still at the helm.

I pray silently, "Dear God…I know that you answered the pleas of the fishermen to still the storm on the Sea of Galilee. This is more than I can bear. I'm not asking you to *still* the sea, but could you just get this wind back to a more comfortable Force 7? Or even Force 8 would feel sane right now. In Jesus' name, Amen."

Now that we can hear each other talk, Phyllis approaches me. "I haven't prayed for so long, I forgot how, but I want to," she says.

"I just finished doing that," I answer. We hold hands and bow our heads. I repeat my prayer with her.

Günter commands our attention. "The first thing we need to assess is whether or not we are in a survival situation. It may *appear* calmer now because the noise is less. But is it safe to leave the boat in irons like this?"

"I think not…" he answers his own question.

"More water, Lois." I hand him another bottle. "Sorry. My mouth feels dry as sandpaper. Adrenalin, I guess." He pauses to take a long swig.

No one says a word.

"During the *Pacific Bliss* christening party in Canet, Jean-Pierre gave me some good advice." Günter turns toward Richard. "He's the founder of Catana. We were discussing heavy weather techniques. He said, 'Run with the wind and the waves as long as you can to lower your *apparent* wind… that's the wind that the boat feels.'"

Richard nods.

off and heave them into the salon. With those actions, the noise level is markedly reduced. *Whew! I can think again.*

The sea boils up to the drain of the cockpit floor. But it has not flooded the cockpit—yet. It just pounds, gurgles, and hisses. At the stern, the dinghy bounces wildly on its davits as each wave rises above it, then slides beneath the dual hulls. Salt water sprays my face, clouding my vision. *What if a rogue wave breaks into the cockpit? We'd be slipping and sliding around like in disaster movies.*

Phyllis manages the inside of the salon, handing towels to the three of us in the cockpit, wiping the floors, and trying to keep the salon free of water as we slosh in and out. The salon, the heart of *Pacific Bliss,* pounds and creaks and groans, teak against Kevlar. *Will the bulwarks hold? They are the load-bearing walls that keep the boat together.*

Back in the cockpit, *Pacific Bliss* seems to be out of control. When gusts hit Force 10, she accelerates to 25 knots. She climbs higher and higher, then hurls down the huge rollers, leaving my stomach at the top. *This feels like a roller coaster ride that will never, ever end.*

Some waves hit *Pacific Bliss* so hard the entire structure shudders at high frequency. The sounds of creaking, bombing, and banging are awful. *Please, God, hold her together. How much more can Pacific Bliss take? We have to slow her down.*

Günter fashions a warp, a device to slow the boat, using our three black docking lines. Bracing himself against the wall of wind, he trails them from the stern

Günter's attention turns to me: "Lois, how much sea room do we have?"

I pry open the salon doors, scan the paper chart secured on the salon table, and rush back to the cockpit. "Well over 200 miles."

"That allows us to run, with the wind at our backs, for a long time, even at 20 knots. We are not in danger of capsizing if we run with the wind and waves…but we *are* in danger like this. You cannot heave-to in a cat. If we stay like this, one of these waves is bound to break over the dinghy and over the cockpit. And if we ram into one sideways, we could flip."

Phyllis goes pale.

Richard's face is serious and set. There is nothing else to say. A decision has been made. Now we need to *just do it*. It is going to be a very long night.

"Richard, you'll have to help Ray. Steer manually every time the compass shows a 30-degree swing from our set course," Günter commands. "Lois, help me pull in these warps to clear the propellers. They didn't help much anyway."

With the engines revving, Richard takes us out of irons. The freight train sound is deafening as the wind resumes its chase. Richard is stoic at the helm, working the boat to keep her running with the wind and waves, keeping both engines on idle just in case we broach again.

Three of us are calm after our talk, but Phyllis remains frightened. She retreats to the salon and curls up into a fetal position on the settee. Since I'm no longer needed in the cockpit, I return to the salon with her and shove the door shut, blocking out some of the fury. She begs me to radio the Coast Guard again.

"I can't imagine what good it would do."

What will I say to them? Come rescue us. We want to leave the ship? I feel safe now, staying with Pacific Bliss. We have no shore, no rocks or reefs to contend with. Even if she flips, we can live on her upside down. She was designed for that. I remember swimming underneath her, pointing up at the red circle between her hulls, a signal for a helicopter rescue. I feel comfortable just staying with the ship. No one but God can help us here.

"Just let them know what's happening with us," Phyllis pleads.

I pick up the VHF. Bad news. I cannot get it to work. Instead of lessening her fears, I have increased them. Not good. There is nothing more for us to do right now but to help the helmsman and captain when they ask for it. I sit at the nav station, watching the hands on the clock move ever so slowly.

How I want this long night to end!

Finally, *my* scheduled watch from 0300 to 0600 arrives. I suit up, donning my life preserver and harness over my foul weather gear. I pry open the salon doors, ready to take over the helm from Richard. He must be exhausted by now. Sitting at our exposed helm station, higher than the cockpit, he has been getting the brunt of the blow and the spray. "I'm ready to take over anytime," I yell.

Richard cannot hear a word. The wind is driving straight toward me. I can barely stand—even under the protection of the hardtop bimini. Richard motions for me to come closer. I force my body forward against the onslaught. Shaking, willing my fingers to work, I clasp my harness onto the cleat near the helm and lean into his ear, "I'm ready."

He shouts directly into my face so the wind cannot steal his words. "No, Lois. You won't have the upper body strength to handle it. I've had to take over manually from Ray two more times. The wind feels like it's easing—just a little. I can keep going."

"What if you have to go? I mean…to the head?"

"I already have…What else could I do? I have to stay right here to manage Ray."

I struggle to unclip my harness. The wind pushes me back toward the salon so fast that I start to trip on the steps. I manage to catch myself just before slamming into the Lexan® door. *Close call.*

Looking up, I notice that Günter has wisely changed the multimeter display above the salon cockpit door from Wind Speed to Wind Direction, to reduce the fear factor. *I understand. I won't tell him the news. The news I also kept from Phyllis.* The last time I had checked the wind speed at the Nav station in the salon, it was 53 knots, and gusting. A steady *Force 10!*

I decide to change our read-out *inside* the salon, at the nav station, to Boat Speed. Not good. We have already reached *25.8 knots top speed!* The fear grips me all over again. *Please God!* I force myself to take a few deep breaths. I check the chart. We are now somewhere between Baranquilla and Bahia Gato, about 60 miles offshore.

A long way to go.

Richard digs in for the long haul, patient and uncomplaining. Günter stays out there by his side. Phyllis lies in a fetal position on the settee.

Shortly after 0300, the wind gradually eases off. Force 9. Then it's down to Force 8.

What a relief!

The waves are still three or more stories high, rolling in from ever-changing directions of a confused sea, but my fears are calmed.

Force 8. This is what I begged for. My prayers are being answered.

At 0500, we reach our waypoint for changing course to Cartagena Bay. It will be a controlled jibe in a Force 8, with the wind to our port side.

Günter forces the sliding salon door open. "All hands on deck." He thinks *Pacific Bliss* can handle it.

Phyllis and I suit up again, braving the wind to receive our instructions.

How can we possibly change course with these huge waves continuing to slam our hull? Should I, as the navigator, recommend that we continue our course to San Blas? Should we bypass Cartagena? But who on board would want to have another night at sea?

I keep my doubts to myself.

With all of us in the cockpit, working like a well-oiled team, we carry off the jibe smoothly. On her new course, *Pacific Bliss* floats like a cork.

We keep the dagger boards up. The noise is like chalk-against-chalkboard times 1000. *Pacific Bliss* squeaks, creaks, groans, and twists, protesting the onslaught of waves against her beam.

During this long night, I had yearned for the dawn. I mistakenly believed that light would lower our anxiety. But now, as wan, amber streaks gradually appear through the clouds, I am grateful that the worst of the storm has occurred in total darkness; we have been spared the trauma of watching wild waves bent on swallowing us alive.

I head for the salon, where I grab a pillow and collapse onto the settee in my foul weather gear.

A few hours later, *Pacific Bliss* enters the quieter waters of the Cartagena harbor. I try the VHF to find that it is magically working again. I attribute the malfunction to the high winds. But I'm frustrated that Club Nautico, with whom we have reserved a berth, doesn't answer my call. Jim and Jo on *Atlas* pick up the call and advise: "Go in anyway, watch for the guys in the dinghy, then follow them."

Thank God for helpful cruisers! Jim had been a calming voice in the darkness, as I talked with him in the wee morning hours before we jibed to reach Cartagena. He told me that the worst would be over, once we had rounded the peninsula and jibed toward the bay. He was right.

By the time we anchor and are routed to a permanent slip, it is past noon. We are one exhausted but thankful crew. And our lady, *Pacific Bliss*? She came through it all with flying colors. We have gained a new respect for her—and for Ray.

Later in the day, we meet Francoise and Bernard, owners of a red-and-white Catana 471, *Adelaide II*, anchored here. They invite us to come on board. Bernard tells us that he has experienced similar, though somewhat lighter, conditions near that same area of Baranquilla—fortunately, with all their sails down. Had we to do it over again, we would have furled the jib to a small triangle size—with the main doused completely. Once we had come upon the storm triple-reefed, however, our options had closed.

We celebrate our survival and arrival with our new French friends by opening our very last bottle of Catana Champagne. Following that, the six of us down two bottles of white Bordeaux. The wine has traveled with us all the way from Canet, secure in our "wine cellar" underneath the cockpit table. Despite all the shaking that went on, they are still quite enjoyable.

Günter asks Bernard, "What *is* the best way to transport wine and champagne over long distances in a rolling, sometimes shaking, boat?"

"Horizontally, of course. Lying down, *comme une femme*."

Like a woman? Ah, those frisky French!

We are elated to be back in port and enjoying wine with cruisers again. Who knows? After our harrowing Force 10 experience, we may never want to leave.

Cartagena, Jewel of the Caribbean
Club Nautico, Cartagena, Colombia

The first day in port, our priority is to take care of our boat. "*Pacific Bliss* has been good to us," Günter says. "We need to be good to her."

Of course! She is a cherished friend to me now, to whom I owe my very life.

Günter and Richard hose down the vessel's exterior from bows to stern while Phyllis and I wash down the interior. Salt is everywhere! One of the foam mattresses was drenched from waves forced through the rubber molding on a side window. The men remove its washable covering and take it to the trampoline, spray it with fresh water, wring it out, and spread it to dry in the hot Caribbean sun. Then they clean out the salt-splashed cockpit locker, hose down the gear, and leave it out to dry. Phyllis and I lug our salt-encrusted clothes and bags of salty towels to the laundry at the end of the dock.

Our chores completed by sundown, the four of us take a stroll beyond the Club Nautico gates. Along the street following the bay, I am struck by the juxtaposition of old and new: Modern high-rises across the bay glimmer golden in the setting sun, peeking behind the time-worn remains of an old, castle tower.

Beyond the ruins, we saunter through the open iron gates of Club de Pesca. We don't get far. A guard approaches us. "Club full, please…all of you, leave."

"Okay, if that's the way you want it," I grumble as we turn back, "we'll spend our Colombian pesos at the much friendlier Club Nautico!"

As we walk the docks back at our own club, the sun turns red-orange and glows through dozens of stationary yacht masts and rigging swaying in the breeze—a wonderful sailor's sunset, safe in port. What a contrast from being all alone at sea!

⚓

After a sound overnight sleep that only safety on land can bring, our crew is ready to explore Cartagena. All of us, that is, except for Captain Günter, who elects to stay behind with his ship. He says he needs to decompress and exchange yarns with the cruisers here; he is not emotionally prepared to transition from sailor to tourist. We, on the other hand, use touring as an escape, not wanting to talk about our adventure just yet.

Phyllis, Richard, and I shop for fresh meats, fruits, and vegetables to tide us over for a few days. Then we walk through the nearby Manga district. Years ago, there was nothing here but Fort San Sebastian del Pastelillo. Now, enormous, stunning mansions, with Moorish details and trim, pack the Manga. We peek through filigreed iron gates, which protect vast courtyards filled with towering shade trees and large wooden furniture. Heavy armor, with intricate scrollwork, covers the windows and doors of magnificent houses.

Back at the club, we inquire about the numerous FOR SALE signs we noticed on mansion gates. We learn that many of Manga's wealthy and aging inhabitants are moving to the more convenient beachfront luxury apartments in the Bocagrande and Castillogrande districts across the Bay.

On our return, we tell Günter what we have seen and, the next day, he joins us on our urban adventures. We taxi to Old Cartagena, then stroll down one narrow, charming street after another, passing carved wooden balconies overflowing with geraniums, ivy, and trumpet vines. I stop to photograph colorful restorations—a blue carved door set into cream stucco; a gnarled and twisted flowering tree artfully flattened between two shuttered and barred windows; a tasteful mural painted on a pale blue wall, framed by a lone palm. The end of one narrow street opens up into a bright, sunlit square dotted with the most amazing metal sculptures I've ever seen: a vendor pushing a cart, four wizened men playing cards, and the sailor hero Don Blas—complete with peg leg and dagger. We realize that the sculptures are part of the Art Museum, housed in another restored building that flanks one edge of the square. One can have dinner served right outside in the sculpture garden!

Cartagena has been declared a UNESCO Cultural and Historic City. The city has certainly made an immense effort to maintain its reputation, despite the fact the country of Colombia has been embroiled in civil war for more than 20 years. The only signs of strife one sees as a tourist are the layers of protection that the city maintains: The first layer is the local guards, standing at street corners and in front of buildings, toting machine guns; the second is the national guards, who protect the city's entrances and exits and more valuable sites; a third layer is not obvious—the plainclothes policemen

DID YOU KNOW?

COLOMBIA

Colombia is the only South American country to have coastline on both the Atlantic and Pacific Oceans. Colombia is also located in both the Northern and Southern Hemispheres. Its capital is Santa Fe de Bogotá, located in the interior.

For centuries, Cartagena has been the stepping-off point for anyone in search of adventure in the Caribbean or about to set off into the interior of South America—a human crossroads. The pace of life in the city depended on whether the fleet was in port at any given time. The burgeoning trade brought great wealth. The city was a meeting point for settlers destined for the Pacific or New Granada. Unfortunately, it was also the first and primary location for delivering African slaves for sale after they had suffered a long and inhumane ocean crossing.

Cartagena also became a cultural exchange. It was the place where wine, oil, fabrics, and books from Europe changed hands. For example, 100 copies of the first edition of Don Quixote were exchanged there. In the words of the historian Rodriguez Frayle: "Cartagena was the gateway through which all of Peru and this Kingdom could enjoy the fruits of all Spain, Italy, Rome, France, India, and all lands and provinces throughout the world where Spain has connections, dealings, or trade."

Don Quixote

Cartagena

Cartagena is a magical place that must be experienced at least once in a lifetime. But a word of caution: Once you come to see her, you will dream about when you can return. From its charming, old, walled city to its historic naval and land fortifications to the posh, modern high rises and its tourist beaches, Cartagena dazzles and thrills. However, this is a city that cannot be devoured; she needs to be savored—slowly and deliciously.

Mark my words: Günter and I *will be back!*

who roam the streets among the tourists, eliminating petty theft. Cartagena is *the* favorite destination of Colombians themselves, favored by lovers, honeymooners, and vacationers alike. And most likely the only city in which they can feel safe.

Leaving the square, we meander past a shop that sells colorful hammocks. A stone-faced guard stands in front. A donkey labors along the street, pulling a cart filled with construction materials. Other donkeys pull street vendors' carts filled with fresh mangoes, huge avocadoes, ice cream, and souvenirs. Günter and I stop at a language school that flies both United States and Colombian flags. There we discover that private Spanish instruction is possible. We just may take classes here, in this wonderful city—someday.

The four of us proceed to the next cobblestoned square. Old-fashioned, ruby red carriages and bored horses rest underneath shade trees. We realize that we need to rest as well. We seat ourselves in a balcony restaurant overlooking a great street scene. There we order gigantic, lime-colored piña coladas, and later, a light lunch. But during our table talk, Günter—usually an eager participant in urban adventures—seems strangely subdued.

His mind is really someplace else. And I think I know where that place is…Pacific Bliss.

On the way back, in the late afternoon, we walk past the sea wall to find Poseidon kicking up his heels again. He forces huge combers to pound against the wall. The palms along the promenade bow to his fury. *I'm glad we're not out there.* Then the realization hits me hard: These sunny, peaceful days are only an interlude; being "out there" again is as inevitable as the setting sun.

We stop to exchange "war" stories in the cruisers' lounge at Club Nautico. "The ABCs-to-Cartagena is one of the top ten worst crossings in the world," one wizened sailor blurts. "It's right up there with Cape Horn and Cape of Good Hope. You just don't hear about it much, because until recently, the Western powers didn't recommend travel here."

"Hey! Cool it," says another. "Don't scare them!" He takes a big swig of his Club Colombia beer. "Most likely, this is the worst situation you will encounter. Ever. In your entire world circumnavigation."

One scraggly Old Salt, an American, has berthed at Club Nautico for a year now. He attempted the passage from Cartagena to Aruba the wrong way—pushing *east* against those so-called "reinforced trades." His yacht broke to bits on the reefs of that cape near Baranquilla. While waiting for his insurance to settle, he took up residence here. Now he has a replacement yacht. She is outfitted for tough passages. Yet somehow, he has been loath to leave port for worlds unknown. Günter wonders whether it has anything to do with the dark-haired, long legged Caribbean beauty that he has seen with that sailor.

Colorful public transportation in Cartagena, Colombia.

The sun sets among the highrises across the bay of Cartagena, through masts at Club Nautico.

February 5: Seated at the cockpit bench sipping my morning coffee, I am updating my journal: "This city is truly a jewel, made all the more precious by the angst preceding our arrival. She has been a delightful, unexpected haven of rest, and after only a few short days, we have fallen in love with her."

Cartagena was the most important Spanish port in the New World for several centuries. Here, God created one of the world's greatest natural harbors, with numerous protected anchorages that could accommodate the largest sailing vessels. This harbor, with its ideal strategic location in the New World, became the western base for the Spanish fleet that gathered the riches of the Indies every other year. Gigantic galleons, full of cargo taken on at Portobelo—a town we plan to visit—could be safely careened here for repairs.

Exhausted from fighting the Force 10 storm, we still had the good sense to enter this marvelous harbor through the Boca Chica Channel, even though our chart showed it as the southernmost entrance to the Bay. "The wider Boca Grande entrance to the north is shallow and dangerous," our pilot book had warned us.

The book also provided the back-story: The submerged rocks filling the channel are the remnants of a sea wall built over two centuries earlier. A number of shipwrecks occurred about that time, including the galleons Buen Suceso and Concepcion, belonging to the Portuguese Navy. These wrecks had blocked off the Boca Grande channel, forming a natural line of defense for the bay. So an underwater wall was added, completing the defensive strategy.

Now, every ship with a deep draft wanting to berth at the city pier is forced to use the Boca Chica entrance. I remember: as we motored through the narrows of Boca Chica the morning of our arrival, we even saw excursion boats headed to those once formidable strongholds of Castilla San José and Fortaleza San Fernando.

After breakfast, the four of us leave the docks to visit the Naval Museum. We walk past display after display, replicas of ships and battles past. I linger at a geographical display of this area of the world, while the others move on. A table-top relief, covered with Plexiglas®, shows how the mountains of Venezuela and Colombia create a virtual wind tunnel that feeds down through the Magdalena River basin and out to the sea. Then below the sea, as the relief depicts, the continental shelf of South America drops off in layers. An especially turbulent area is created at—guess where—Baranquilla! Now the geography and topography become clear. Not only did we encounter the typical "cape effect" while rounding Baranquilla, we also encountered the high waves and confused seas that resulted from this "wind tunnel effect." And all of that combines with the convulsive outflow of Magdalena, the mightiest river on the Spanish Main.

Why didn't the cruising books warn us about that? Why all the text and talk about avoiding drug runners, but not the dangerous seas?

As I stand there transfixed, Phyllis comes to get me. "Lois, what are you doing?"

"Just thinking… about how we got into that mess out there."

Our crew is deep into reviewing the naval battles of yesteryear. I turn to join them. It turns out that the history of this city is as troubled as the temperamental Caribbean Sea that slams into her walls: The city of *Cartagena del Poniente* was founded by Spanish expeditions in June 1533. At that time, she was a marshy island called *Calamari*, inhabited by Yagu Indians living in adobe huts. This natural port, with two bays, quickly became a point of entry for merchandise and passengers destined for the interior. It also became the first line of defense for the new kingdoms of Granada and Peru. As a result, Cartagena, from its very beginnings, was prone to attacks from pirates and mercenaries who sought to break the stranglehold of Spain and to steal her wealth.

Eleven years after she was founded, Cartagena suffered her first pirate attack. The city was celebrating the wedding of one of Governor Heredia's sisters, and in the noise and din of the party, a French pirate—along with a Spanish pilot/informer—stole all the money and goods belonging to the inhabitants and razed the fledgling city. Numerous victories and defeats followed, affecting the very way the city was run. The city begged the Spanish crown for fortifications, to no avail.

Attacks continued.

In 1559, seven ships, commanded by a Frenchman, Martin Cote, landed a thousand men, who defeated 500 native archers and then destroyed the city. Shortly afterwards, yet another Frenchman, Jean de Beautemps, attempted a landing. But this time, the furious citizens of Cartagena drove him and his forces away. Then ten years later, Cartagena defended itself successfully again, this time from the forces of John Hawkins, an English aristocrat and sailor.

As Cartagena moved into the 17th century, it finally came into its own as a commercial port with massive fortifications.

Our group moves to an excellent diorama display that shows the route of Spain's fleet of galleons. First, the fleet would sail from Spain to the Caribbean ports of Santo Domingo, Puerto Rico, and/or one of the islands in the Lesser Antilles. Then, it would split in two. One group of ships would sail to Veracruz, Mexico, for supplies. The other group would sail to Portobello, Panama, where its ships took on the plundered riches of Peru and parts south. These stolen treasures had been transported earlier by mule all the way from the Pacific port at Panama City through the jungles of the isthmus

The varied architecture of Cartagena.

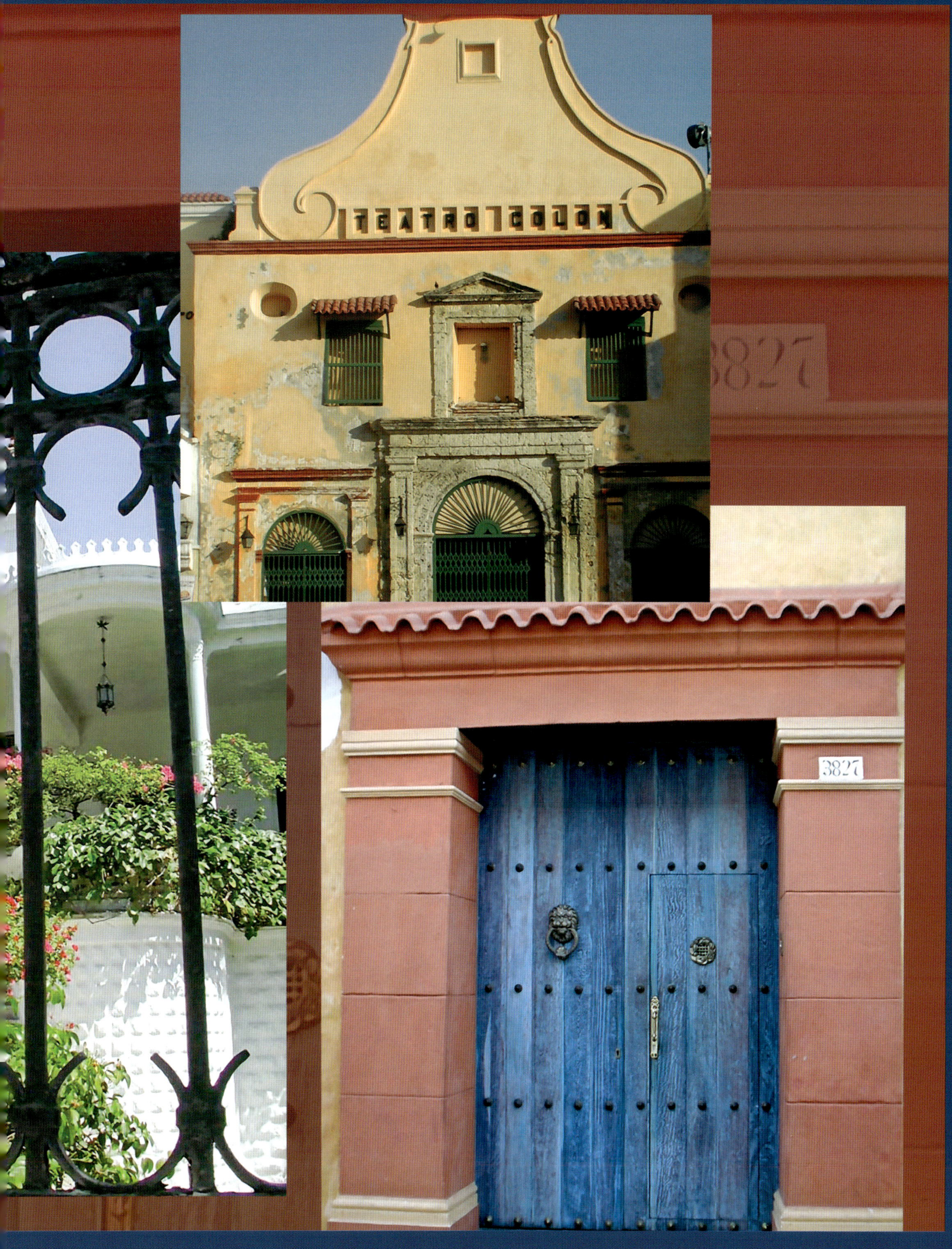
TEATRO COLON
3827

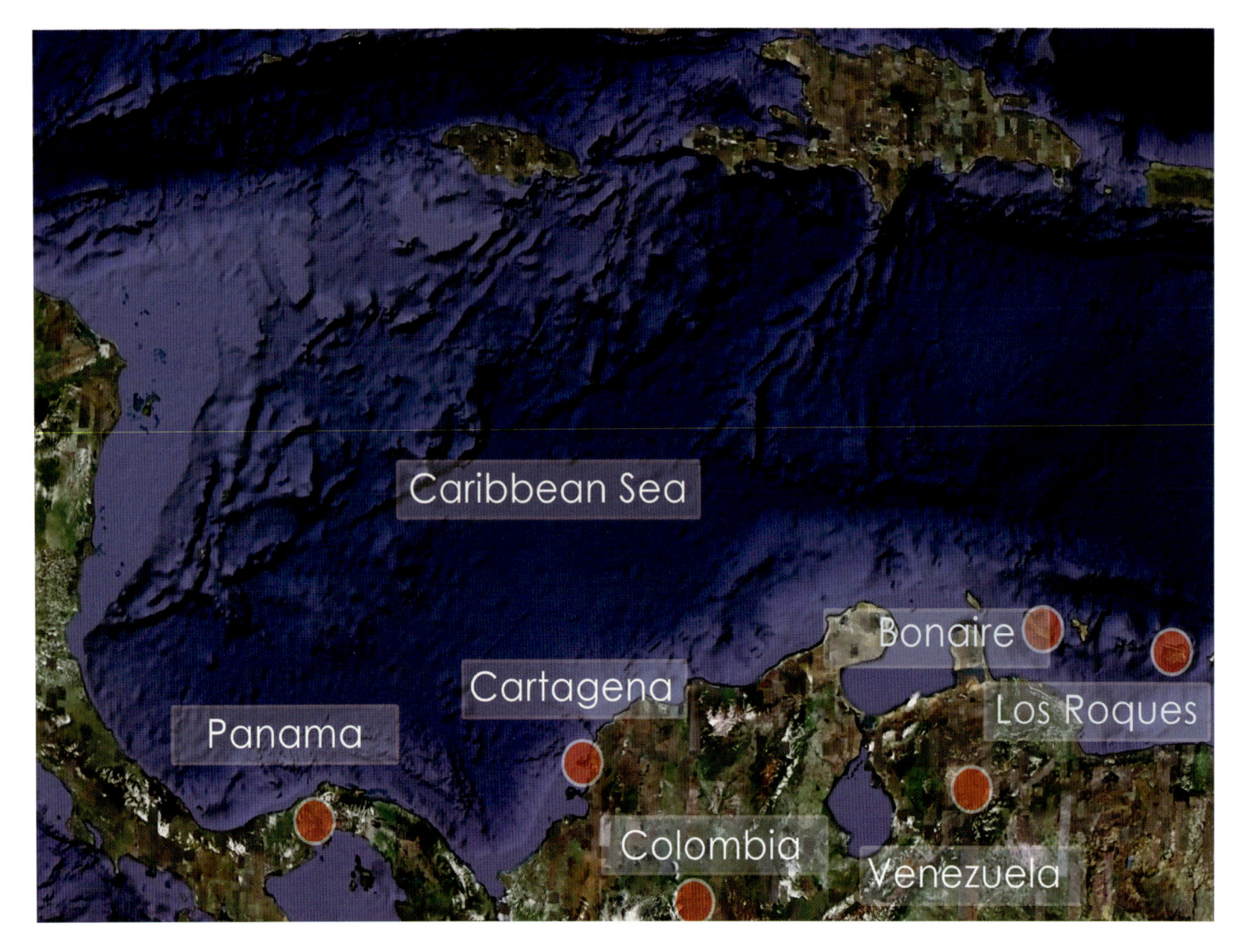

to Portobelo.

Once back in Cartagena, the fleets would take on passengers and freight from the New Kingdom of Granada and then sail northeast to form a huge convoy in Havana. Then, the entire convoy would set sail for Spain, heading north of the Antilles to take advantage of the Gulf Stream currents. It was quite an operation, with the merchant ships protected by warships, all designed to fill the treasure chests of Seville.

No wonder our crew has been entranced by this history! These displays breathe new life into the naval battles of yesteryear.

The next display we see features the local hero, Blas de Lezo, an amazing sailor. Don Blas had a wooden left leg. He lost his leg at the age of fifteen while fighting a sea battle off Malaga, Spain; he was blinded in one eye while defending Toulon; his arm was limp from a bloody battle to rescue Barcelona from the English. All this before he reached the age of 25!

He had arrived in Cartagena with more than 40 years' naval and military experience. He had served the Crown on the high seas the world over. And by 1740, he had twice routed the fleet of Admiral Vernon. Then on March 13, 1741, three ships, their sails puffed with pride after sacking Portobelo, appeared off the city. They were the vanguard of Vernon's third fleet: 100 war vessels, frigates, and transport ships carrying 8,000 soldiers and 12,000 sailors. Cartagena had only a motley collection of 3,000 soldiers, militiamen, native archers—and the crews of Blas de Lezo's ships.

A David vs. Goliath moment!

Vernon's first plan was to avoid the Boca Chica entrance (the southern entrance that *Pacific Bliss* sailed through). He landed in Boquilla, seven kilometers away. Then he planned to control the surrounding area, bringing the city to its knees via starvation. But landing was difficult in the marsh, so he gave up that plan and, instead, laid siege to Boca Chica directly. This caused Blas' forces to retreat and the English then entered the inner bay.

Elated by this triumph and certain that the city would now capitulate, Vernon dispatched a ship to London with news of the fall of Cartagena. In London, commemorative medals were cast.

Lois and Phyllis in the old city of Cartagena.

An embarrassing miscalculation.

Back in Cartagena, the tides of war were turning. For a while, the English flag flew on abandoned La Popa Hill, and the English controlled the islands of Manzanillo and Manga. But the detachments continuing to land at Boquilla suffered heavy casualties. Thirty-five hundred English fighters attacked San Felipe fort. Don Blas, with only 500 men, forced them to retreat, then turned to attack *them*. Five hundred fighting English men were lost in that battle. Completely demoralized, the English were never able to dominate the fort. Finally, Vernon set sail, never to return.

However, the victory was bittersweet. Blas de Lezo died shortly afterward; shrapnel wounds claimed his life. While Cartagena celebrated, she also mourned the death of her greatest champion.

Now that we know the story, we stumble upon more statues and sculptures of this peg-legged hero than a boat has barnacles.

⚓

On our last evening in Cartagena, Günter and I tour the restored San Felipe de Baraja Castle on Lazarus Hill. We see yet another sculpture of Don Blas; this time in stone. It fronts the castle. We climb tiers of stone steps to the lookout. Cartagena is spread below us in the setting sun, her rooftops sparkling like a million jewels. We sit on a bench near a small chapel. It is windy, yet peaceful up here. We talk about the next phase of our voyage, the sail to the San Blas Islands, still another tribute to the Cartagena hero.

I dread another night at sea.

I turn toward Günter. "I know this sounds hackneyed, but I feel that I've lost my innocence…and I don't know whether or not I'll get it back."

"I know…I understand." Günter puts his arm over my shoulder, pulls me toward him, and hugs me tight.

Sculpture of Don Blas a local hero, in the plaza of the Old City.

Old wooden boat in Cartagena harbor.

A Mamitupu islander asks to have her photo taken.

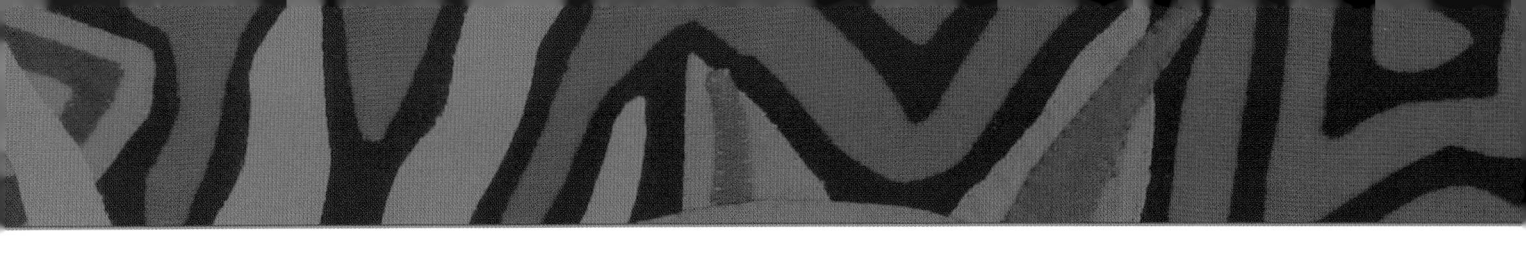

CHAPTER 8
THE SURPRISING SAN BLAS ISLANDS

Ordeal or Adventure? Introspection under a Full Moon
The Gulf of Darien, Colombia
9° 37.8' N, 77° 47.5' W
February 8, 2001

Some say the sea is cruel. I agree. I say it is without mercy. Freedom at sea? Independence, managing your own municipality? Ha! Leave the shore, and you leave behind a certain degree of freedom; you must live by Poseidon's rules, pawns to the sea god's whims. And you're left with a burning question: Is the cruiser experience worth the loss of control over your life?

At the starboard helm, on my favorite 0300-0600 watch, I strive to renew my relationship with *Pacific Bliss* and the sea. I would love to regain that camaraderie with her that I felt during those blissful night watches of our Atlantic crossing: the shared wind against my cheek and her sails, the small vibrations in the rigging that she senses along with me, the rumble of the water sloshing her hulls, which I hear and she feels. I trust her. She came through the storm just fine, but I don't have the same emotional connection with her that I had before the storm.

During our five days of decompression in Cartagena, the moon had continued to grow. Now, it is full and complacent, with a pale sheen that fades whenever clouds pass by. The seas are still unpredictable. *Pacific Bliss* has been reined in much too tightly, double-reefed already. Our crew fears another Force 7-to-Force 8 escalation.

Attitude, the Difference between Ordeal and Adventure. I look down at this inscription on my tee-shirt from *Lats and Atts,* short for *Latitudes and Attitudes,* a California sailing magazine. *What is my attitude now, this first overnight since our Force 10 ordeal?*

Leaving the safety of port has been difficult—with each of us compelled to face those raging demons within. This short hop across the Gulf of Darien would have been a breeze before our night of terror, before we lost our innocence.

"Life is either a daring adventure—or nothing at all," I whisper my favorite quote, the one from Helen Keller. *Hmm. This has been a key maxim for my life. Should it be? Must it always be like this? Must I always live life on the edge?* Rollers slap against the hulls of *Pacific Bliss* as she heaves onward, while answers elude me like a school of slippery eels.

I try talking out loud to *Pacific Bliss*, feeling a little foolish. "Do you hear me?" She fails to answer. Maybe she's just an inert hunk of fiberglass after all.

Cruisers at Club Nautico had assured us that the southern part of the Golfo de Darien would pose no problems. "You will face none of those horrific winds and high seas there." Even so, we agonized. After a discussion fraught with emotions, the four of us decided to ease our nerves. Instead of our original plan of sailing directly across the gulf to the San Blas Islands, we decided to sail to Isla Tintipan. And that daysail would be followed by this single overnight. I checked and re-checked the NOAA website at the internet café a few blocks from the Club. It called for 25-knot winds and 9-12 foot seas, with swells still rolling in toward Darien from that cruel point off Barranquilla. Religiously, we followed all of the weather nets, as well as our on-board Navteq®. Everything confirmed the forecast. We knew in our hearts that *Pacific Bliss* could handle these conditions easily.

But could *we*?

125

Fisherman's family portrait Mamitupu, San Blas.

As usual, we played our ritual *Amazing Grace* as we set sail. This time, though, we bowed our heads in silent prayer: Please, God, keep us safe…and don't make us go through another Force 10 storm. *Amazing Grace, how sweet the sound…*

Our sail began yesterday under hazy, gray-blue skies and a benign Force 4 wind. It was an ideal sailing day, but my nervous stomach refused to calm. I became riveted to the display panel in the cockpit, a knot forming in my gut whenever a gust brought the multimeter display to a Force 6 or more, however intermittent. We sailed all the way close-hauled with a full main and jib, an easy voyage of only 47.4 miles. At 1730, we dropped the hook in a sandy bottom with good holding at 18 feet. The anchorage was deserted except for an occasional fisherman in a *panga* (a narrow boat) off the reef at the point. During dinner, we sat around the cockpit table in uneasy silence. I felt relieved, but the relief was only temporary.

"What's on your mind?" Phyllis prodded Günter.

"I'm thinking of every little thing that could go wrong."

"Like what?"

"For example, those fishermen could board the boat while we are all asleep…or the anchor might not hold, or the wind could pick up at night…" Günter worried out loud. "We'll need to set an anchor alarm."

If Captain Günter is concerned, how should we feel?

We continued our subdued discussion. We worked out what time to pull anchor in the morning so that—sailing overnight—we would arrive in San Blas in the daylight, with time to spare. Richard and I spread out the charts, carefully checking the waypoints we had entered before leaving Cartagena. Then we conferred with Günter again. It would be 171 miles to our charted waypoint, the wide entrance to the Cays Hollandes channel. At an average speed of 6.9 knots, we should arrive well before dark.

Shortly after 2000 (8 p.m.), we bid each other goodnight. Our customary *joie de vivre* had disappeared. A new respect for the awesome power of the wind and the sea had, indeed, replaced our innocence.

That morning, we awoke to a dead calm. We had set our departure for 0940, but when we performed our take-off procedures, we found that our flow-driven knot meter wasn't working. Richard dove underneath the starboard hull to scrape off the algae. That action freed the little paddle wheel, which is driven by the motion of the water. But our progress, which was then hampered now by coral heads rising 12-30 feet above the sea floor. Consequently, it was almost 1200 before we cleared the San Bernardo islands on a 285° heading toward the San Blas—a much later than anticipated start.

"We have got to get it together," I confide to *Pacific Bliss*. "I can't control Poseidon, but you and I can be a good team again."

To get through to *her* core, I turn off Ray, our autopilot and brains. I seize the leather-covered wheel to hand-steer, sensing the force of the waves on the rudder and the pull of the sails as they envelop the wind. In *my* core, I can feel the ship respond as she surges ahead. Once again, *Pacific Bliss* and I are one.

The moon bids adieu as the sky gradually lightens. This first overnight has come to a peaceful end. My spirit brightens. My attitude swings from binding apprehension to eager anticipation.

Another country. Yet another adventure. After all, isn't that why we continue on?

Exploring the Hollandes Cays
9°32.7' N, 78°53.9' W

During the late afternoon, we spend long, precious hours zigzagging, trying to find an opening through breakers in a NNE Force 6 wind. Foaming whitecaps top long rollers from the NE. My stomach returns to full alert. At the nav station, I note 200 on the Trip Miles Indicator; already, we are more than 30 miles over our estimate for this leg to the San Blas islands. Soon it will be dark. Finally, we find our opening, dodge through the protective, fringing reef, and anchor at 24 feet. We are near Tiadup, the only inhabited island in these remote cays. We are now in Panamanian waters.

I am totally exhausted; I sleep fitfully this first night in Panama. The calm waters in the cozy anchorage belie the crashing of waves against the reefs in the sea beyond. All night the wind wails through the window netting in the master cabin. My uneasiness escalates.

We haul anchor at dawn's light, intent on finding a better anchorage. Inside the reefs, the sailing is superb. We sashay in a Force 5 NNE wind, averaging 9 knots. Up at the pulpit seat on forward lookout, I am completely dry—not one splash of salt water accompanies the wind against my cheek.

By mid-afternoon, we turn into Cayos Limon. Phyllis spots a cruising powerboat plopped right in middle of the shallow channel. "A stinkpotter!" I fume. "Now, how are we going to work around that big lummox and into the deeper anchorage?"

But my worry is unnecessary. We manage to maneuver to the side of the vessel in the narrow, eight-foot-deep channel. As we pass, a man and woman wave from the stern. My frustration turns to joy. These are Jim and Jo, the cruisers from *Atlas*, who consoled us during our night of terror! Ensconced on a 40-plus foot Nordhavn trawler, with a deep draft, they could proceed no farther. *Pacific Bliss,* however, eases past them, with the dagger boards up, over the shallow sand bank, and into the bay. We anchor in the sand.

Günter and I dinghy over to thank our new friends for their support during that long night. "That's what cruisers do," Jim says. We stay with them for an hour and are

The Art of Mola-Making

The Kuna consider the art of making molas to be an integral part of their culture and important to their ethnic identity. When a Kuna woman marries, her husband usually moves into the home of her mother and lives with her female relatives and their families. The women in the family share the household responsibilities by allocating duties according to age. The oldest women take care of the heavy work such as cooking, a smoky and time-consuming job. Younger women care for the children, haul water, wash clothes, and hull rice. Girls also watch the younger children. This division of tasks by age enables women from their late teen-age years through middle age to spend many hours each day making molas.

Women who sew molas behave much as western women who knit. They sew while traveling, visiting, or by themselves. In villages larger than the ones we visited, a constable walks through the streets shouting "Mor maynamaloe" (go make molas), to bring women to the gathering house. There groups of women sit together sewing while listening to a visiting chief chant about the history of mola-making and women's arts.

Young girls are encouraged to sew as early as they seem interested, usually at the age of three or four. By the time they are five, they usually make sewing a part of their play, just as our children play with dolls. They begin by sewing small scraps of material together or by cutting pieces of cloth that the household that women in the household are working on. By the time they are seven or eight, they are sewing designs on a small piece of cloth for practice. As they improve, they allowed to stitch on small areas of "real" molas.

On the Panamanian mainland, molas sold by the islanders to retail outlets are fashioned into handbags for resale to tourists.

The process of mola making is often described as embroidery or appliqué. It is actually a distinct technique in its own right. The basic sequence is draw, baste, cut and sew.

Photos courtesy of UCLA Fowler Museum.

Mor gonicat, many colors, are the most complex and most popular molas. These are commonly used a part of the blouse.

Molas are sold to tourists as is on the remote islands of the San Blas archipelago. We framed one of ours for the wall hanging shown here.

1. Draw the design on the top layer.
2. Baste carefully along the line and cut about 1/8" along the basted line.
3. Fold under about 1/8" along the cut edge of the top layer and sew the folded edge to the base layer with fine hidden stitches using matching thread.
4. Repeat the process for more layers.
5. Colorful molas with filler motifs require additional steps, including a wide range of finishing touches.
6. Completed fish mola, commonly used as a panel on a blouse.

Mother, daughter, and new puppy, San Blas Islands, Mamitupu.

grateful when they give us what will later turn out to be a most valuable contact: the card of Peter, the agent they used to transit the Panama Canal.

One of the saddest sights in the world is a wrecked boat careened on a reef, the seas washing over its disintegrating hull. All night, our view is of a wrecked Halberg-Rassey monohull on the reef extending between two of the islands. The next day, to escape the sight, we visit the one inhabited island, named *Robinson's Cay* after a well-known English-speaking local. There we meet the tattered Mr. Robinson himself. He recounts the story of the shipwreck. The story begins—as usual—with a sailor coming in too late in the day to see the shallow seas and reefs. He had missed the correct channel, the one we came through. The rest of the story is memorialized on the reef for all to see.

We spend a couple of delightful days just hanging out in the Cays, beachcombing, swimming, reading, and relaxing. Refreshed and rejuvenated, we are ready to move on through a safe opening in one of those protective, yet dangerous, reefs.

Coming of Age in Mamitupu
9°32.84' N, 78° 58.04' W
February 10

We have chosen Mamitupu as our destination, using a recommendation in our guide book. As we reach the waypoint to turn toward the island, Phyllis is positioned at one bow and Richard at the other. They direct Günter and me through another shallow, eight-foot channel. Anchoring here, in a brisk wind, becomes another challenge: We want to position *Pacific Bliss* away from the reefs, yet close enough in to obtain some shelter from the wind, while allowing for adequate swing, if the wind should change.

This is clearly a one-boat anchorage. We are fortunate to be here, wedged near Mamitupu, an island so small that we can see three-fourths of its shoreline. Thatched huts crowd the island's perimeter; tall coconut palms and spreading breadfruit trees grace its skyline. Crammed into the center is a large *congreso* (meeting house) as well as a basketball court.

Fifty feet from our stern sits an island home, built precariously upon a small *motu* (sand-bar island), protected from the sea by a waist-high wall of stones. The bamboo house is no larger than our 43-foot catamaran. Should our anchor drag, we would demolish it. To our port, we have an unobstructed view of the village life of Mamitupu. Off our starboard pulpit seat lies the picturesque island of Korbiski. The principal activity here is the docking of the local, island ferry.

The ferry now being unloaded must have drawn passengers from the entire island chain! All morning long, it disgorges its load. The passengers step into *cayukos*, large dugout canoes, rowed by muscled, tank-shirted

DID YOU KNOW?

The Kuna Indians of San Blas

The San Blas Archipelago consists of some 360 islands, including 60 that are homeland to the indigenous Kuna people. "We have an island for every day of the year," they say. Although their territory includes the narrow strip of land between the sea and the peaks of the Serrania de San Blas, almost all the Kuna live on the Archipelago, a chain of coral atolls that runs the length of the forested coastline like a string of pearls.

The Kuna people are the second shortest in the world, after the pygmies. They have the highest rate in the world for albinism. The society is matriarchal: The line of inheritance passes through the women. A young man, after marriage, must live in his mother-in-law's house and work for several years under apprenticeship to his father-in-law. Divorce is uncommon, although it requires no more than the husband to gather his clothes and move out of the house. The daughters of the Kuna people are prized because they will eventually bring additional manpower into the family. Ironically, the boys love basketball.

Officially, the islands are part of Panama, but as of 1925, after the Kuna Revolution, the islands have been administered as a "country within a country," led by the Kuna themselves. They are rich in tradition, following their own customs. Their laws enable them to preserve their natural environment and heritage. The Kuna have a custom for every event and happening in their lives. These customs are passed on to their children through dances and chants and are also documented in their molas, squares of cloth decorated with reverse appliqués.

Mola Masks

Bamboo dwelling, Hollandes Cays.

Indians. They deliver precious cargos of gifts and food, and proud Kuna ladies, to Mamitupu. Disembarking girls and women are costumed to the hilt. They wear dresses sewn with colorful molas—squares of cloth decorated with reverse appliqués—and orange print headscarves. Jewelry covers them from head to toe.

I sit here in the cockpit watching the action, feeling like I'm living inside a *National Geographic* photo spread.

A raggedy, weathered Indian paddles up to *Pacific Bliss* in his dug-out canoe and humbly introduces himself as the owner of the home on the motu to our stern. He displays one mola after another—each sewn by his wife—and apologizes that she cannot come to us herself because of her lame leg. I choose a mola in a tropical fish pattern. The dominant greens and blues will complement the Australian Barrier Reef bedspread in our master cabin. Then, I select another square of fabric, a turtle in a multi-colored reef, that I plan to frame and hang in our home. Phyllis also purchases a few molas. Before long, we send the shy, gentle man happily on his way.

Next, a dark, tank-shirted fisherman from the main island of Mamitupu appears at our stern with his catch. He introduces himself as Antonio. He says he learned English years ago, as a single man working the coconut plantations on the Panamanian mainland. After we negotiate for our evening dinner, Günter inquires about his family. He is proud to have a grown family. His son and daughter-in-law have a little girl who is his delight.

"Antonio, why are all the canoes coming to the island?" Günter asks. "What's happening?"

"Oh, they are here for Coming-of-Age Ceremony for my niece. She turns 12 today. Our relatives come from many islands." He sweeps his rough worker's hand like a fan. "Do you want to come for celebration? Big party. This afternoon. Right after hair cutting."

"Hair cutting?" Phyllis asks.

Antonio explains the day's festivities: they are the culmination of puberty rites, which begin with an ancient purifying ritual. For three days his niece has been isolated in a small hut. This is a protective enclosure, painted black from the juice of the *genipa* fruit (a large berry) to guard her from evil spirits. Attendants have bathed her with salt water several times a day. The isolation rite will end with a hair-cutting ceremony, signifying her entrance into adulthood and her readiness for marriage. Then the entire village and extended family will celebrate her coming of age with a big feast and plenty of *chica*.

"We don't have *chica house* here," Antonio adds, "so we use *casa de congresso*." He explains that *chica*, a fermented mixture of sugar cane juice and corn, has already been brewed in large vats for this special occasion.

After Antonio leaves, we enjoy lunch around our cockpit table, right in the midst of Kuna Indian life. Children paddle up in their small dugout canoes, curious about the big ship that is our home. Teen-age boys splash and play alongside *Pacific Bliss,* cavorting like dolphins.

Lois towers above the grandmothers in Mamitupu.

If we fail to acknowledge them, they gain our attention by overturning their canoes, riding them upside down, then righting them again.

Later, we watch the ceremony on the beach through our high-power binoculars. Kuna women surround the niece. Every so often, the group parts, and we can see the face of the slim, raven-haired girl at the center. She bravely holds back her tears. An attendant performs the rite of passage by cutting the girl's hair. Long chunks of ebony drift to the sand and scatter slowly to the sea. The attendant wraps the standard orange print scarf over the girl's thick short hair. She is a woman now.

It is time to lower our dinghy, *Petit Bliss*, to go ashore.

Let the party begin!

⚓

I had purchased paper tablets, colored pencils, and crayons in Cartagena. Usually, the best way to assure an even distribution of gifts is to give them to the elders of a village. Since the Kuna Indian society is matriarchal, I assumed that the gifts should be given to the grandmothers. Wrong!

We leave *Petit Bliss* pulled up onto the sand. Antonio is waiting for us. "Antonio, will you direct me to the houses of the grandmothers?" I ask.

"Follow me."

Scores of Kuna children crowd around me, pushing and shoving to get even closer. The grandmothers and great-grandmothers command the inner circle. As I pull the gifts from my bag, one of the grandmothers commands, "Give to me!"

I look down at her. She is a full head shorter than my 5'2" height. But she is no lightweight in spirit! Her eyes are stern and steady and her stance aggressive. I know that she will not take no for an answer. Realizing my mistake, I hand over all of the gifts in my hands, still protecting those in my bag. She grasps the gifts with greedy hands. Then she turns her back to me and shows them to the other matriarchs, ignoring the mothers and children. I stand by silently. Finally, she turns back to me with a brusque thank you.

Will she share my gifts with the island's families? I think not.

As we leave the grandmothers' huts, I sneak one set of supplies to Antonio, whispering, "For your family." With an audible sigh, he jams the gifts into the pockets of his trousers. I get it. The grandmothers will probably *sell* the supplies—just as they hawk the intricate molas embroidered by the island's women. These matriarchs are tough businesswomen.

The docile men of the San Blas, having married into their brides' families, are confined to fishing and harvesting coconut—all the while showing off their beautiful women. The men wear practical tank tops, shorts, and sandals.

Trading Molas in the Hollandes Cays.

Strikingly beautiful and festive, the women and girls dress like royalty. They wear bright-colored blouses with puffed sleeves and intricate mola panels on the fronts and backs, combined with darker print wraparound skirts. A special sign of beauty is their face painting: a thin black line running from the forehead to the bridge of the nose so that it will appear longer. Gold earrings and gold nose-rings are common. Intricate beadwork, called *unni*, adorns the women's arms, from wrist-to-elbow, and legs, from ankle to just below the knee. The head scarves are always the same: bright orange with a small print design.

As we walk through the village, the younger women are eager to point out their mothers, their mothers-in-law, and their grandmothers. The grandmothers carry around bottles that look like white rum (perhaps *chica* poured into old rum bottles). They tend to hang out near their houses. All the women proudly show off their babies, all dressed up for the celebration. The little girls are already displaying the wealth of the family, wearing gold bracelets and necklaces or breastplates, the best their fathers can afford.

Phyllis maneuvers close to the honored birthday girl, who is now wearing the standard orange scarf as well. On the sly, Phyllis hands her a bag filled with cosmetics and a pair of earrings. Taller than the grandmothers, the girl lifts her bag high above the reach of the crowd and then moves away to look inside. The sudden smile that floods her face says it all.

I managed to sequester a package of crayons. Now as I take the children's photos, I hand out one crayon to each child. Not that they need coaxing! They all crowd around me *begging* to be photographed. *Thank God I've converted to digital!* When a few teen-age boys discover that they can see their image in the back of my Nikon, the word spreads. I become the Pied Piper traipsing through the island village, followed by a troupe of boisterous, laughing children.

"Where are the Kuna men?" Günter asks. This question is soon answered.

Antonio takes us to the *congresso,* where the men are heavily into drinking *chica*. Inside the dimly lit structure, groups of sweat-soaked men stir vast cauldrons of steaming rice, the staple food for the feast to come.

After walking through the village, we spend some time conversing with Antonio's family. I ask whether I can take a family photo. Antonio meticulously sweeps the sand in front of his bamboo house. Then he arranges plastic chairs before the door. The entire family poses for a formal photo, taking the event very seriously. The resulting image reminds me of the sepia photos of my grandparents, posed woodenly for the "professional" photographer. After obliging them with formal photos that I promise to print out, I ask a special favor: May I take a candid photo of Antonio's daughter-in-law, granddaughter, and the new family puppy? The photo turns out perfectly and tugs at my heartstrings. I know this is one photo I will treasure forever!

The children of Mamitupu have been waiting. Now they swarm the beach to see us off. As Günter and Richard launch our dinghy to motor back to *Pacific Bliss*, I continue to snap photos of children, tears streaming down my cheeks. I don't want to leave them.

My day with these islanders is the very essence of cruising. THIS is what I came for. Ordeal or Adventure? Daring adventure or nothing at all? All I know is that for this day, I have braved the ordeal of a Force 10 storm. For more days like today, I will brave the entire world. My attitude has changed forever.

Back on *Bliss*, I am reminded of another quote from Helen Keller:

"No pessimist ever discovered the secret of the stars, or sailed to an uncharted land, or opened a new heaven to the human spirit."

A Kuna Leader Speaks to His Followers Concerning the Quincentennial Celebration of Columbus' Discovery of America

Now then, we are sitting together here. We sit listening. We sit here feeling our pain. We sit here knowing our sorrows. This five hundredth anniversary that is coming, this great day that is coming, it is our pain. Why is it our pain?

When the Europeans came here, they abused us, you see. They beat our grandfathers, they killed our grandfathers, they cut open our grandmothers, you hear. They came here and killed our wise men, you see. So now they say, "Celebrate the day," you see. "We discovered this land." But we say, "They didn't discover it." Well, we've always been here…

Therefore this day that is coming, they're coming to celebrate the day of our grandmothers' and grandfathers' death. Our pain, you see. As for them, they feel happy…

Cacique Leonidas Valdez
February 1992

Children of Mamitupu.

137

THE LAND DIVIDED   THE WORLD UNITED

"Far better it is to dare mighty things, to win glorious triumphs, even though checkered by failure, than to take rank with those poor spirits who neither enjoy much nor suffer much, because they live in the gray twilight that knows not victory or defeat."
Theodore Roosevelt

138

Chapter 9
Pacific Bliss Transits the Big Ditch and Heads Up the Creek

Struggling Through the Shoals
February 11, 2001

The four of us awaken to heavy skies sodden with mist. Angry waves slap against the shores of Mamitupu. It is not an auspicious day to begin a new adventure. We are, however, tired of this constant swaying back and forth at anchor in this tenuous location between the motu and the island; we have had enough of the ubiquitous wind groaning and howling, interrupting our sleep; we want to leave. Now. Portobelo, our next destination, is 171 miles away. We plan to sail part way, then anchor again.

Antonio struggles against the wind to paddle his dugout canoe from the island to *Pacific Bliss*. Steadying his wobbly *cayuko* against the swim steps, he reaches for the portraits of his family that I have printed out for him and placed into a zip lock bag. Haltingly, he expresses his thanks.

"Thank *you*, Antonio," I reply. "*You* are the one who did so much for *us*."

He nods, smiles, and heads back to shore.

After he leaves, we sip our coffee, ears glued to the SSB. Discouraging weather reports are coming across the Panama Net. The forecast is for four days of continuing overcast conditions with high seas. It blankets the entire area. The ABCs, back where we came from, have 14-foot seas all the way to Cartagena. Even the usually placid Gulf of Darien is riled up.

Five yachts are waiting it out in the lee of Tiburon Bay, on the Panamanian mainland only one and one-half miles away. We decide to join them. Again and again, we venture out from our cozy salon into the cockpit to see whether we dare to leave. Each time, we are beaten back by another Force 7 gust. Finally, there is a break. We all rush to our assigned posts to haul anchor and gun the engines fast—afraid of being slammed back into the fisherman's frail, thatched-roof house on the motu less than 50 feet way. The family waves good-bye from shore, oblivious to their danger. The wife with the lame leg holds her baby while she waves with her free hand. Two other children tugging at her skirt grin and then wave timidly as we motor past them.

In Tiburon bay, *Pacific Bliss* plops like a bloated whale among four monohull sailboats and a one stinkpotter. Sheltered from the merciless wind by the coastal ridges of Puerta Playita, our mood improves. Life is good again. We can finally relax without one of our crew being on "anchor watch." My thoughts wander to the book, *Little House on the Prairie,* which I treasured as a child. I understand now what Laura Ingalls Wilder meant. How that Kansas wind would howl! It would blow unceasingly across the empty plains. Here, the constant wailing of the wind makes me uneasy and grates on my nerves. I am certain that long-term exposure would bring on depression. But these stoic San Blas Indians seem to take it all in stride. I guess that is all they know.

We shower, and tidy up the boat. Then we discuss our plans going forward. Keeping to our schedule—based on a quick passage through the Canal and reaching Golfito, Costa Rica, by February 19—is now out of the question. Phyllis and Richard agree to a sensible alternative: to fly out of Panama and see Costa Rica on their own. We are relieved to have such a flexible crew.

Günter changes the subject. "*Pacific Bliss* can take

Shoals on the way to Tiburon Bay.

these 25-knot winds, day after day, just fine…but her crew needs to be rested and alert. I don't know about you, but I'm exhausted."

"We're also ready to crash," Richard says as he heads for the port hull. Before long, we are all asleep. After lunch, we fall into our bunks for a second nap.

Later, Günter and I dinghy over to the boat named *Soggy Paws* to meet Stacy, the "weather woman." We have become familiar with Stacy's well-modulated voice giving the daily weather report on the Panama Net. We have looked forward to meeting her. This is our opportunity to find out, first-hand, about the "weather windows," the ideal times for departure. Stacy bends her tanned, lithe frame over the back of their 46' monohull to help us tie up *Petit Bliss*. Her curly and carefree, strawberry-blonde hair blows in the wind. We climb over the transom and around the wind vanes to the crowded cruiser cockpit. I note the wooden pulpit stand next to the steering station. This contains their SSB and VHF radios, the ones Stacy uses to transmit her weather reports. Then we descend backwards down the hatch into the salon.

"This is where Stacy fell only a few days ago and injured her wrist," says her husband Dave, a tall, lean man with a mustache and a receding hairline. After obtaining crucial weather reports, we engage in cruiser talk for hours. Upon hearing our Force 10 story, Dave replies, "That one, to Cartagena, is one of the worst passages in the world."

"Then why is that not mentioned in the cruising guides?" Günter asks.

"Because, until recently, Colombia was not even *considered* as a cruising destination. Too dangerous. Drugs and pirates." Dave describes how *Soggy Paws* recently hugged the coast of Venezuela and Colombia all the way to Cartagena, that very coast we were warned to avoid!

"Weather, drugs, or pirates…sometimes there is just no safe way to go," I conclude. "One just has to go for it."

We finish our first sundowner and go on to the next.

"Everyone here in the bay is spooked…" Dave admits. "We're waiting for a weather window that just may not ever happen. We all stuck our necks out the other day. Reached the high rollers inside the shoals out there. Had to turn back."

⚓

I awaken the next day to find the groaning Navteq® weather forecasting system at the nav station disgorging mountains of paper, all in curly rolls three inches wide. Reinforced trades are forecast throughout the Caribbean as another high pressure system stacks on top of the current high. "20-knot winds today and tomorrow, then up to 25 knots for the remainder of the week," I announce as everyone enters the cockpit for their Colombian coffee fix. We listen to Stacy's report on the Net, which confirms our forecast.

Over a breakfast of scrambled eggs, shredded cheese, and grated potatoes, I hold forth as the ship's navigator and weatherwoman. "It will take us two days to get to the Canal, anchoring along the way. If we go today, we can be there before the stronger winds hit. Otherwise, we're holed up here for a week."

Everyone agrees that we should head out. To the sounds of *Amazing Grace,* which we may need today, we head for the dreaded Escribanos Shoals. The crews of *Soggy Paws* and the others wave as we pass by. We have transmitted our intentions to go for it, promising to radio back reports along the way.

Why didn't they act on their own weather window? Was it that bad when they ventured out there before? I wonder what we have in store for us. Worst case, we could always turn back to this protected bay.

As we motor out of the bay, we listen to ongoing chatter on the VHF. The women are discussing what ship stores they have left and what treats they will bring to the potluck on *Athena* tonight. "Comfort talk," says Phyllis, always the psychologist. "It's a way of getting over their fear. Did you notice that the guys take a different tack? They just ask for the facts. What is the wind out there? How high are the seas?"

"Perhaps the little group will splinter and a few will venture out after all," I reply. "I think the women are just biding their time, waiting for the men to make up their minds."

The wind and waves hit us square in the face as we leave the shelter of the bay. "It's all relative," Günter says. "We endured the square waves of the Med. They were shorter and steeper than these. We can do it."

With both engines full bore, burning lots of diesel, we make 5-6 knots against 8-10 foot seas. The wind is steady at 25 knots, the sky 95% overcast and brooding. After rounding Punta San Blas, we are able to set sail with reduced canvas: two reefs in the main and two-thirds of the jib rolled in. Under sail, *Pacific Bliss* glides over the rollers instead of taking them head on. "It's not so bad, once you round the point," Günter radios back. But the boats in the bay are not budging.

With the churning shoals to our starboard and the wild breakers slapping the shore to our port, the power of the sea is breathtaking, awesome, and exhilarating. *What an adrenalin rush! What a ride!* We drop the hook in our plotted anchorage, but it is rolling, windy, and only 25 feet to the nearest reef. We exchange looks, shaking our heads. No, we cannot sleep here. With all hands on deck, we haul anchor swift and smooth. I plot another anchorage, near the mouth of a Panamanian river. This night, there are no sunset, no moonrise, and no stars. But the anchor holds, and we are safe. We spend the night at *Bahia de Nambu de Dios*, in the hands of God.

The Faded Glory of Portobelo
February 13

We awaken to the chirping of birds. Egrets walk proudly along the riverbed as we pull anchor to sail to Portobelo. By 1300, we are already near the ancient port. Because the ground is worn smooth from centuries of sailing ships, our plow anchor fails to hold. We give up on anchoring near the town to try a second anchorage recommended in our guide. It has an excellent view of Fort Fernando. But that ground also fails to hold. Finally, on our third try, the anchor grabs; now we are facing the ruins and well-groomed hills of San Fernando.

Portobelo. *Puerto Bello*. Beautiful port. The town still carries the name that Columbus gave it back in November, 1502. He came back to his beloved bay the following April and had to abandon one of his ships, the *Vizcaina*, in a cove nearby.

Seventy years later, the gentleman buccaneer Francis Drake hung out in the San Blas Islands (1572-1573), assaulting every ship that came close. Portobelo was a favorite destination of his. He returned with a large fleet 20 years later as "Sir Francis," after being knighted by Queen Elizabeth I for his part in defeating the great Spanish Armada. On his last trip to the Caribbean in 1596, searching for Spanish loot, Sir Francis Drake was stricken by a tropical disease. On board his flagship *Defiance,* in this very bay, Drake rose from his sickbed to don his armor so that he would die as a soldier. He was placed into a lead coffin and buried here at sea.

My excitement grows as the men launch our dinghy. I look forward to exploring this port that so charmed the seaman who discovered America. It is a long dinghy ride to this historic garrison town, giving us ample time to enjoy the expansive bay. I can picture an armada anchored here, a longboat from the fleet rowing over to the mouth of the river near our anchorage to fetch fresh water. On banks of that river, long-legged birds search for food. The scene reminds me that mighty Portobelo, with a treasury of gold and silver famed throughout the Spanish Main, was just a jungle outpost after all. No man dared travel the royal road alone from the city's gate after nightfall. Along the streets crawled snakes, toads, and iguanas. Native wildcats prowled the suburbs carrying off fowls and pigs—and sometimes an occasional child.

What a setting for adventure!

Here in 1668, pirate Captain Henry Morgan led a fleet of privateers and 450 men against Portobelo. He captured and plundered the town for 14 days, stripping it of nearly all its wealth—raping, torturing, and murdering on a grand scale. In 1739, the port was again attacked,

The faded glory of Portobelo, a world heritage site.

this time captured by a British fleet commanded by Admiral Vernon. The victory was acclaimed throughout the British Empire. Many streets and settlements in Britain as well as the Thirteen Colonies were named *Portobello* (spelled the British way with two l's).

We tie up *Petit Bliss* at the dilapidated dock, hand a few quarters to each of three rag-tag boys, about six or seven years old, who agree to watch our dinghy for us, and we head for the town.

The World Heritage Site of Portobelo is a big disappointment. The decrepit cross slung into the unkempt grass against the ruins of the old fort says it all. *Where is the excitement of silver flowing from the warehouses into the streets? Where has all the glory gone? The locals could have banded together to make it a museum, a tourist site, with the Canal so close. Clearly, awareness of the value of this historic site is missing.*

We wander along the dusty streets trying to find the "personality" of the town touted in the guidebooks. Less than a thousand people live here now: descendants of the Spanish and Indians; descendants of the Spanish and African slaves; and Africans. But the only "personality" we discover is that of the Spanish-Indian proprietor at the little restaurant where we stop for an early dinner. He makes us an excellent meal from the stores he has available: consommé with *yucca* (a starchy root endemic to this area), fresh fish, rice with fried coconut, and cold Coronas. With our limited Spanish and his "*poquito Ingles,*" we laugh with him and share our stories.

Outside, the wind whips up the dust and trash as we pass a group of children hitting a ball with a stick. No baseball bats here. We pass a tourist stall, but no one is in charge. We try to enter the parish church of San Felipe, one of the oldest buildings in the town still in use, but are turned away because we are wearing shorts.

The church houses the carving of the Nazarene of Portobelo. It is an effigy of Jesus bearing the cross, hewn of wood from southern Spain more than 300 years ago. Called the "*Black Christ*" the image is reportedly one of the most revered icons throughout Panama. Legend has it that this Christ arrived in Portobelo aboard a sailing ship bound for Cartagena, Colombia. However, when the galleon sailed from Portobelo, it was sunk by a fierce storm. The carving packed in a box washed up on a nearby beach. Townspeople found it. Later, a cholera epidemic ravaged the Isthmus of Panama. The people of Portobelo prayed that if the epidemic would pass them by, they would celebrate their deliverance each year. And so was born, in 1821, the annual "Feast of the Black Christ."

Our last sightseeing stop is the old customs house along the waterfront. Standing here, surveying the long forlorn structure, I am reminded that Portobelo had been a market town as well as a fortress. When the town was at its prime, it was known as the emporium of the riches of two worlds: the Old and the New. After Pizarro began his plunder of Peru, gold and silver poured through the jungle trails and were traded here for goods from Spain and Europe. The town sprang to life every year during the trading fairs, which continued for 40 to 60 days. Imagine the excitement! I can see it now: The square facing us is crammed with goods. Merchants erect booths of cane and tents made with discarded sails from the tall ships. Travelers crowd the guesthouses. And windjammers fill the bay.

Portobelo now is only a shell of its romantic past.

We dinghy back across the famous bay to *Pacific Bliss*, my head filled with what *was*, not what *is*. Soon, though, reality must set in. Tomorrow, we sail to the Panama Canal.

Entering the Panama Canal Zone
9° 24', 79 °55' Cristobal Entrance

We are all on deck. We have decided to sail perpendicular to the shipping lanes. "First, we can go faster," Günter explains. "Second, the other ships can spot our white sails easier in this haze."

Phyllis and I scan the area with binoculars. "I spot three… four…five…no, *six* freighters ahead in the haze," Phyllis shouts.

We douse our sails, then proceed between the buoys. Once we reach the freighters, we realize that they are just sitting there, anchored in their designated waiting zone. *Pacific Bliss* is the only yacht in the channel!

We proceed toward the famous Panama Canal Yacht Club (PCYC). I had imagined it to be the meeting place of sailors, merchants, and tourists, the happening place where yarns are spun and deals are done. We motor past the club, a long, dilapidated, wooden building, its paint peeling. No! We must have the wrong coordinates. *Surely, this run-down, seedy-looking structure cannot be the PCYC of my expectations: a refuge from the wind, a lively networking hub, and a comfortable center for R&R before our transit of the Big Ditch.*

We motor on, eventually stopping to ask for directions. We learn—yes, that was it! Günter turns *Pacific Bliss* around while I call the Club, Channel 68 on the VHF. There is no answer. Perhaps it is siesta time. We stop at the fuel dock to find out. There is no room at the club for visiting yachts, we are told, unless we cannot motor under our own power. All the yachts docked here are out of commission; they cannot move.

My dreams are dashed. There will be no water or electricity hook-up, no hot showers. We are directed to Sailboat Anchorage F, called The Flats. Three times, we try to anchor in the murky, debris-filled location before our plow anchor finally catches. I pray that we are not hooked permanently into the mess at the bottom.

We dinghy back to the PCYC. Our first impressions are magnified tenfold. We find seats at one of the 50s-style tables. They are not replicas of an age gone by; this is for real. A few other tables are scattered around the unpainted concrete plaza. A few yachtie families with kids—all hot, dirty, and disheveled—are having beers and cokes while waiting to use the two pay phones. It is not an encouraging sight.

Back at The Flats, Günter falls halfway into the yucky water while getting out of the dinghy. He has bruised his hip. But a few rum drinks, a couple of ibuprofen, and Phyllis' special Chinese patch dull the pain until nothing matters.

Tomorrow is another day.

Crime-ridden Colón

Crime in Colón is rampant; however, Carlos, our cabbie, has adopted us and vows to keep us safe under his care. "Do NOT leave the Yacht Club on your own," the swarthy man commands. "I will take you everywhere and wait for you. You do not walk the streets here—even in the daylight."

Carlos knows the cruiser routine well. He takes us to Immigration, where our passports are stamped and we are asked to provide multiple copies of our crew list. He takes us to the ATM and then to the store for provisions. He helps us arrange for the requisite long, dock lines and old, car tires needed for our passage through the Canal. He even thinks ahead to bring materials—garbage bags and packaging tape—to wrap the tires so that they won't blacken the sides of our boat. Our thoughtful Panamanian is worth every dollar we pay him.

The one problem Carlos can't solve is the exasperating electrical outages that occur at the Yacht Club. During one day, the power goes out three times. It is the very day we want to catch up on e-mails to friends and relatives. When the electricity is finally on, the hard drives for the internet computers crash. "This is typical here," says the blonde, blue-eyed internet assistant. "Nothing works in this country. Too much corruption."

Jim and Jo, the cruisers on *Atlas*, had recommended an expediting agent. His name is Peter. He joins us at the air-conditioned bar attached to the sweltering Yacht Club facilities. Life is looking up! While most yachties wait five to seven days out at The Flats, Peter can cut that wait to two days, and only one day for the transit. He will "grease the skids" for $500. In addition, we will pay the usual $500 fee to the Canal Transit Authority.

Our chores done, we have time to spare. Carlos, our cabbie, takes us touring to overlook the locks we will soon pass through. Mesmerized, we watch a huge cruise ship being pulled slowly through the locks with less than a foot to spare on either side. We try to imagine

1. Overturned dugout canoe, with the old fort in the background, Portobelo; 2. The old customs house; 3. A typical fishing vessel.

Lunch with Carlos, our driver, overlooking the Chagras River in the Panama Canal Zone.

how it will be when we go through. Will we be in the locks with a ship this huge?

Lunch at the locks is special. We are seated outside, at a table overlooking the dammed Chagras River that forms a lake high in the middle of the Canal. What a marvel of engineering! I am eager to learn more.

Pacific Bliss Transits the Big Ditch
February 19

Multiple alarms rouse all of us well before dawn. I splash cold water on my face, then run a pint or so into the sink for a quick sponge bath. The teakettle sings. Richard is already in the galley making coffee. This is our big day. By evening, we will finally enter the placid Pacific.

A canal pilot is scheduled to board at 0500. The young Panamanian line handlers we had hired, NG and Alfonso, have spent the night on board. With a flurry of activity, the six of us ready the boat for the transit. All is set. But we cruisers always find something to worry about. Our anchor has held faithfully in the mucky mud of the Flats throughout our stay. Will we be able to pull it up? It may be stuck in all that mess at the bottom. The six of us wait and worry in the dark.

A PCC (Panama Canal Corporation) launch motors through The Flats at full speed, barely slowing as it delivers our pilot. With one agile leap, the stocky man in the white cap lands flat-footed onto the deck of *Pacific Bliss*. Without even touching the fenders we have put out, the launch steams back to the Canal.

I'm impressed!

The anchor breaks loose with a giant sucking sound. Richard and I brush off all the mud, plastic bags, and debris clinging to the anchor and the chain. We high-five, relieved to be finally leaving The Flats. The pilot directs Günter at the helm as we motor along. As dawn breaks, we arrive at the entrance to the Gatun locks, awaiting further instructions.

The Gatun locks we see straight ahead tower over seven stories high, with walls about five blocks long. Our spirits are soaring.

Two monohulls, *Mallory*, flying a French flag, and *Iwalani,* flying a nautical version of the Stars and Stripes, join us. The three yachts will be "nesting" through the locks, our pilot explains. Nesting is rafting two or three boats together so they go through the locks as a unit. When the three yachts are nested, the yacht with the best ability to maneuver the group will be sandwiched in the center. *Pacific Bliss*, with its two engines, is chosen for this position.

There are four possible methods of navigating the locks in a sailboat: (1) nesting, (2) center chamber, (3) side tie (against the sidewall), and (4) alongside a PCC tug. (When the Admeasurer visited *Pacific Bliss* a few days before, he explained these approaches to us and checked off the ones we were willing to use. "The more options you allow, the higher will be the odds of going through quickly." We approved all approaches except for the sidewall tie, which has reportedly damaged quite a number of small vessels.)

The Panama Canal, connecting the Atlantic and Pacific Oceans, extends northwest to southeast for 80.5 km (47 miles). Three sets of locks raise and lower vessels over the Continental Divide. These are: (1) the Gatun locks, (2) the Pedro Miguel locks, and (3) the Mira Flores locks. While going through the Panama Canal, *Pacific Bliss* will be raised and lowered 85 feet. The Gatun locks will raise us the entire distance. After going through Gatun Lake and Gaillard Cut, we will enter the Pedro Miguel Locks to be lowered 31 feet. One mile later, we will enter the Miraflores Locks to be lowered the remaining 54 feet to the Pacific Ocean. Each time a ship goes through a lockage, 52 million gallons of water are used.

Our pilot is the most senior person of the PCC officials on board the three yachts, so he takes command. Projecting a calm demeanor gained from twenty years of experience, he directs the three yacht captains and the two PCC advisors on the other yachts through a meticulously planned rafting procedure. Our crew follows the pilot's commands to the letter, putting bow lines, stern lines, and spring lines in place, attaching our boat to the two on either side. We add eight fenders and five tires to protect the port and starboard hulls. Our pilot instructs all three captains to keep their engines running.

The Gatun Locks. Finally, a canal official high on the walls above signals us to move lahead. We follow *Danae*, a Panama-registered cruise ship, into the first set of locks, keeping our distance. *Danae* is secured in the locks by *mules*; these are locomotives attached by steel cables that bring the ship along. Each cable exerts a pull of up to 40,000 pounds. Despite this strength, they do occasionally break. The pilot instructs Günter to motor forward behind *Danae's* churning wake.

The Gatun locks consist of six chambers. Workers poured three thousand cubic yards of concrete every day for two and one-half years to complete them. Our little raft of sailboats is like three tiny peanut shells, lost in the enormity of these concrete locks and the huge luxury liner, whose passengers look down at us.

Messenger lines, long ropes with pieces of lead wrapped into the end, are thrown by lock line-handlers to the two outside boats; the crews then cleat them to their boats. Now each of the four corners of the nested flotilla has a messenger line attached. The handlers on the lock walls high above walk forward as Günter motors slowly using both engines. After the nested raft is in place behind the cruise ship, the handlers secure the lines to huge bollards attached to the canal wall.

The gates close slowly behind us. Water is forced through a hundred holes in the lock floor. As the water rises and the surface swirls, passengers on *Danae* look down at us, the Lilliputians, and wave. The line handlers up on the dock wall take up the slack in the lines. After fifteen minutes, when the lock is filled, the handlers slip the lines off the bollards, freeing the nested boats from the canal walls. Then Günter motors to the next chamber and the process is repeated.

The three sailing yachts remain nested until we exit the third chamber. Altogether, we have been lifted 85 feet! Our anticipation builds. Like a curtain opening for Act II, the doors of the locks open slowly from the center to reveal the dramatic vista ahead—a vast, deep-blue lake surrounded by jungle. Lake Gatun. At the time of its creation, it was the largest man-made lake in the world. And we will sail it! Here we are, in the middle of the grand canal that joins the two great oceans of the world—the Atlantic and the Pacific. I can't begin to describe the excitement I feel!

Lake Gatun. Our crew unties the bow, stern, and spring lines. We are no longer nesting; *Pacific Bliss* is free again. We motor slowly out of the locks.

I glance at my watch: It is only 0810. The PCC wants vessels to make the fastest possible time through the lake. We have convinced our pilot that *our* fastest time is not with our two engines full bore, but under full sail. Günter commands us to hoist the main and unfurl the jib. *Bliss* is in her element, under full sail, making between 8 and 10 knots.

The two monohulls head for the Banana Cut, a narrow shortcut between lush islets. They are motor sailing. Our pilot wants us to stay in the main channel through the lake. Günter turns off the engines and we enjoy a wonderful sail of 20.5 miles. We sail past the Barro Colorado National Monument, an island operated by the Smithsonian Tropical Research Institute. A tropical moist forest, it contains more than 60 troops of howler monkeys, 366 species of birds, 30 species of frogs, 22 species of lizards, and 40 species of snakes. The 15-square-kilometer island contains a complete biological station with laboratories, libraries, and living accommodations for scientists.

Right after the island, as we pass buoys 35 and 37, we meet the monohulls that left us at buoys 5 and 7. Despite their motor sailing through the shortcut, *Pacific Bliss* is right behind them.

I take the helm for the first time during our transit. I love the challenge of trying to pass the monohulls under sail. We round the buoys of Bordada Bohio, Bordada Buena Vista, Tabernilla Reach, and San Pablo Reach. I pass one yacht, but then we all lose our wind. At 1020, we douse the sails and motor along, with wind at less than 14 knots, but right on the nose. Soon we spot the village of Gamboa ahead on our port. Most sailing vessels spend the night here in Gamboa Reach. But luckily, we don't have to: We left The Flats before sunrise; we can sail and motor faster than the minimum 8-knot speed; and we have a licensed pilot on board who got us through the locks, so far, in record time.

The Gaillard Cut. We motor through The Reach and enter a nine-mile-long channel, which had been carved through rock and shale. It is called the Gaillard Cut. Because of recurring landslides, this cut was one of the most difficult challenges in building the Canal. Contractor's Hill, on the west bank of the canal, was sliced from 410 feet to 370 feet to stabilize the earth. Even so, landslides still occur, the most recent in 1987. The canal section north of the area was widened from 300 feet to 500 feet to allow large ships to pass each other. Because even larger ships are being built today, another widening is in process. Dredging vessels run back and forth. Earth moving equipment lines the banks. The work seems endless.

Pedro Miguel Locks. We have sailed and motored 31 miles since the Gatun locks. Now, we are about to enter the Pedro Miguel locks.

Our pilot leaves us via a PCC launch and another man, wearing mirrored sunglasses, jumps on board. He introduces himself as José, a Grade 2 Advisor. José is a light-complexioned Panamanian, all pumped up, full of adrenalin and himself—quite a contrast to our pilot, so cool he never did give us his name.

José stands near the helm, alongside Günter. "Do you have connections?"

"Why do you ask?"

"Because you had a Senior Grade A Pilot on board."

Günter shrugs. "We hired an agent; maybe that's why."

José quickly takes charge. This slightly built man is into control, big time. "*Pacific Bliss* will be the lead boat," he puffs himself to full height, still shorter than Günter. "*We* will control all of the operations of the three boats. The lines will be thrown only to us."

The two monohulls are behind us, coming up quickly.

"I want *Pacific Bliss* and *Iwalini* to raft together. Then you enter the locks against the wall, pulling along *Iwalini*. When that French boat comes up, she will move into place between *Pacific Bliss* and the wall…I want all of us into the locks before that freighter back there arrives. He will come into the locks behind us."

What a contrast with the Gatun locks procedure! Our first pilot had directed all three yacht captains and had supervised the entire nesting operation, explaining not only what to do, but exactly how to do it. José, however, gives vague directions and spends most of the time on his cell phone acting important. *Pacific Bliss* is the only yacht using her engines, so there is less maneuverability. We have to pull the rafted *Iwalini* into the locks, then away from the sidewall to fit the other boat alongside. Soon, it becomes evident—even to José—that controlling the lines from the center does not work. We lend our Panamanian line handlers to the other boats to handle the lines from each side.

Eventually, we are in position and begin to move toward the front of the locks. As the three nested yachts move ahead, a messenger line thrown down to *Iwalani* catches in the walls of the locks, turning the entire raft sideways. It is high adrenalin time. The entire raft could crash into those walls! The crew of *Iwalani* wedges a fat fender between the boat and the wall to prevent damage to their boat. Our line handler, now on *Iwalani*, jerks the stuck line loose. Günter guns the engines, and we are back in position. A close call!

The giant freighter comes into the locks and creeps up to our stern. The gates slowly close. The locks begin to empty. We drop 31 feet before the gate slowly re-opens. Since we are all nested nicely, the captains ask José to allow us to move the one mile across Miraflores Lake to the Miraflores locks as a raft.

José agrees. "Full speed ahead, both engines."

"Hard on the boat," Günter mumbles, suppressing his frustration with José. But he proceeds as instructed.

Miraflores Locks. This last set of locks consists of four chambers. Each lane holds two chambers. While the Pedro Miguel locks dropped us 31 feet all at once, the Miraflores locks drop us the remaining 54 feet in two steps.

This time, our transit is uneventful. As the gates open from the last chamber, the water level inside and outside is the same, but the heavier saltwater outside of the gates sinks down under the fresh water and into the chamber, and the fresh water on top surges out. We can see the long snake-like tongue of the current rushing out of the lock, churning the blue of the lake with the teal of the Pacific.

Upon exiting, José commands, "Full speed ahead."

What else would we expect from him? Safely out of the locks, we are all relieved to un-raft, independent cruisers again.

I dash to the nav station to check the chart for the location of the famed Bridge of the Americas. We will need to exit to the Balboa Yacht Club from the channel at buoy 15 ½. I come back on deck, we round the bend, and there it is. What a breathtaking view! The bridge spans the Isthmus of Panama in grand style. Built in 1960 at a cost of $20 million, the mile-long, non-swinging design was an engineering breakthrough for its time. The suspended span in the center is a single tiered arch, which we will pass underneath, with 204 feet clearance at high tide. The graceful structure—

Crossing the
BIG DITCH

Gatun Locks.

Gaillard Cut.

Miraflores Locks.

The gates open to the vast blue Pacific and the Bridge of the Americas.

149

Phyllis and Richard, ready to depart from Balboa, Panama.

curving steel ladders and trussed triangles—reminds me of DNA diagrams used in biotechnology presentations.

We motor to the club's floating dock, take on water and fuel, and motor over to our assigned mooring. After enjoying a cold beer, our Panamanian line handlers depart. Tula, another Panamanian, helps us secure our mooring.

Phyllis, Richard, Günter, and I sit silently in the cockpit of *Pacific Bliss* as the sun sets over the mountains flanking the Bridge of the Americas. It has been one long day. Each of us needs time to let the impact of this day sink in. The sky turns to blood red, then to purple. Günter opens some beers. Then the cheering begins. We did it! In 12 hours and almost 50 miles, we have transited The Big Ditch into a very different ocean, the peaceful Pacific.

The wind and seas seem calmer here. The air seems fresher…cooler. Or is it just my imagination?

As for *Pacific Bliss*, she is rocking and rolling less. She deserves a rest—and a good cleaning with fresh water, inside and out. I know that she will delight in this ocean and provide her owners with many Moments of Bliss. Why? Because this ocean is part of her name; she is our serene lady, *Pacific Bliss.*

The next day, it is time for Phyllis and Richard to catch their flight to Costa Rica and home. We hug and kiss and tearfully bid adieu.

For the first time on Voyage One, Günter and I will make passages alone. We have mixed feelings, relishing our personal space but knowing that we will miss this wonderful couple that has become like family to us.

During the following evening, at the Balboa Yacht Club, we hear rumors of bad news flying among the cruisers there: A tugboat in one of the locks somehow came loose and smashed into a small sailboat, jamming its mast through to the bottom. The yacht sank, and several sailors on board were injured. The accident occurred the day after our transit.

Thank God we came through without a scratch.

Panama City and *Panama La Vieja (the Old City)*

"…and I maintain that Panama will be easier to make, easier to complete, and easier to keep up than the Suez." Ferdinand de Lesseps

Günter and I stare at the bust of Ferdinand, a huge sculpture set atop a marble base in the deserted French Plaza of Old Panama. It is one of almost a dozen statues, and all the statues here are backlit by the searing sun. We swelter under a cloudless sky, and there is no place to buy refreshments, no chance of taking refuge in an air-conditioned building. The museum that depicts the French struggle is closed as tightly as that chapter of French history, when the French finally gave up building the Canal and the Americans took over.

This extraordinary French venture had lasted more

MESSING WITH BOATS

Part IV
by Günter

We said good-bye to Phyllis and Richard here in Balboa. We had become like a little, close-knit family, sharing experiences that will last a lifetime. Peter, our agent, arranged their flight to Costa Rica and back to the States. He has been a great help to us.

Kudos to Tula. He is the dark, broad-shouldered Panamanian I hired for a few days. Well worth his weight (which is considerable) in gold! Knows yachts well, and certainly how to clean them. *Pacific Bliss* is the shiniest she has been since she was brand new in Canet. Boat soap, Never Dull, and lots of muscle have worked wonders.

No longer on a schedule, we stayed at a mooring at the Balboa Yacht Club for a few extra days waiting for our yacht broker, David Renouf. He was on his way through the Canal, delivering a new 47-foot Catana, Le Chatou Fou, "The crazy kitten," to the west coast of California.

He told stories of going through the Strait of Gibraltar in 40-knot winds, then hitting 44- knot winds again from Curacao to the Panama Canal Zone. Speaking of high winds, he asked whether we had checked our rigging after the Force 10 storm.

"No, not yet," I said.

He offered to check it for me. I cranked him up the mast in the bosun's chair with Lois on lookout. Fortunately, David proclaimed the rigging 100% safe. It hadn't budged a bit. That gave me all the more confidence in the integrity of *Pacific Bliss*. Looks like she can withstand high winds more than we can, David's advice for "next time:" Use a handkerchief of jib to control the boat, and no main.

"Had we had some warning of the high winds on the way, say at Force 8 or so, we could've turned into the wind and doused the main," I answered. "Once we were into a Force 10, the only way would have been to physically pull down the main, and even the electric winch couldn't take it." At any rate, we don't intend to have a next time! No way!

I added that we are happy with our boat, and will take our time bringing it back to San Diego for warranty repairs. Our only concerns now are being north of Cabo San Lucas by June, before the hurricane season begins, and completing my increasing TO DO list before our warranty expires. The boat has a ten-year structural warranty, one year on the rest.

Church door, Panama La Vieja.

than a decade and had cost them 1,435,000 francs, about $287,000,000 in U.S. dollars back then. That amount was one million francs more than the cost of the Suez Canal, far more than had ever been spent on any one peaceful undertaking of any kind in the history of mankind.

We have been attending to *Pacific Bliss* maintenance by day and reading David McCullough's *The Path Between the Seas* at night. We learned that as many as 22,000 lives were lost during the French fiasco. "It had indeed been such a blunder on such an inordinate scale, a failure of such overwhelming magnitude… that nobody knew quite what to make of it; and as time went on, the inclination was to dismiss it as the folly of one man, Ferdinand de Lesseps, about whom markedly different views evolved," McCullough wrote.

Since today is Sunday, a well-deserved day of rest, we want to make the history we've been reading about come to life by visiting this French Plaza. We did not expect that all would be closed. No life stirs here at all, except for one Panamanian family, dressed in their Sunday best. The parents sit under a spreading, chestnut-like tree while their children play, seemingly oblivious to the heat. We explore the rest of the Plaza in a somber mood. We read detailed inscriptions about those who died here, the words carved on memorial stones. Then we wander over to *Casco Viejo*, a World Heritage Site that is still being restored.

Our guidebooks have told us that Panama was the first European settlement on the Pacific coast of the Americas. It was founded in 1519, four centuries before the building of the Canal. This city served as the starting point for the expeditions that eventually conquered Peru's Inca Empire in the 16th century. It also became a stopover for travelers crossing the isthmus to those famous fairs in Portobelo.

To walk through Casco Viejo is to stroll through more recent history. When the French attempted to build the Panama Canal in 1881, they also built homes here. French architecture contrasts sharply with the earlier Spanish structure. Buildings, side by side, can be over three hundred years apart in age. Amazingly, nothing seems to clash, despite a wide variety of styles and income levels. Laundry hangs over ramshackle railings, yet iron balconies are full of well-maintained geraniums, potted plants, and bougainvillea vines. We pass by Caribbean, Art Deco, French, and Colonial styles in a site of fewer than 800 buildings. Using our travel guide, we spot The Salón Bolivar, the renovated Cathedral, the National Theatre, and the Iglesia San José.

Now if only we could have an iced coffee on a rustic balcony overlooking the ocean! But that's asking way too much.

DID YOU KNOW?

PANAMA

In the country of Panama, things are not always as they seem.

Which direction did Pacific Bliss go through the Panama Canal from the Atlantic to the Pacific? You might think of the Canal as the path between the east and west. While the Pacific Ocean is generally west of Central America and the Atlantic Ocean is to the east, the journey through the canal from the Atlantic to the Pacific is from northwest to southeast. This is a result of the isthmus's "curving back on itself" in the region of the Canal. Look at the map. The Bridge of the Americas at the Pacific side is about a third of a degree of longitude east of the side near Colon on the Atlantic.

Which direction did we sail before rounding Punta Mala on the Pan-Pacific coast to head north to San Diego? Because we made day hops, following the Panamanian coastline, we turned to sail southwest after transiting the Canal, then we turned southeast to round Puerta Mala (the same direction we traveled through the Canal). After we rounded the peninsula, we headed in a northwest direction up the coast.

Before we entered the boundary between Panama and Costa Rica at Cape Burico, which direction did we sail? We first sailed south to round the Punta Burico, then northwest up the coast again, eventually entering Golfo Dulce in Costa Rica.

What U.S. time zone does Panama follow? Panama is on the Eastern Standard Time zone (EST), five hours behind GMT (Greenwich Mean Time), also called Zulu time.

Panama Canal, Gatun locks.

Panama City skyline.

The week we spend moored at the Balboa Yacht Club seems to fly by. On February 28, we head up the Panama Coast for Costa Rica. Our destination: Bahia de Chame, only 28 miles away, a quick day-hop. We enter the buoyed channel to meet the Colombian tall ship *Gloria*. She is in full regalia, motoring slowly toward the Canal. At first, she appears to be flying banners from her many spreaders (horizontal spars) but as she approaches, we realize that those "banners" are the crew, standing on the many spreaders—all the way to the top! Additional crewmembers are balanced on the bowsprit, which hangs far over the prow. What a breathtaking sight!

We pass by a quarantine anchorage, in which over 25 freighters with potentially dangerous cargo are anchored. They wait patiently to transit the Canal from the Pacific to the Atlantic. Amongst such large vessels, we are considered relatively unimportant by the Canal authorities. We pay only $500 to transit the Canal. Yes, this fee will increase to $1350 shortly, but so what? The PCC can charge $100,000 for each of these waiting freighters.

This day is sunny and hot, with the typical Panamanian haze. By mid-morning, the deck scorches our bare feet as we scramble to locate our flip-flops. In a NE breeze of less than 7 knots, we motor slowly along.

We spot Isla Taboga, called the *Flower Island*, which was a common resort getaway for Panamanians when the French were building the Canal. Yellow fever and malaria convalescents escaped to the island to recuperate in the "better air." At that time, it was thought that turning over so much dirt had stirred up the "bad vapors." The prescribed cure was fresh air and clean surroundings.

We have progressed in our reading of *The Path Between the Seas* to the American role in the Panama Canal and the larger-than-life figure of Teddy Roosevelt. He had a different view of the Canal than Lesseps and nearly everyone else. While others talked of the Canal as a dream of Columbus, a giant step forward in the march of civilization, and a boon to world commerce, Teddy thought of it as the vital—the indispensable—path to a global destiny for the USA. According to McCullough, "He had a vision of his country as commanding power of two oceans, and these joined by a Canal built, owned, operated, policed, and fortified by his country."

Roosevelt was well aware of the tragic experience of the French. But in his own mind, the memory of American losses in Cuba was uppermost. During the Cuban war of 1898, the number of American troops who died of yellow fever, malaria, and typhoid fever was 13 times greater than the number killed by the enemy. Roosevelt declared that solving the sanitary and hygienic problems of the Canal had to take priority over the engineering problems. Consequently, he enlisted the help of Dr. Gorgas, who became his right-hand man. Gorgas began a massive (and controversial) program to wipe out mosquitoes from the isthmus. The success

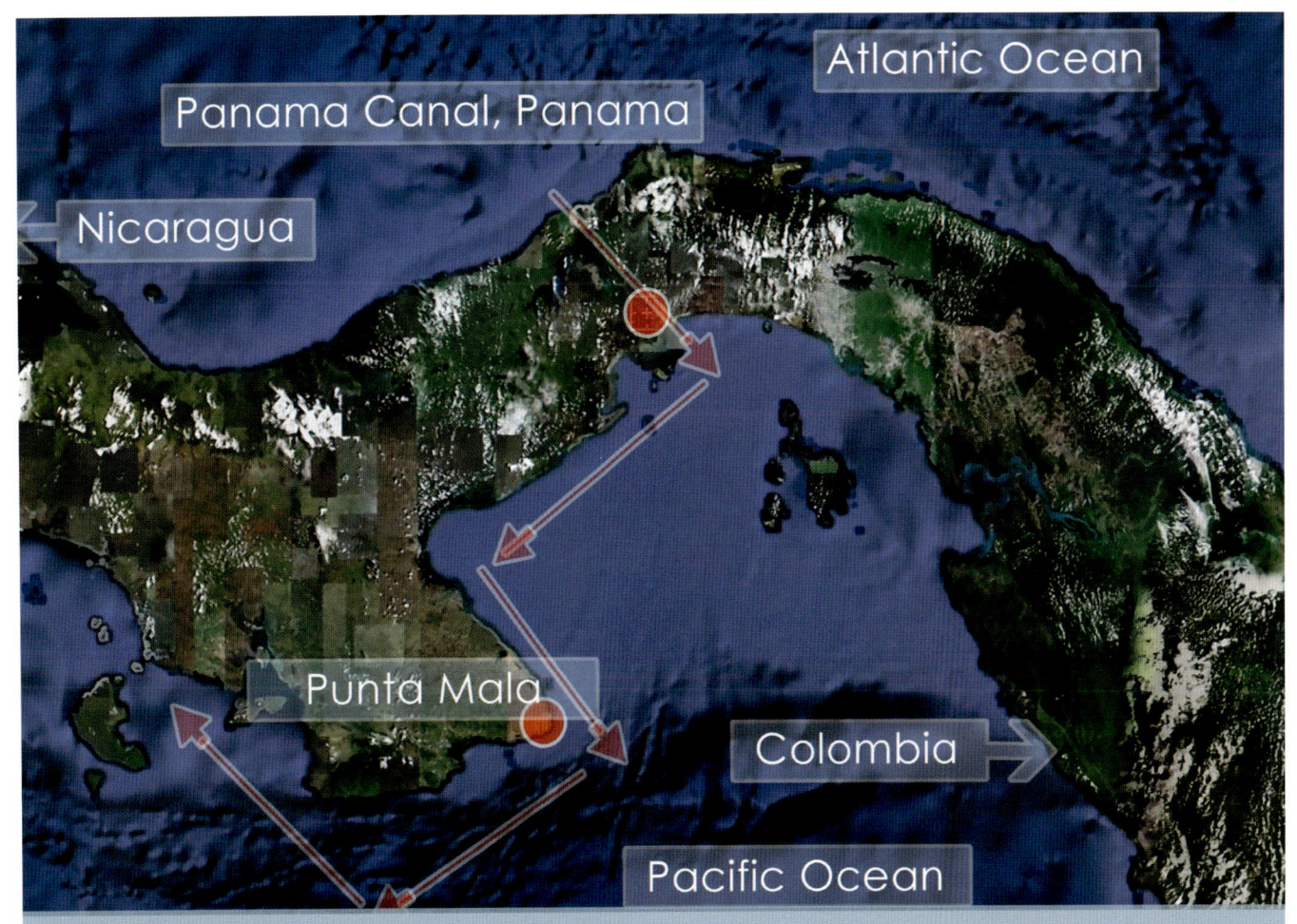

Rounding Panama challenges one's sense of direction.

of his effort allowed the construction of the canal to proceed and to fulfill Roosevelt's dream.

A ferry motors by. It is loaded with passengers on the way to Tobago to enjoy fresh pineapples on its jasmine-scented sandy beaches. Flocks of pelicans and a few snowy-white great egrets fly over *Pacific Bliss* as she passes the island on her port side.

We sail on, far beyond the famed Canal Zone.

Up the Creek and Down to the Depths
March 2

Day sailing up the coast of Panama is uneventful, until we near the conical-shaped Pan de Azucar and Isla Ensenada anchorage. This location, shown in the *Panama Cruising Guide*, has a white-knuckled approach. The passage is only five feet deep at low tide and with that comes the risk of grounding. We make it through, then the depth increases rapidly to 20 feet, which now makes it difficult to anchor. After several attempts, we set the anchor in the lee of the convex-shaped Isla Ensenada. Our bow faces the island. By the time we retire, the NE wind we had while anchoring changes to N and by 2300, it changes to NW. We have turned around 180° and now our stern faces the shoreline.

The Wind Speed at the nav station shows 20 knots, Force 5. For the first time, Günter sets the new GPS/anchor alarm, which we purchased in Panama City. Although the shore appears to be sandy, we sleep uneasily, fearing that the anchor will twist with the changing wind and finally break loose.

Dawn finally arrives. We haul anchor and head for a more protected location. We choose Puerto Aguadulce, up a river over 75 miles away. It will be a long day's sail, but should be worth it. We look forward to a good night's sleep.

The winds along the coast are variable, ranging from NNW Force 4 to Force 5, then back to NNE Force 4, finally down to Force 1. We douse the sails and motor along a sea of cobalt glass. I enter into the logbook, "Flaky wind today, now F0, no wind." Aeolus, King of the Winds, takes up my challenge with a vengeance: He calls on Boreas, the furious North Wind, who rises rapidly from F4 to F6, then gusts to F7. By the time we spot the estuary, *Estaro Pablo Blanco*, leading to the river, Boreas is huffing and puffing at 33 knots, pushing frothy whitecaps against the shore.

We snake through the buoys guiding us into the main channel of the Aguadulce River. Then we wind slowly through the narrow river channel on a rising tide at depths averaging about 14 feet. The banks are lush jungle-green, dotted with white specs. I point them out as we pass by. "Egrets, one of my favorite birds!"

DIGGING THE DITCH: THE PANAMA CANAL

One picture equals a thousand words. Looking down at the Panama Canal during our land tour was incredible. And motoring through those massive locks was better yet! But it is the rest of the story that photos alone cannot explain.

That all this was begun in the early 1900s, without the benefit of the modern earth moving equipment and project management tools we now have at our disposal, makes the story even more mind-boggling. Imagine the smothering heat of Panama at 9° latitude! (Our crew consumed seven gallons of water during our one transit day.) Imagine the rains, the mud, the insects, and the diseases! At the bottom of the Cut at midday, the temperature was seldom less than 100 degrees. More often it was 120 to 130 degrees.

Yet when the work under Goethals was at its height, the United States was excavating at Panama the equivalent of the entire Suez Canal every three years! In fact, the 37,000,000 cubic yards of earth and rock removed in the one year of 1908 was nearly half as much as two successive French companies had succeeded in digging at Panama in a total of seventeen years.

Gatun Locks.
The construction of these locks took four years, beginning in 1909. Visitors who stood on the concrete floor during the last stage of construction, before the water was turned on, would lose their sense of scale. The walls, 1000 feet long, rise to 81 feet, higher than a six-story building. Looking down at these locks during our tour was like looking down at a level street five blocks long—with a solid wall of six-story buildings on either side! A single lock, stood end on end, surpassed the height of the Eiffel Tower in those days. (One lock we transited was compared to the height of the two World Trade towers, still standing in early 2001.)

The Gaillard Cut.
The Culebra Cut (now called Gaillard, after U.S. Major Gaillard) is the most remarkable part of the Canal. The remarkable feats of building of the Gatun Dam and constructing the locks pale in comparison to excavating the nine-mile stretch between Bas Obispo and Pedro Miguel. The heroic struggle at the Cut lasted seven years, from 1907 through 1913, when the rest of the world was at peace. In the dry season, the tourists came by the hundreds, and later by the thousands, to stand and watch from grassy vantage points hundreds of feet above it all. Special trains were arranged to bring them in. Imagine men in white shoes and pale straw hats, ladies in ankle-length skirts, carrying parasols for protection against the tropical sun. Lord Bryce of the time called the spectacle the "greatest liberty ever taken with nature."

The journalists tried to make sense of the statistics: 15,700,000 cubic yards in 1907, and an incredible 37,000,000 in 1908. They attempted to translate the amounts into pictures that their readers could understand. If the United States were flat, and a canal was dug from coast to coast that measured ten feet deep by fifty-five feet wide, this would give you only fifty miles of the Panama Canal. The amount of dirt dug out would be enough to build a Great Wall of China from San Francisco to New York. A train of dirt cars carrying the total excavation at Panama would circle the world four times at the equator. The dirt would be enough to build sixty-three pyramids the size of Cheops. The aggregate depth of the dynamite holes drilled in an average month at the Cut was 345,223 feet, more than 65 miles. In the same average month, more than 400,000 pounds of dynamite were exploded. The statistics went on and on

Pedro Miguel Locks.
At Pedro Miguel and Miraflores, the engineers used cantilever cranes so enormous that they could be seen for miles rising above the jungle. Five million sacks and barrels of cement were shipped from New York to build all the locks, dams, and spillways. Sand was dug from the Bay of Panama and rock was quarried and crushed at Anton Hill. Building anything so large out of concrete had never been done before.

The fundamental element in all the design—structural, mechanical and electrical—was water. The buoyancy of water would make the tremendous lock gates virtually weightless. Water would lift and lower the ships. The power of water falling at the Gatun spillway would generate all the electricity needed, even that needed to run the towing locomotives, called mules. The force of gravity would raise or lower the water level in the locks. The water would merely flow from the locks above, e.g. Milaflores Lake or Gatun Lake, or flow out into the sea-level channels.

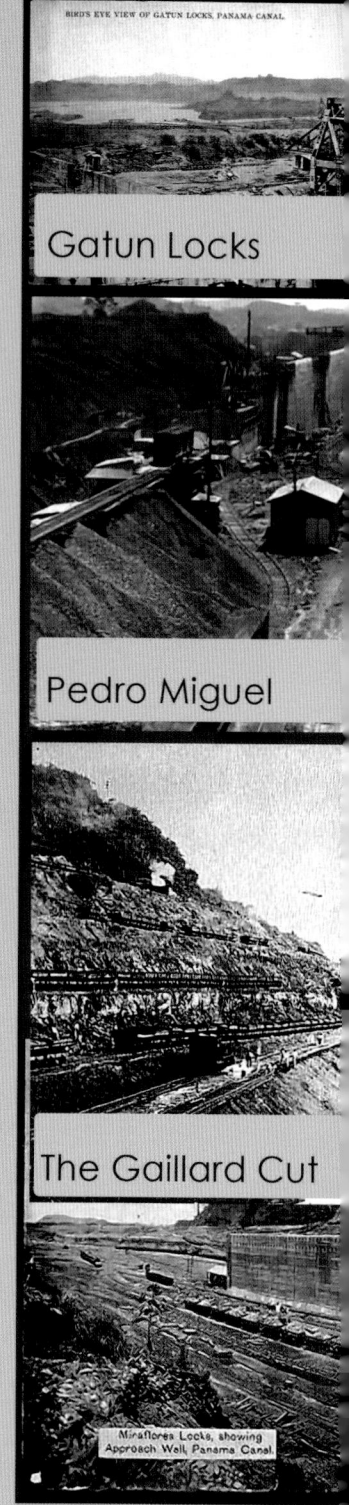

Theodore Roosevelt

Miraflores Locks

Miraflores Locks.
The width of the lock chambers would be 110 feet wide to accommodate the largest battleship then on the drawing boards, the Pennsylvania, with a beam of 98 feet. (The largest commercial vessel then being built was the Titanic, with a 94-foot beam.) On the Pacific side, where heavy silt-bearing currents threatened to clog the entrance to the Canal, the engineers designed a breakwater that would extend three miles across tidal mud flats.

Photo credits: Panama Canal History Museum, Panama City, Panama; U.S. Library of Congress
Text based on The Path Between the Seas, by David McCullough

Eight miles up the river, we come upon a huge and seemingly out-of-place commercial dock. To our surprise, a freighter sits there, tied up to an extremely high mole. This must be *Puerto Aguadulce*.

The *Panama Cruising Guide* advises us to anchor around the first bend in the river, supposedly only 10 feet at low tide. But as we round that bend, the river increases to 24 feet deep! According to the directions, the river narrows to almost nothing around the next bend. We proceed on, and attempt to anchor there in shallow water, but the current is too strong. The current is flowing *up* the creek, due to the incoming tide. We make two more attempts at anchoring. Then we spot some workmen on shore who motion for us to turn back towards the commercial area.

"*Donde?*" Where? Günter yells.

"*Ahi.*" There. (That's what I think they said.)

The men dash in and out of the mangroves lining the riverbank as we slowly proceed back down the river. Then they direct us to a rusted platform on top of one of three sets of huge log pilings.

"*Aqui?*" I shout from the bow of *Pacific Bliss*. They nod in unison.

Here? What if our beautiful new CAT gets scratched against the wood and rusty metal? Well, we wanted a place to sleep without fear. And despite what the guidebook says, anchoring in the middle of the river here is out of the question.

Here we go. Another adventure. Did I actually ask for this? This search for adventure is crazy. Or am I crazy? I'd go for a little Bliss right now.

"Lois!" Günter snaps me to attention. "Get out all the fenders we have and put them on the starboard. Quickly."

I stretch into the locker. I grab all the fenders I can reach and heave them all out onto the net. Then I climb down inside to retrieve the rest. I rush toward the lifelines. I have never attached fenders so fast.

"And get the dock lines ready to throw."

"Captain, if you will recall, you are down to only one crew. Me."

"You're not crew. You're my partner."

"Well, then, I advise you to go back out into the river to give your partner some time to set up."

Günter turns *Pacific Bliss* back into the river; together, we prepare the dock lines. By knotting two dock lines together, he fashions bow and stern lines that will reach out to the other pilings. Then he takes the helm and closes in again. I heave the lines, one by one, up toward the workers standing at the platform. Günter and the men attach a spring line to the platform, allowing for plenty of slack. These workers—about five of them now—appear to know what they are doing.

Günter asks about the tide differentials. No one speaks English, so the exchange is completely in Spanish. He turns toward me. "I think they said five feet." The men leave the site. We grab a snack and turn in, exhausted.

In the middle of the night, we learn the truth about those tide swings. I wake at 0200 to go to the head. I peek out of the side window and cannot believe what I see! Hundreds of snails and barnacles cling to algae-covered posts pounded into the muddy riverbed! My bleary brain focuses on the reality. The platform is evidently high above us. Maybe the Panamanian workers were saying that the *depth* of the river would go down to five feet. Or maybe *they* were talking in meters and *we* in feet. Whatever. The tide swings here are obviously far more than five feet! Before climbing back into my berth, I pray that the tide will turn soon, and that we won't end up sitting on the bottom in the mud.

The next day, *Pacific Bliss* gradually rises up toward the platform on top of the pilings. High tide, we discover, is 12 feet. A dark-haired worker in a faded blue shirt and navy jeans introduces himself as Baliera and offers to take us into the nearby town of Aguadulce to obtain supplies. We accept the kind man's offer immediately. We plan to lower ourselves and our supplies back down to the deck before the river is too low to do so.

Baliera explains that he works at the sugar cane factory on shore and that this loading platform belongs to the factory. Operations are slow right now, which is why most of the workers are standing around idle, watching us. He drives us past the docked freighter where long wooden electrical poles are being unloaded and stacked at the terminal. Beyond that, it is a few miles into the town.

Aguadulce appears to be a prosperous industrial center. The town boasts polymer factories, a fertilizer factory, and a clean, well-developed commercial district. Baliera gently shepherds us to the food market, a separate produce market, the bakery, and an ice store. Yes! Block ice, and for only 25 cents a bag! It will melt after a few days because we are currently using our freezer as a fridge to conserve power. But what a treat it will be until then!

On the way back from town, Günter asks about how to pay for our stay. Baliera stops at the port captain at the freighter dock. We understand, with our limited Spanish, that Aguadulce only gets about one yacht per year. The port captain, accustomed to commercial vessels, admits that he does not know how much to charge a cruising yacht; he decides to charge us $12 for our two-night stay.

Back at the cane factory's platform, three other workers pull on the spring lines to bring *Pacific Bliss* closer to the platform so that we can lower our supplies down to the deck. What friendly, helpful men!

The architecture in Panama City is a mix of Caribbean, French Art Deco, and Colonial.

Pacific Bliss ties up to pilings at the sugar cane factory at Puerto Aguadulce.

I get up during our second night on the river to go to the head. When I flush, yucky, mucky river water comes back into the bowl. We are at the bottom of the river, again.

Right before dawn, an army of mosquitoes decides to invade us. We are forced to shut the boat as tight as a clam. Our fans circulate the hot, humid air while we hide inside. *What on earth are we doing here?* After spending two days and two nights descending to the river bottom and rising to the top, I don't need another day and night here to find the answer. I am not Jonah—stuck below the surface of the sea! It is time to blow this pop stand.

The dependable workers at the sugar cane factory arrive right at 0615, as promised. They cast us off, waving and cheering us on.

The river shimmers, soft as purple satin in the early-morning stillness. Fishermen paddle their pangas, the swoosh of their oars slicing through the silence. Birds swoop from the mangroves to serenade us as we motor around the bends. We reach the sea once again, and the sun peeks over the riverbanks, then explodes into a glorious halo of gold. We have a renewed lease on life. It is a wonderful morning to be leaving one adventure, yet anticipating another.

Bliss and Romance in Unexpected Places

We motor past the churning mix of fresh and salt water at the head of the estuary. Then we hear a loud thump.

"We must have hit something." Günter stops the engine and we take a look around. "Nothing here." He dons his diving mask and fins and heads on down.

"Yep. We have slammed into a net attached to a drum," he calls up to me. "Fortunately, there does not appear to be any damage."

Crisis averted, we motor sail for 83.8 miles. When we finally arrive at our anchorage, Ensenado Beneo, we are dead tired. We drop the hook at 2020, after 8 p.m. But by 0630, we are underway again. It seems to take forever to round Punta Mala. The good news: There doesn't seem to be any *Mala* (bad luck) here. In fact, a school of dolphins—a sign of good luck—appears to escort us on our way. Later, we spot a group of sea turtles with birds on top, catching a free ride. We anchor in Naranjo Cove after another 66 miles. The following day, we motorsail another 57 miles to another anchorage, Bahia Honda, recommended in the *Panama Cruising Guide*.

Dodging in and out of the islands and the mainland, following our plotted course, we enjoy a wonderful sail under powder blue, partly cloudy skies. Günter is relaxing up at the bow. Ray, our faithful autopilot and now our third crewmember, is in charge. The day goes smoothly until mid-afternoon. Suddenly, our plans are thwarted big time.

"Lois, what is that up ahead? It looks like clouds rolling all the way across the next channel! Am I seeing things?"

I put my book down and rush to retrieve the binoculars from their usual place inside the salon door. "Gray, churning roll-clouds. All the way across!"

Günter rushes to the cockpit. "I'll take the helm. You go check the charts. See whether you can find a convenient bay to turn off. I don't want to hit a squall right in the middle of the next channel."

I find that we are opposite a large bay that appears to be shallow all the way across, although it is not a designated anchorage. "We can head into that bay to your starboard."

"Great. Take the helm and turn into the wind. We'll douse the sails and motor on in."

We motor into the vast bay and set the anchor right in the middle. Then we sit together in the cockpit and stare back toward the sea. The squall races past the channel, kicking up the waves on shore. But we are safe and snug in an uncharted bay.

The storm clears. We relish this wonderful break from our sail-at-dawn, anchor-by-dark routine. We have an early dinner and then sit in the cockpit together, sipping our best wine and watching a stunning light show. The setting sun scatters its afterglow on a panoply of clouds: puffy cumulus, cumulonimbus, high-flying wisps of cirrus. The bay is deserted, without a boat or another human in sight. The wind calms. *Pacific Bliss* swings around, then bobs contentedly. We move up to the trampoline. Before long, we are naked as jaybirds.

"Where do you get that 'jaybird' expression?" Günter asks, his hands cupping my breasts. "We don't have that expression in German."

I giggle and snuggle against his chest. "It's folk slang from the Midwest, I guess. We have a blue-and-white bird called blue jay, or jaybird. The young birds tended to get rambunctious and push each other from the nest. They were real mean."

"Well, I'll be gentle."

"I know you will."

Purple clouds fade to black as we lie there on the net afterwards. The cool, tropical air from the sea below tickles our bare buns through the woven strings.

"Want a blanket?"

"That would be nice. For the top, anyway. Just a light one."

Günter brings the afghan from the settee along with two more glasses of wine. The moon rises, almost full now, above the jungle on shore. Soon we are nested, side by side, fast asleep.

I awake with a start. The sound is like nothing I have ever heard, a kind of braying, like that of a hoarse donkey. The guttural sound comes again, clearly from the jungle. I listen more closely. It seems like more of a throaty, pulsating roar than a bark. *Do they have wolves out here in the tropics? I don't think so*. Günter is now wide awake as well. Because we can't identify the noise, we decide to retreat into our cabin to shut it out. We remain there all night long.

The day dawns sunny and bright, without a trace of clouds. As we sip our coffee, two dark men in ragged clothes pass by in a panga, headed toward the jungle. There appears to be a settlement there after all. It is

DID YOU KNOW?

AN UPSTAGED GRAND OPENING

In a tragic turn of history, the long-anticipated opening of the Canal was dwarfed by a new heroic effort. No world leaders graced the bow. Instead, the beginning of World War I filled the front pages of the newspapers, while the official opening was buried at the back.

The first oceangoing ship to transit the Canal was a lowly cement boat. The grand opening was performed perfunctorily by the steamer Ancon. Until the close of the war in 1918, traffic was light, only four or five ships a day. But ten years after it was built, the Canal handled 5000 ships a year. Ship widths increased until the Queen Mary, launched in 1936, was the first ship too large for the locks. The Canal now handles about 40 vessels per day, 14,600 per year. In 2014, the Canal will open its sluices with a new series of locks, so that ships wider than 110 feet wide at water level can use the Canal. The new set of locks will stretch that limit to 180 feet at the base and 160 feet at the top. You can view ships going through the Canal at http://www.pancanal.com

President Woodrow Wilson, in 1913, pushed a button that sent a signal via telegraph to blow up the center of the dike that would mingle the Atlantic and Pacific waters.

Moonlight underway to Costa Rica.

Günter steers *Pacific Bliss* down the Rio Aguadulce.

obviously a primitive one without electricity, since we saw no lights at night.

We stay anchored in the bay, using time to catch up on boat chores. Günter calls me into the port engine compartment to help him change the oil. Using the hand pump is a slow, sweaty operation. By the time we complete the job on one engine and crawl into the starboard engine compartment, the sun is straight overhead, blazing into the open hatch.

Evening brings coolness—and more wine and romance. But this time, we decide to be romantic inside. Strange sounds—low and resonant—are already coming from the shore. But we are too involved to care.

Our next port will be in Costa Rica, a country with 25 species of animals, 9000 species of plants, and 900 species of trees.

Who knows what we'll find (or do) there.

Church tower serves as a navigation aid entering Banana Bay, Costa Rica.

Chapter 10
Slogging Through Central America: Costa Rica and El Salvador

Out of Our Depth
8 ° N, 82 ° 47.5' W
March 8, 2001

We are on an overnight sail to *Golfo Dulce*, the Sweet Gulf. We approach *Punta Burica*, at the tip of a triangular peninsula that divides Panama from Costa Rica, and, already, we are in trouble.

"How can this be?" Günter asks. "It is supposed to be over 100 feet deep here, not 18. Do you think the point goes farther out than the chart shows?"

I stand beside Günter at the helm. "I can't imagine that our chart would be off this much."

Günter pulls back on the throttle. *Pacific Bliss* slows to a stop. The idling engine breaks the stark silence of the Pacific. The ocean is smooth as opal, dark as squid ink. I look around. We are alone in the universe, except for the man in the moon; he seems perplexed as well.

Günter narrows his brows accusingly. "I thought you plotted a wide berth for this cape."

"I did. Is it possible that this is an uncharted submerged rock?"

"I doubt it. Maybe our depth gauge is off. Lois, let's resolve this the way the ancient mariners did. Help me get out the lead line from the storage locker."

I comply, and Günter slowly drops the line as I read off the depth. "Five feet, ten feet, twenty feet..."

"Keep reading." He continues to drop the line. Near the end of our 100-foot line, there is *still* no clunking sound to indicate the bottom.

I pull the line in, and Günter steers farther out to sea. He gives *Punta Burica* a larger berth than I had plotted. In fewer than 10 yards, the depth meter reads 100 feet, which is what it should be. Dumfounded, we round the point and continue to motor throughout the night on glassy seas.

By morning, the sun rises hot and high. It turns the immense gulf ahead into a lake of sparkling emeralds. I squint to distinguish the red and green colors of the channel buoys. Then, I spot the crazy reflectors on shore that double as a church tower. We line them up and head on in to Banana Bay Marina.

A dock man directs us to moorings right in front of a wooden structure, which, on huge stilts, sprawls over the bay. We tie up and high five. Here's to Costa Rica and civilization! It has been ten days since we left the Balboa Yacht Club. And for many days now, we have not spoken to anyone but each other. Now it's time for cruiser talk.

Yarns and Characters
8 ° 37.3 N, 83 ° W
Banana Bay Marina

A bedraggled cruiser dinghies over to *Pacific Bliss* from a small monohull anchored nearby. Günter motions him on board. Dennis introduces himself while we ply him with coffee, juice, and Dutch Royal Dansk butter cookies. He fills us in on the local scene. "Dennis, this is the guide book we are using." I flip open our well-worn *Cruising Ports: Florida to California via Panama*. "Here it instructs cruisers to announce one's arrival on VHF Channel 16, and then to anchor in the quarantine area, near the commercial pier. We are supposed to pick up the immigration officers in our dinghy so they can inspect our boat."

"Wrong!" Dennis slams his bare arm on the cockpit table, almost spilling his juice. "Forget waiting

Banana Bay Marina, Golfito.

for authorities. They won't have the energy in this heat to 'inspect' your boat! Besides, the Port Captain's office has air conditioning now. They're just sitting there watching TV in the cool. And that agricultural 'inspection' it warns about here? That is just a paper questionnaire—although they will charge you $35 for it." Dennis' insight proves the value of cruiser talk.

After settling in, Günter and I tie our dinghy to the Banana Bay Marina dock. We soon fall in love with this little haven, where everything is colored yellow and white, from the exterior trim to the cheerful décor inside the bar and restaurant. All the rooms are delightfully cool, with white ceiling fans humming overhead.

Hungry for more cruiser talk, we have come to the right place. The advice and good-natured help from other cruisers proves to be enlightening. They explain that depth problems in this region are a common occurrence. Large swarms of fish cause the meter to read as if they are the bottom.

Later in the day, after we check in, Dennis joins us again, with his partner. Her name is Casey; I can't help but notice her wild and curly hair. They invite us to join part of a larger group enjoying sundowners at the Land & Sea. This is a funky yacht services and travel agency, located nearby. First, we drop off our laundry and check our e-mail. Then we join them at the bar.

"We planned to leave Costa Rica yesterday," says Casey, twisting a strand of hair around a finger. "But obviously we haven't left yet."

"How long have you been here?" I inquire.

"Six years."

I stare at her, surprised.

"We live on board *Anastasia*, our ketch."

"I guess that's what happens in some of these ports."

We find no shortage of interesting characters in Banana Bay. Their tall tales keep us occupied for hours. One weathered, scraggly cruiser spins this tale about a "lady" who turned into a sailor the hard way.

Günter and I lean forward on our barstools, taking it all in.

Lady Turned Sailor. "See, this lady's boyfriend of only a few dates had invited her to meet him in Bermuda and to help him sail his boat back to Massachusetts…" The storyteller takes a swig of beer, the foam sticking to his unruly beard.

"She was at the point in her life where she could use a little adventure, so she accepted his invitation and flew down to meet him. She stepped gingerly onto the yacht in her high-heeled sandals, flowery sundress, and newly-coifed hair. Now, this was the first time that she had ever stepped onto a sailboat of any kind. Get the picture?

"Understand…the Captain's buddy was already on the boat as crew for the trip. They would leave the next day. The captain told his girlfriend that she could learn to crew underway.

"The first day out of port they ran into a fierce Atlantic storm. It raged on for three days and three nights. Since the Lady didn't know how to sail, the two men took turns at the helm. Finally, they were exhausted. They could take no more.

"'Here, you'll have to steer,' the Captain said as he lashed her to the helm station. He stayed there a few minutes to make sure that she could stay the course. Then he went down below to join his buddy. Both crashed onto their bunks. Totally wiped out. They didn't show topside for twelve hours.

"During that time, the Lady had peed in her pants, but damned if she hadn't become a sailor!" The storyteller slams his fist on the bar, sloshing his beer over the rough wood.

"So, the storm calmed down. She took her turns faithfully during the remainder of the voyage. They were finally coming near their port. There was to be a huge welcoming party…

"Now, there are two look-alike harbors along the Massachusetts coast. The first is littered with vessels that have crashed into the rocks and shoals. The second is the 'real harbor.' Our Lady was at the helm, heading toward the second one. Suddenly, her friend's buddy grabbed the wheel and insisted the first harbor was the correct one. He took over the helm--and promptly added their ship to the vessels piled on the shoals."

The storyteller pauses dramatically for effect, and then breaks into a huge grin. "But they managed to pull it out," he said, "and they eventually went on to the party by land. Now, during the party, the lady met the captain of another boat, this one headed toward Nova Scotia. It was scheduled to leave the next day, and it was short on crew. 'Can you possibly get your gear and be here in the morning?' he pleaded.

"Well, she thought for a few minutes. 'Sure,' she said. 'Why not?' And there she went, off on another adventure. Years later, our Lady was still sailing but, now, in the tropics. As a matter of fact, she told this story right here, at this very marina." The storyteller waves his hand to encompass the bar.

One of the old salts on a stool laughs, "That's a good one." He signals the bartender. "Worth another round of beers, I'd say."

Innocence Is Bliss. "I didn't know anything about sailing either when we started out," a tough-looking woman in a sailor's cap begins. "Such innocence I had back then. It was true bliss."

Another round of beer appears like magic.

"In the beginning…I was in love…and so I just trusted my man to get us through anything. And knowing this, he never leveled with me. In retrospect, I must've been quite a burden.

"The voyage down from the Washington coast, along the coastlines of Oregon and California, can get very rough. But I was naïve then…didn't even know the difference. I'd never sailed the ocean before, just the bays."

She pauses to scan the assembled cruisers, some sitting on barstools, some standing around, some dirty, some spruced up, but all with one thing in common: Each is holding a mug or bottle of beer. "One time during our passage, my man looked a little tense at the helm," she continues with her story. "I peeked out from the hatch and saw that the waves were very high and the boat was tossing up and down. I thought I'd cheer him up, so I went down below to bake a fresh casserole and dessert. The stove was a gimbaled model; it was swinging this way and that. Half the time, I was losing my balance. Finally, after managing to put the casserole into the oven, I stirred up a batch of cookies. Now picture this…I was sitting on the floor, the bowl propped between my legs so it couldn't slide away!"

The group explodes with laughter. Many of the monohullers have been there, done that.

The cruiser adjusts the brim of her cap and recaptures the attention of the motley group. "Later, after I began to understand such things as Beaufort Force levels, my amazed partner told me that we had been in a Force 10 storm with over 50 knots wind!"

Though they tried for the rest of the evening, no one could top that story.

⚓

During lunch at the marina our second day in port, we meet a charming, gray-haired, retired couple, Dwight and Fran Fisher, from Washington State. They are heading south toward Panama on their Fisher 30 ketch, aptly named *WE THREE*. "When we talked about our plans before we left," says Fran, "our friends asked, 'Aren't you too old for cruising?' We decided to set them straight. So, we have begun a website for cruisers over 60—or couples with a combined age of 120—called www.seniorsoffshore.com. Would you two qualify?"

She is being diplomatic. Of course, we would!

Later, after our siestas, we dinghy over to their ketch for sundowners and the requisite boat tour. Their space is cozy and cute—and much too small for us. As we dinghy back to our own boat, I realize that I would go as crazy as a caged goose living in such a tiny space. We tie up to the stern, at the swim ladder. From there, I view the spaciousness between the hulls of *Pacific Bliss* in a new light: *The lightness of being… The openness of freedom…The gracefulness of wings spread wide. This is what it means to sail on* Bliss.

Hell-holes and Crime

Banana Bay is part of Golfito, and Golfito is a "hurricane hole." A hurricane hole is a sunken lake or round bay, completely protected from the wind, where yachties can safely leave their vessels during the hurricane season. In cruiser talk, a hurricane hole is called a "hell-hole," and hell holes are damned hot.

While sailing the cold and stormy Med, I had never imagined feeling so hot that I would not be able to sleep. And in the Caribbean, I'd never imagined that I would ever complain about a lack of wind. But here, at night, we can manage living in the "hole" only with fans blowing directly on our naked bods. And in the afternoon, since fans merely stir the hot, humid air, wearing a muumuu with nothing underneath is being overdressed. Entertainment is watching rivulets of sweat drop from Günter's glasses, onto his nose, and into his mustache. We lie in our bed after lunch with the shades down, misting ourselves from a squirt bottle. Even when we do fall asleep, we awaken on sweat-soaked sheets. We stare listlessly at the clock, waiting for sundowner time, so that we can sit in the air-conditioned bar and find some relief. Sundowner time seems to come earlier and earlier each day, as we struggle to survive "the hole."

Our one-mile trek to the grocery store for provisions can only occur in the morning, and even then, it is a wet proposition. By the time we lug our supplies back to the marina dock, load them into our dinghy, unload them into *Pacific Bliss*, and store them away, we are drenched. Except for escaping a hurricane, I would *never* want to be in such stillness and humidity again.

Unemployment has been high and crime rampant ever since the United Fruit Company pulled out of Golfito a few years ago. The marina employs a night watchman to protect dinghies and motors from "disappearing" at night. He helps somewhat, but even so, theft is still common.

The government has tried to solve the unemployment problem by establishing a duty-free shopping area at the northern end of Golfito. But it is thwarted by its own red tape. Few cruisers take advantage of the duty-free bargains there. In order to buy something there, one must obtain a permit one day, and then return the following day to shop. Bureaucracy is alive and well in Costa Rica.

Günter and I fantasize about flying to San José and staying in an air-conditioned hotel for a few days. But we're concerned about crime here. We don't dare leave *Pacific Bliss* by herself. So instead of San Jose, we opt for the local jungle tour.

In Search of the Howler Monkeys

All that cruiser talk in Golfito has helped us to identify those strange sounds in that uncharted anchorage in Panama. Apparently, they were neither the barks of dogs nor the howls of wolves. They were the calls of the howler monkeys. Some say these monkeys are the loudest land animals on earth. Howler calls can be heard from three miles away and are used to mark their territories.

We also learned that these monkeys live in troops of 4 to 18. Each troop maintains its own territory, ranging from 3 to 25 acres. Troops are led by a dominant male. This tough guy will kill all the infant monkeys when he takes over (so females will mate with him).

Howler monkeys weigh between 8 and 22 pounds. "How can such a loud, throaty sound come from such a small animal?" I asked during one of our cruiser talk sessions.

"It all comes from the throat sac of the male monkey," a helpful cruiser responded. "The sac resonates. Like an echo. That amplifies the call throughout the jungle."

I found that these noisy creatures live only in the canopy of Central and South American rainforests, and since we don't plan to return to South America, I'm determined to see them here.

The monkeys howl only at dawn and dusk. We line up a private tour—by boat, jeep, and finally on foot—that will arrive in Puerto Jimenez, on Peninsula de Osa, just before dawn.

José, a short, wiry Costa Rican, is our driver and guide. When we arrive at the peninsula, I tell José about our Panamanian experience hearing the howlers for the first time. "So forget the flora and fauna for now," I add. "We *must* see a real howler monkey."

"Oh, you'll see one all right," he says. "But you'll hear them first. Then we'll just follow the sound."

I tramp alongside Günter and José through the dark jungle. The sun's thin rays barely penetrate the thick underbrush. On other treks, I might have raved over the lacy evergreens and fiery red heliconia growing in the wild. But today, I am on a mission.

"There are over 200 species of heliconia native to the American tropics," José rattles off in a low, yet authoritative, voice, "and we have more than 40 of them here in Costa Rica."

I have absolutely *loved* these red tropical flowers, since Günter flew me to Hawaii to meet him there during our dating years. On our honeymoon in Bali, another special place, Günter fell in love with tropical flowers as well. After our return home, we fashioned an eclectic area in our condo, replete with an indoor fountain, a parrot hanging from the ceiling, and a profusion of tropical flora. We called it our *Bali Corner*. There, we grow the deep red flower known as the "Heart of Hawaii." The flower's real name is anthurium, a word we can never remember, so we call them "love-flowers," because of their thick, yellow stamens. When one dies, I always make sure to buy another. Symbolically, I don't want *our* love to die! I grow other tropical flowers and plants there as well—orchids, bromeliads, and yes, even the heliconia we see here.

Ahead, the rising sun casts its rays deeper into the jungle, lighting the way. What a wonderful photo this would make! Shadows and sparkles and on the bark of bamboo. Vines, strangling acacia trees. Back-lit plants, hanging on other plants.

But I am on a mission. Mostly, I'm looking up. Not at the sun, but at the lush jungle canopy, searching for anything that moves.

"I'm afraid that they've already gone back to sleep," Günter whispers.

"No, they do sleep a lot, but they'll wake up and yell when you tramp into their territory, no matter how quiet you think you are," José murmurs.

Suddenly, we hear a bark, like that of a terrier.

"What's that?" I whisper, not wanting to scare away whatever it is.

"Oh, that would be a female howler. It's only the males that have the loud cry. He'll be close by though. I know there's a troop of them because I come here all the time. This troop has a couple of adult males, half a dozen females, and a few babies."

Günter and I trek along behind José. We're well off the path now. I try to keep up without tripping on the matted underbrush. *I could never find my way out of here. We're not even carrying a compass.*

José turns back to see how we are doing. "Let's keep going. We're getting close."

Suddenly, the canopy ahead rustles and crackles. There is an ear-splitting, pulsating roar.

"That's it!" Günter exclaims. "That's the howl we heard in that Panama bay."

"Quiet!" José commands. "That's the male. Let's try to get close enough to see him…there, straight ahead." We walk quickly, inevitably cracking old twigs and dead leaves.

The howler retreats, and then yells again from farther ahead, warning us not to encroach upon his sovereign territory.

I can feel my chest, sticky and wet, clinging to my cotton blouse in the still, humid air. I can hear my heart thump.

"There! High up in the tree to your left." Quickly, I aim my camera to where José is pointing. Way, way up there is the female. I can barely distinguish her gray-brown coat from the tree branch. But I manage to make out a hairless face and a deep, jutting jaw. In a moment, the monkey's long, prehensile tail grabs the next branch. She swings even higher and out of range.

Mission accomplished: I've seen my howler.

We turn to head back toward the gravel road where the jeep is parked. Along the way, José teaches us more about our photo prey. "You know that these

DID YOU KNOW?

COSTA RICA

The four million people of Costa Rica are known both as "Ticos" and "Costa Ricans." The dominant religion is Catholic. Spanish is the dominant language. Unlike many of their Central American neighbors, present-day Costa Ricans are largely of European descent. Few of the native Indians survived European contact.

Ticos are short, so chairs and sofas are built about 6-8 inches lower than furniture from the USA. This was fine for me, but if you are tall, you will find that the act of just getting up from a comfortable seat might be an effort. Costa Rica has a coffee culture. It is not uncommon to give coffee to babies (in their bottles, along with milk) and to young children. (I wonder whether that stunts their growth.)

Children take their father's name, but add their mother's maiden name to their full name. Costa Rican women do not take their husbands' last names. The woman uses her full maiden name for life. This makes life easy: There's no need to change national ID cards and drivers licenses. While we say in English, "She had a baby," or, "She just gave birth," the Costa Ricans say, "Ella dio a luz," or, "She gave light." Cool!

Instead of saying "my other half," Ticos often refer to their significant other as their "media naranja," or the other half of their orange. Tangerines are called mandarins. Limes are limónes. And you can't buy lemons.

In Costa Rica, the Spanish word for pedestrian is "Target." One must be careful here. Pedestrians seem to have no rights. The meter in a taxicab is known as the Maria… apparently a loose reference to the honesty of the Virgin Mary.

Christopher Columbus landed here in 1502. The Spanish optimistically called the country "Rich Coast." When they found little gold or other valuable minerals, they turned to agriculture. Costa Rica joined other Central American provinces in 1821 in a joint declaration of independence from Spain. An era of peaceful democracy began in 1899, the first truly free and honest elections in the country's history. Costa Rica is an amazingly stable country given the trials and tribulations of surrounding countries. The literacy rate is 96 percent.

1. Epicytes (plants hanging on plants); 2. Exotic flowers are common to Costa Rica;

3. Lois and Günter in front of the Puerto Jimenez yacht club sign; 4. A howler monkey (Photo courtesy of Flickr.com); 5. Anthurium.

Günter finds a juice bar, and a California hippie, in the Costa Rican jungle.

monkeys 'howl' to mark their own territories. But did you know that when a foreign troop of howlers enters an established territory, they howl at each other to negotiate their boundaries?

"Yes." He answers his own question. "They can accomplish that from distances of up to one mile and never even meet!"

On the way back, José spots a three-toed sloth. In contrast to the howler, it sits there calmly while I take his photo. And yes, I can confirm that he does have three long claws on each foot!

The sloth is the world's slowest mammal, so sedentary that algae grows on its furry coat, so lazy that it doesn't know when it's dead. Sloths spend nearly all of their time aloft, hanging from branches with a powerful grip. Dead sloths have been known to retain their grip, remaining suspended. Sloths sleep in trees, and sleep a lot they do—some 15 to 20 hours every day. Even when awake, they often remain motionless. At night, they come to life for a while, eating leaves, shoots, and fruit from the trees—and sucking water from juicy plants.

"Don't expect him to come down, no matter how much we disturb him," José says. "Do you know, sloths even mate and give birth in these trees? The baby clings to its mother as she moves. She can turn her head almost full circle to watch the baby. Looks weird. Extra vertebrae in her neck."

"Can they walk on land?" I ask.

"Not very well. They sort of drag their bellies across the ground. But if they fall from a branch over a river, they can actually swim."

"What do they sound like? Have you heard them?"

"It's a very high-pitched sound…not like the howlers, of course. Sounds like ahh-eeee. That's why you'll hear locals calling them *eyes.*"

Günter turns toward me and grins. "Ahh-eeee. Good we didn't hear *that* sound in that Panama anchorage."

Now that the sun is high and the fauna are sleeping, we have ample time to pay attention to the flora. The jungle's emphasis on wanton sexuality and reproduction is unbridled. We wander beneath tall palms with long, narrow pods that hang down suggestively. Heart-shaped love-flowers, some with purple stamens, cover the jungle floor. Hairy-stemmed spires of tall, white, bulbous flowers stretch toward the sun. Wild banana plants with imperial purple blossoms block our path. Yet, in the midst of this profusion of raw jungle joy, pastel pink orchids timidly show their faces—wiry, delicate, and feminine.

Günter points out a pure-white, primrose-like flower. It seems tame, rather incongruous, like it should be in an English garden. But who knows what is compatible in this bizarre place?

When we reach the seashore, the surf's up. The beach is deserted, wild, and wonderful. Driftwood sculptures streaked with ebony erupt from coal-black sand. One wave-worn tree trunk twists and arches like a serpent about to strike. Günter and I sit together on a gnarled log, staring vacantly into the sea, wondering what the Pacific will take us to next.

We rouse ourselves to stroll towards Puerto Jimenez and the jeep. Along the way, we come across a wacky shack, sporting a Coca-Cola sign, set in a clearing of black sand. José introduces us to the lady who runs this strange concession. She could double as a '70s-era California hippie. White glass beads adorn her cleavage. Giant tattoos sprawl up and down both arms. She stands at a ramshackle counter covered with piles of oranges, pineapples, and bananas, alongside a giant juicer. Multicolored glass beads frame the doorway to the storage area behind her. After we order, she joins us, and the four of us sit around a red, plastic table, sipping cold Coke Classic from straws inserted into dusty green glass bottles. The camaraderie is instant. Soon, we are all laughing and telling stories like old friends.

Speed Bumps
8°32.5' N, 83° W
March 18

We anchor overnight near the fishing village of Puerto Jimenez. But we're up early, and by 0600, we are already underway. We leave Golfo Dulce behind and round the Peninsula de Osa, passing the jungle where we had searched for the howlers. We continue motoring along the Pacific coast of Costa Rica on a calm sea, with less than a 6-knot breeze. By 1000, the salon is scorching. Ray is in control of *Pacific Bliss*.

Anticipating that the salon will heat up even more, I whip up our lunch early and load it into the fridge. I am dripping with sweat; I dash down to the head for a quick sponge bath. As soon as I splash cold water all over my naked bod, I hear a loud thwack against the side of the starboard hull. Quickly I throw on a sarong and rush to the helm. Sixty feet. Plenty of depth. No rocks or debris. Whatever it is, it didn't hit our prop! I check out the port and starboard hulls. No logs are floating about. *What could have made that strange thumping sound?*

And then I see it, a *huge* turtle, slow and methodical, swimming away from the starboard hull. We must have dazed him, but there he is, still lumbering along.

The sailors in Costa Rica call these turtles "speed bumps." We had seen quite a few turtles before, but we have never hit one—until now. Usually, we spot them easily because birds catch rides on their backs.

There are four sea turtles common to Costa Rican waters: the Olive Ridley, the Hawksbill, the Pacific Green Turtle, and the Leatherback. I doubt that I saw a leatherback because that one has a huge, barrel-shaped body. I'm assuming it was the smaller Olive Ridley.

We arrive at Drake's Bay at 1600, after 61.5 miles of motoring. Soon it is sundowner time, a sailor's favorite time of day. We bring two rum punches, an assortment of chips, and a bowl of fresh guacamole forward to the net. We sit there for hours, enjoying a fantastic evening light show. Act I: Look to the stage on the west. The hot sun finally retires for the day, a fiery golden globe that dips into the vast, empty Pacific. Act II: Look to the opposite stage, toward land. The afterglow scatters daubs of color onto the clouds, like an impressionistic artist's palette. Act III: Look above. The color purple paints our world.

Günter slings his arm over my shoulder. "Sunrise… Sunset. You could make a photo album just with these."

I snuggle into his teddy-bear chest. "I feel so fortunate to begin and end my days this way… It's like being in the presence of God."

The next day, motoring from Drake's Bay to Quepos, I make a positive identification. I am sitting at the starboard pulpit seat, scanning the horizon for fishing nets, my binoculars handy. "There's a Leatherback, for sure!" The turtle's huge, barrel-like shell protrudes over the glassy, cobalt sea as he slowly paddles away.

Morning March in Quepos
9°25.7'N, 84° W
March 20

I awaken to a pre-dawn glow. The sky is pale red against the mountain ridge; the night lights of Quepos still glimmer against the sandy shore. The wind has shifted 180 degrees during the night, as it often does here. As the land cools, the afternoon land breeze changes to a sea breeze. The 50-plus fishing vessels moored here have all changed direction in sync, like marching soldiers. Yesterday afternoon, when we anchored here, they all faced the sea. And *Pacific Bliss* took up the rear. This morning, they are lined up facing the shore, with *Pacific Bliss* in the lead. This is what makes living on board interesting: One's environment is constantly changing, even when anchored.

The action begins at 0600, as the sun breaks brightly over the mountains. Caravans of sport fishing boats proceed to the dock, met by groups of men in white tee-shirts and jeans. Günter and I view the industrious scene, while leisurely sipping our coffee in the cockpit of *Pacific Bliss*. This morning, we plan to take it easy

SEA TURTLES

There are four sea turtles common to Costa Rican waters:

1. The smallest is the Olive Ridley Turtle, with adults weighing up to 45 kg (100 lbs.) and measuring up to 75 cm (2'6"). The back of the head, shell, and flippers vary from dark green to bright yellow, but most of them are olive green. The plate protecting the bottom of the body is yellow. These turtles travel far offshore. Their food consists of shrimp, crab, sea urchins and snails, for which they may have to dive as much as 150 m (almost 500'). They nest along the stretch of the Costa Rican coast near Drake's Bay. During the arribada, thousands of turtles clamber ashore in a frenzied search for a nesting site. Some turtles are injured in the foray, many nests and their contents are destroyed as the beach becomes an egg-spattered war zone! Bahia Huevos ("bay of eggs" in Spanish) is named after such a nesting site.

2. A medium-sized turtle, the Hawksbill, weighs from 35 to 75 kg (77 to 165 lbs) and measures from 65 to 95 cm (26" to 36"). The backs of the adults have streaks of reddish-brown, black and yellow on an amber background. These turtles are seldom seen here outside of their nesting areas; one of these is Playa Curu, Costa Rica. This species of turtle is endangered; unfortunately, its shell has been used for ornaments and jewelry. In Mexico and Japan, juvenile Hawksbills are polished and used as wall hangings.

3. The Pacific Green Turtle is larger than the Olive Ridley, averaging about 80 cm (32") in length and weighing from 65 to 125 kg (143 to 275 lbs.). Its carapace (shell) is very narrow, highly arched, smooth, and narrows toward the rear. The hatchlings have a dark grey/green carapace. This turns to brown spots as juveniles and to medium brown to dark olive as adults. Some green turtles are famous for their extensive migrations; those, which feed off the coast of Brazil, swim to nesting beaches on Ascension Island, some 1400 miles distant. The Green Turtles on the Pacific coast, however, appear to live year-round in the same general area. All of the green turtles are classified as endangered largely through decimation for the restaurant trade in the U.S. and Europe. Though protected, many nests are destroyed by poachers in search of eggs for sale as food and as an ingredient in cosmetics.

4. The most amazing turtle in these waters is the giant Leatherback. It has a huge body that is shaped like a barrel, encased in black leathery skin, with five ridges. It is the largest marine turtle and in fact, the largest reptile in the world today. These monsters of the sea grow from 1.5 to 2 m (5 to 7') and weigh from 260 to 600 kg (700 to 1600 lbs.) Leatherbacks are amazing creatures. They can be found nesting on tropical beaches bordering the Atlantic, Pacific, and Indian oceans. In the non-nesting season, they travel as far north as Canada, Iceland, and Norway and as far south as New Zealand and Peru. (They can maintain a body temperature up to 10 degrees centigrade above that of the surrounding water.). They can travel as much as 6,000 km (2,727 miles) to feed in waters as deep as 500 m (1,640'). Their primary food is jellyfish. Leatherbacks are still exploited for their oil, which at one time was used as a caulking material for wooden vessels. Their oil is still used in cosmetics and as lamp fuel.

and lazy. Later, we will find out what else there is to see in Quepos.

Locals of this town boast that it is one of the top ten sport-fishing meccas in the world. Fishermen catch yellowfin tuna, marlin, dorado, wahoo, and amberjack. Sailfish, however, are the big prize. Offshore fishing thrives here from December until April. Depending on the size of the vessel, the equipment on board, and the experience of the skipper, a day's fishing trip can cost from 300 to 1000 U.S. dollars.

Pacific Bliss is one of only three sailboats occupying the anchorage. Before we checked-in with the Port Captain yesterday, we met the owner of one of the other sailboats. He charters small tourist groups here. The second sailboat is a large ketch that is obviously chartering tourists as well. We watch as it transports about 20 passengers, all decked out in bright orange life preservers. They have returned from a three-hour sunrise sail—motoring, of course, since there is no wind. Chartering is not a bad business at $55 or so a head for three hours!

I refer to my guidebook: The town's name comes from the Quepos Indian tribe, which inhabited this area at the time of the Spanish conquest. By the end of the 19th century, that population had disappeared; European diseases, internecine tribal warfare, and slavery had decimated the native communities. Farmers from the highlands then colonized this area. Typical of many ports here, bananas became the primary export. When the banana production declined because of disease, African palm oil became the next export. Now, sport fishing and tourism provide the bulk of Quepos's income.

By afternoon, we have had enough of leisure. We go ashore to investigate what inland tours might be available.

The Rainmaker Tour with the *Oh, My God* Bridge

At the Quepos fishing dock, we meet the tour van. We will travel about 14 km inland to visit the Rainmaker, a new ecotourism project that opened in 1997. Visitors walk through the rainforest canopy on a series of suspension bridges, which are attached to the largest trees in the forest. A 2000-hectare preserve, Rainmaker mimics aerial walkways in Asia and the Peruvian Amazon. It represents the first such project in Central America.

As the van takes us inland, we bypass bridges under construction by going around them and over dry creek beds—quite a lumpy ride. We bump over one bridge I'd rather go around! A pile of red rust, it creaks and groans under the van's weight. Günter asks the driver to stop so I can photograph a sign that says, DANGER. CROCODILES. DO NOT SWIM HERE.

After arriving at the preserve, we enjoy a fruit-and-juice snack under an orange-and-yellow canopy. There we meet three women, part of our tour group. Our guide, another José, introduces himself. He is a dark-complexioned Costa Rican naturalist who completed his graduate degree in Ames, Iowa—of all places.

The five of us walk past a man-made "Walden Pond" and then through a magical rainforest canyon. Wooden walkways and bridges protect the canyon floor. A pristine stream tumbles down a series of boulders and rocks from a divided waterfall.

After a mile or so, we are already dripping with sweat. José points to a rope swing hanging over a shallow pool at the bottom of the falls: "Jump in!" Günter and I are wearing swimsuits beneath our clothes. We accept the invitation, quickly peeling off our shorts and shirts.

Günter takes the first jump from the rope swing. I follow. With a whoop and a yell, we plunge wholeheartedly into the bracing cold, refreshing, and restorative spring water. The two younger women follow our example. Their mother, whom they address as "grandmother," stays on the bank. She rejoins us, and the group climbs several hundred steps to a tree platform.

Once there, we spot a suspension bridge through the thick jungle. It is high, high above, spanning the entire canyon. Grandmother points to the bridge and gasps, "Oh, my God."

José is smug. His slight frame puffs to full height. "Yes, it is called the *Oh, My God Bridge*. Everyone says this. Now you understand why." He pauses. "The bridge hasn't opened yet, but we are going up there. You'll get to see it…firsthand."

"We can't go on it?" I ask, disappointed. I'm in a rare, daring mood today.

"Well, the inspector is due today. It's ready…It's scheduled to open in four days. We'll see…Maybe we'll be lucky."

We stow our backpacks on the first platform and meander through a maze of smaller footbridges and platforms. Posted at every stop is the maximum number of people allowed. To play it safe, José divides our small group into groups of two. We peer into the dense canopy, searching for animal life. We spot some striking, cobalt blue butterflies. Then we spot an indigo hummingbird. Finally, through his binoculars, Günter focuses on a toucan with a massive yellow bill. He hands the glasses to me. "It's flying to the top of a tree high over that canyon. Seems to me that big bill would make it too top-heavy to fly!"

I have to agree.

Promotional brochures feature these toucans. Every souvenir shop in Costa Rica sells replicas of them. According to José, actually spotting one of these birds is rare.

We see other birds, but no mammals. "Animals are best seen in the early morning hours. Or at dusk," says

The rainmaker tour

1. A dual waterfall; 2. DANGER. CROCODILES. DO NOT SWIM HERE; 3. Günter gazes at the tropical wonders;

4. The Oh My God Bridge; 5. Lois swings from a rope and drops into the dual waterfall pool.

José.

I glance at my watch. It is now 11:00 a.m.

As we trek higher and higher, we glimpse the new suspension bridge through the forest. It beckons to us—grand, glorious, and tantalizing.

I cannot stand the thought of coming this far, and not getting on that bridge. But I'll keep quiet—for now.

We arrive at the final platform before the bridge. We look into the deep canyon. Awesome! We are now 25 stories above the canyon floor.

I turn to José. "How long is it?"

"This bridge is 310 feet long. It is the longest and highest suspension bridge of its type in the world," says José, pride written all over his brown face. "You would have to go to the Amazon or to the Orient to walk on a bridge like this."

That does it. I must walk across this bridge!

"Could we just go on it, just for a little way?" I beg, throwing all caution to the forest far below.

"I'm thinking of allowing each party to go halfway."

Why only halfway? That is strange. But I don't want to rock the boat.

"Lois, you go first," commands José. "When she comes back, Günter, you go next."

For the first time, I question what I am doing. *You asked for this. This is the point of reckoning. You know full well, Lois, this bridge hasn't been tested yet.*

But I cannot renege now! With baby steps, I walk cautiously to the middle of the bridge, gripping the woven, bamboo fronds that make up the "lifelines." I inhale deeply. Then I dare to look down. Twenty-five stories down. *Oh, my God!*

The waterfalls and the trees on the canyon floor look as small as the miniature world one finds in Lego Land.

From the platform, now half a football field away, Günter takes one telephoto and yells to me. "Wave!" I loosen my grip and stand bowlegged. Like when I do the "cat walk" on the boat. Slowly, I edge toward the middle of the single-lane walkway. The footbridge wobbles and sways. The shaking sends shivers up my spine. But any residual fear is drowned by my elation. *I did it!*

My pace increases as I walk back to the safety of the platform. When I reach it, I exhale, unaware that I had been holding my breath most of the way.

Günter walks confidently to the middle. *No fear there! He used to climb mountains.* I snap his photo.

José convinces the three women to brave the bridge as well. They are hesitant, but courageous. They return with triumphant smiles on their faces. Now we retrace our steps back to platforms and across wimpy footbridges, which have shrunk in comparison to the *Oh, My God Bridge.* On the way back, José explains that the pathway on the other side has yet to be completed. That's why he had us walk only halfway across! We end our tour under the canopy, welcoming the shade, and we're rewarded with cold drinks made with fresh pineapple.

If you ever have the good fortune to travel to Quepos, Costa Rica, you would be crazy to miss this tour!

The Punta Leona Trots
9 °42.5' N, 84 °4' W

We are the only boat anchored in this bay near Punta Leona. We are here because we have made plans to meet Saverio, a savvy diplomat with the Italian embassy in San José, Costa Rica's capital. Saverio has corresponded with us by e-mail ever since he first surfed our *www.pacificbliss.com* website last September. He is considering the purchase of a Catana 431. Because here are no Catana dealerships within thousands of miles, touring ours gives him a rare opportunity to evaluate one firsthand.

We dinghy to shore to meet Saverio for breakfast. He is accompanied by his striking girlfriend—a black-haired, brown-eyed, Costa Rican beauty. After eating and getting acquainted, we bring him and his Costa Rican girlfriend back to *Pacific Bliss*. Upon boarding, our visitors present us with a "care package." It is filled with items that a cruiser needs: (1) a package of floppy disks, (2) a 12-volt fan for the nav station, (3) a spatula for scraping barnacles, and (4) rechargeable batteries for our portable, back-up GPS unit. Grateful, we thank him for his thoughtfulness.

Showing our boat to this charming couple reminds us of all the reasons why we fell in love with *Pacific Bliss*. Günter points out the mechanical and electrical features and options. I point out our custom modifications: the built-in computer desk, the footwear storage we added underneath the bunks, and the silverware-and-glassware storage unit under the salon table.

Like the many travelers and yachties we have met along the way, Saverio is an interesting character. He has spent most of his life in countries other than his native Italy, where his father still lives. He has traveled around the world by land; now his dream is to repeat his adventure by sea. By day's end, we have established an easy rapport.

⚓

The rest of our stay in Punta Leona goes downhill. Onshore, a large resort area offers sprawling motel-like rooms, three bars, numerous restaurants, and a large swimming pool. None of this interests me, because I want nothing more than access to the internet. The only

1. A fisherman hands over his catch; 2. Activity on the fishing docks, Quepos.

Costa Rican Beauty.

internet service available to us is dial-up, which is found in the resort's reception area, near a noisy bank of pay phones. They offer no computers. One must bring his own laptop and connect it to a phone line—and they call that "service!" We return to *Pacific Bliss* and pack our laptop into its waterproof case. Then, we dinghy through the surf toward the shore. Just as we are about to beach…Splash! A breaker swamps our dinghy. Our bags are drenched. The floor is flooded. Our clothes are a salty mess. But nothing is damaged other than our egos. After this, we conclude that bringing in the laptop by dinghy—even in its waterproof case—is not something we want to risk.

I look forward the touted internet access at Barillas Marina in El Salvador, the next country; supposedly, one can take a laptop to their *palapas*—little tables with thatched roofs, wired with internet and phone connections. *Now that will be progress! If that actually happens.*

"Well, this will be our last night *here*," Günter announces. "Let's get underway at dawn's light."

Midnight brings on cramps and diarrhea that last throughout the night. For hours, I'm confined to the starboard head while Günter dashes to one port side.

By mid-morning, we recover enough to motor 20 miles across the Gulf of Nicoya to Bahia Bellena, our next destination. Safely anchored there, we never leave *Pacific Bliss*. We read, sleep, and lie around listlessly close to the heads, trying to recover.

The next day, we feel slightly better. We slog on to Bahia Carillo with the goal of refueling. This secluded bay has a difficult reef-and-rock entrance and must be approached in full daylight, preferably at low tide so that one can see the reefs. Despite our malaise, we manage to navigate the entrance. We arrive to find everything closed on shore. We spend yet another day on the boat.

Günter becomes my hero again. And he has scraped knuckles to prove why. Still as listless as a Costa Rican three-toed sloth, he wills himself to dive under *Pacific Bliss* to scrape the gunk off the stalled knot meter. He gathers the energy to scrape the tenacious barnacles off the rudders. He even cleans the bottom of the dagger boards.

The water is super-rich and clouded with nutrients. Günter reports that the underwater visibility is less than two feet, clear enough for cleaning, not for swimming. How we long for crystal clear water!

There *are* Costa Rican islands that have such a clear marine environment: One is Cocos, 300 miles away. We dare not go there. Sailing that far offshore is not recommended because of the threat of *Papagayos*, strong winds that can extend from Quepos, Costa Rica, all the way through Guatemala. We recall the advice in our cruisers' guide: "Hug the shoreline."

Here, in this deserted, God-forsaken bay, I fall into my first bout of depression. I long for a "real home," not this crowded yacht. Our condo in San Diego will be like a mansion compared to this! I agonize over the many miles of coastline yet to come, the never-ending little bays and anchorages that we must pass, until we are finally home.

Life seems to be laughing at us. We are living on the water, yet cannot snorkel in the water. We are living on a sailboat, yet haven't raised the sails since our adventure "up the creek" way back in Aguadulce, Panama. There is always the threat of wind, of dangerous Papagayos, yet there is no wind.

I try to relate our predicament back to my tough days in the business world. What did I do then? Yes! I rallied the troops with such sayings as, "In the confrontation between the river and the rock, the river always wins—not through strength, but through perseverance."

Why not now? Like all those turtles we encountered along the way, we must keep on slogging, even though it seems uphill at times.

Bloody Flamingo Marina
March 27

Scratch that complaint about not having enough wind! That's apparently true in central and southern Costa Rica. Now that we are in *northern* Costa Rica, we have periods of too much wind. We enjoy one day of great sailing. Then the next day, the wind is right on the nose, as we motor into port, both engines at full bore. We approach the Flamingo Marina bucking Force 6 winds, only to find that there is no dock space or moorings available in the small, protected harbor behind the breakwater. It is too late in the day to motor on. "You can pick up one of those moorings *outside* the breakwater," the dock master yells, cupping his hands against the wind.

Picking up a mooring ball in a 26-knot wind, gusting to 30, is quite a feat. Boat hook in hand, I bend over the bow and stretch way down, a difficult maneuver for someone as short as I, even in calmer seas. After a number of attempts, I manage to grab the mooring. But the wind is driving the boat backward, and fast.

Günter rushes forward from the helm and grabs the line. He struggles to cleat it off. Barnacles clinging to the mooring line slice his flesh. He refuses to let go and wins the battle, with blood flowing all over him and the boat.

"You should have worn gloves," I chastise him, as I carefully dress and bandage his hand and fingers.

"There wasn't time to get them from the anchor locker."

"You should have let the line go."

"We already tried three times. I was determined to get it this time."

"I know. But you paid the price."

Persistence and determination, wearing down the boulders in the stream. Günter has it. This I know. Or, is it just plain stubbornness?

We dinghy to the dock where I can finally drop off our laundry. But we are too late to buy ice for a well-deserved cocktail. The iceman on the dock sells ice from 6 a.m. to 2 p.m., then locks up the chest. The office doesn't have a key. Typical! In addition to this, the marina has no eating facilities, and of course, no internet. We have been yearning for some camaraderie with other cruisers. But there's no such luck there, either.

"There's a restaurant at that hotel up the hill," the marina man informs us.

Maybe tomorrow. Our primary interest now is provisioning. Our goal is to buy food to last us for a week, until we arrive in Barillas Marina in El Salvador. *Barillas. That destination is beginning to sound like the Promised Land.*

The marina man points across the bay. "There's a store over there. You can take your dinghy."

I squint over the surf to the whitecaps beyond. I cannot see the store. It will be a long, wet dinghy trip in this wind. We'll save that challenge for tomorrow.

⚓

The next morning, with wind whipping up whitecaps, we brave the trip across the bay. We provision and load up the dinghy. By the time we return to *Pacific Bliss*, our food is wet, but packable. We release the mooring and top off both tanks at the floating fuel dock. We now have food as far as El Salvador and fuel as far as Mexico.

During our sail up the coast, the SSB conversations are dominated by the issue of where to fuel in Costa Rica. Many yachties have been forced to go to the gas stations near small towns along the coast, a complex process that can involve many trips. They must fill jerry cans on shore, load them into dinghies, then return to their yachts to pour the gas into fuel tanks. Where our nine-year-old guidebook, *Charlie's Charts of Costa Rica,* says there is fuel, often there is not. According to the guide, only four cruising destinations along western Costa Rica have fueling docks. One of them, Bahia Carillo, was closed when we were there. Two others, Golfito and Puntarenas, involve going 30 miles each way into a large gulf. Some cruisers, headed south to Panama, skipped both of those fueling opportunities. Now the cruisers are frantic, searching for fuel along the mostly-deserted stretch of Panamanian coastline to the Canal. Thank God we had enough foresight to avoid their problems!

The farther we cruise, the more we realize that cruising takes not only persistence, but strategic and tactical planning as well.

Costa Rica is a wonderful destination for tourists. Every hotel offers an inland jungle "ecotour." Expansive resorts perch on spectacular bluffs. Swimming pools overlook the crashing surf. For resorts, the purpose of the sea is an all-encompassing view. But for cruisers, the country offers nothing. Fuel is hard to come by. Provisions are difficult to obtain.

I look forward to checking out and moving on.

Exiting Costa Rica and Finding New Friends
10 ° 33.4'N, 85 °42' W
Playa del Coco

The customs facility here in Playa del Coco is barely a step above a shack. Familiar with the slow wheels of Costa Rican bureaucracy by now, Günter and I sit side-by-side on the unpainted wooden bench, patiently waiting to be called to the rickety counter.

I study the couple next in line. The tall, dark-haired man is smooth-shaven and well-groomed. His short-sleeved shirt neatly tucked into long, tropical-weight pants. The woman with him is cute and petite. She wears a red-and-white striped sheath with matching red-duck sports shoes. These are not your average *American* cruisers, most of whom are independent and belligerent. Most don't dress as neatly as these two: Instead they usually wear shorts, tees and TEVA's, even to customs and immigration offices. And they do this, despite the guide books' advice to show respect for local authorities by dressing properly.

Günter and I dress somewhere in between: shirts and long pants to show respect, but sandals, rather than socks and closed-toed shoes.

Before we can reach the counter, the officer puts up a CLOSED sign. It is obviously siesta time. And it seems as if the entire town will go to sleep for an hour or two. Günter and I get up to leave, and we find ourselves walking alongside the neatly dressed couple into the dusty main street. The man turns toward us. "Do you know how long they will be closed?" His accent is distinctly French; his English pronunciation is perfect.

"No idea," Günter responds. "Do you want to have lunch while we wait? There's supposed to be a good restaurant down this street."

Thus begins one of those friendships that I sense will last a lifetime.

The couple introduces themselves as Jean-Claude and Claudie. Their yacht is a ketch called *Makoko*, after a place in Nigeria where Jean-Claude managed a brewery for a time. They talk of a flat in Paris and a summer home on the French Riviera. We hit it off immediately, laughing and joking. By the time we decide to return to Customs, a new line has already formed. But we take it all in stride as we talk the time away. They are heading

Drying out roof tiles, El Salvador.

Proprietor showing clay bowl made from the mud of the lake.

north to Mexico on a schedule similar to ours. We make plans to meet again in the Bahia Elena anchorage because we have agreed to sail together along the coast of Nicaragua to El Salvador.

After we complete customs, I decide to tackle the Costa Rican internet system one last time. From the main street, I enter a facility called an internet café. It has no food, no soft drinks, and no water. In short, it is not a café. It is just a small, dusty room with three computers. I try to transmit my Rainmaker story for our website. Without warning, the computer crashes; the electricity is off.

"It should be restored any time," the clerk says.

I check back periodically, but three hours later, I give up. We return to *Pacific Bliss,* anchored in the bay.

Networking in Bahia Elena, the Stepping-Stone for Nicaragua and El Salvador
10 º 55' N, 85 º47' W

We motor sail across the Gulf of Papagayo under a tropical haze. When we arrive in Bahia Elena, a group of sailboats and one large motor yacht are anchored there. The anchorage is stark and dramatic, protected on three sides by rugged cliffs and rolling hills. I recognize its overwhelming beauty from a description I read in Herb Payson's *Blown Away.* This is a cruising book, written in the '70s, about casting off the lines in San Diego and heading for the South Pacific. Interestingly, it is one that Günter and I discovered that each of us owned when we merged our books, our households, and our lives.

The wide bay is an ideal resting point for cruisers before or after tackling the Gulf. Heading north, the navigation is easy. There is just one waypoint, the Lempa Shoals. This waypoint is on the route past Nicaragua, and we will turn at this point into the river that leads to the Barillas Marina.

We set the anchor in the bay, and a sailor on one of the monohulls calls me on the VHF: "Lois of *Pacific Bliss*! I know you from the Net. You are invited to a potluck on board *Heather,* that Grand Banks 46 anchored here. Guess where they're from? San Diego."

"Can *Makoko* come too? They're the Super Maramu just anchoring now."

"Of course."

What a wonderful way to exchange news of ports and anchorages going north! Of the six yachts represented, three of us—including a small monohull called *Namuka*—are heading north, the other three, south. The conversation changes from French to German to Spanish to English, but everyone seems to follow it all. After my first glass of wine, a three-woman "delegation" approaches, asking me whether I can "take over" as Net Controller one morning per week.

"We started this SSB Net in Mexico," one says. "But now we are heading south out of range. You're heading north. You'd be perfect."

"Why me?" I ask.

"We've been listening to you already, reporting your position. You have a good radio voice. You'll do fine."

"But I don't know the procedure…the order of things."

"Not a problem. We have a cheat sheet right

Lois purchases a cane in a stall near El Salvador.

here."

How can I refuse? Besides, it should be a valuable learning experience, as well as a way to facilitate a group of cruisers who can keep in touch with each other. Communications and buddy boating will become essential for our safety: Heading north, we face the threat of fierce winds—Papagayos, Tehuantepeckers, and finally, the Baja Bash. It will be one long slog.

One Hand for the Boat: Accident at the Shoals
13 °07' N, 88 ° 25' W
April 1, but this is no April Fool's joke.

We follow our buddy boat *Makoko* along the Nicaraguan coast, as we hoist, then reef, our sails in variable winds. The evening brings shifting winds and lumpy seas. When off watch, I cannot sleep. By morning, we are coasting along on benign, following seas. *Makoko*, with a convenient, all-electric winching system, raises dual spinnakers of red, white, and blue, the colors of the French flag. We on *Pacific Bliss*, with our own spinnaker not so accessible in the sail locker, are content to sail along, wing-on-wing.

By 0755, we are off the Gulf of Fonseca, still 37 miles from the dangerous Lempa Shoals. We spot a sailfish, massive fins gliding along the surface of the gently rolling sea. Later, a school of dolphins joins us. They travel ahead for hours. At 1250, I make a VHF call to the marina to relay our position and to confirm the mooring reservations for *Pacific Bliss* and *Makoko*.

"We'll send a panga to meet you at the shoals in approximately one hour," the marina replies. "Wait for our call-back. It's quite a difficult passage to make on your own, zigzagging through the shallows and reefs."

Closer to the waypoint, we understand what he meant. We would never dare this on our own! At the estuary, the raging surf crashes into massive boulders. It appears impossible to navigate to the river beyond. We stop and wait. I grab my camera and begin to shoot photos. Günter, at the starboard helm, watches for the panga.

"Here he is! He's motioning for us to follow him. Lois, take these binoculars."

Günter guns both engines to get through the boiling mess. I've just let go of the cockpit table to reach for the binoculars with my left hand. My camera is still in my right hand. *Pacific Bliss* lurches forward, bucking across the shoals. My foot slips on the salon steps. Down I go. First, the back of my head hits the square corner of the teak cockpit table. Then, I land on my right hip on the stairs. My arms are straight up. I'm still holding the binoculars in one hand and the camera in the other.

"Are you okay?"

"I think so. I've always been hard-headed."

"Climb up to sit beside me on the helm seat. Stay close to me. In case you have a concussion."

We follow the panga along the river for a while. Then it speeds ahead. We hang back, taking our time, motoring past sugar cane farms, primitive fishing villages, and mangrove shores lined with egrets and herons. Children grin and wave as we pass. I go back

185

On passage from Costa Rica to El Salvador.

into the salon to get my camera again. All seems fine. About 10 miles up the Lempa River, about 30 yachts are tied to moorings along the shore. Apparently, "the forgotten middle" of Central America, Guatemala and El Salvador has been discovered by cruisers.

Günter slowly idles to the mooring ball. My injury forgotten, I reach out to pick up the mooring. I get it on the first try. "Not bad, eh?"

"Way to go," Günter congratulates me.

From our mooring, we have a great riverside view. "Look! They really do have thatched *palapas*. And cruisers are sitting there with laptops. Finally, I can send off my e-mails."

"Fine. Let's close up the boat and launch the dinghy." We go into the salon. I shut the hatch above the settee. Then I reach to shut the other hatch above the nav station. "Ow!" A sharp stab in my lower back, above my right hipbone, causes me to scream in pain. I cannot move. I fall onto the settee. Günter comes to help me. I still cannot move.

"Maybe it will be better later. I'll launch the dinghy by myself," he says.

I never do get over to those elusive *palapas*. This first night after the accident, Günter helps me undress, then leads me to the head. He tries to put me back into our bed, which must be accessed from the end. I cannot hoist myself up. I cannot crawl to my pillow. Next, we try the guest/crew cabin in the port hull. I can barely make it up and down the steps. But there, I can at least access the bed from the side. Günter tucks me in and places the hand-held VHS unit on the nightstand. "You call me when you have to go to the head. Or if you need anything at all," he orders. Then, he returns to the starboard side.

Four tablets of 200 mg Advil, taken through the night, barely dull the pain.

After what seems like an endless night, 0800 finally arrives, and the Net is on. Günter has helped me up the stairs to the nav station. I stand there, now, with the control in my hand; I still cannot sit. Fortunately, this is not my day to serve as Net Controller. When the controller asks whether there are "medical emergencies," I explain my situation. There are no doctors among the thirty or so cruisers here, but a nurse on another yacht answers my plea. "Sounds like the sciatic nerve," she says. "I had that once. I'll bring over the kidney belt I used. It should speed your recovery. At the least, it will allow you to move without so much pressure." She brings the belt immediately.

Claudie also dinghies over to supply me with a stash of pain killers.

Standing at the laptop, I compose an e-mail to my doctor in San Diego, asking for his recommendations.

Günter dinghies to the marina to send it off. The internet actually works here. Too bad I cannot experience this miracle for myself! He brings back comfort food and chocolate from the marina restaurant.

⚓

After three days, I can manage only to climb down the swim steps and into the dinghy for a visit to the marina.

Claudie and Jean-Claude come to visit me on *Pacific Bliss*. "We plan to take a little tour to San Salvador,

Along the river to Barillas Marina, El Salvador.

"This is the last bloody fish I'll deal with," says Günter.

the capital," Claudie begins. "We want to visit some villages along the way…" she hesitates. "Do you think you are up to it?"

I can't bear to leave El Salvador without really seeing it. So I agree to go, despite my pain. Part of the attraction of this country is that it's so small you can drive from east to west in just seven hours, north to south in four, hopping from beaches to colonial towns, mountain lakes, and volcanoes—all in one day.

Our friends hire a car and driver. In the morning, the four of us take off along a blacktop road to the hinterland. Our first stop is an open-air market. I gravitate to the colorful hammocks strung across one booth. Then, I come across a display of handmade crutches. Günter bargains for a wooden crutch with a stunning carved handle. The combination of the kidney belt and the new crutch allows me to walk without pain for the very first time since the accident.

Touring El Salvador

El Salvador is a poor country with a history of sadness that never seems to end. Poverty, unemployment, a 12-year civil war, and natural disasters—all have left their mark on this society. We drive past hundreds of flimsy shacks clinging to the muddy banks of polluted streams. Our driver, Elena, points out that the forests have been emptied of all animals—even the monkeys. They were killed to feed the revolutionary army. "The war ended in 1992," she says, "but the jungles still suffer the aftermath."

Despite its sad history, El Salvador remains a beautiful, resilient country; its natural wonders cannot be defeated. Near the coast, we drive through broad valleys and beaches of black volcanic sand. Inland, the road winds around rugged volcanoes to deep, blue, mountain lakes. I long to see the cloud forests in Parque Nacional Montecristo-El Trifinio or the moonscape on top of Volcán San Miguel. But I won't be able to see these and many other wonders of El Salvador on this brief, two-day trip.

As she drives, Elena tells us about the war as it really was: terrifying because her family was ousted by the revolutionaries, thrilling because she lived through it, boring because it seemed to go on forever (throughout most of her childhood), confusing because the landowners were not all bad and the revolutionaries not all good, and sad because of how it scarred her country forever.

We drive past San Salvador. It is a city of about two million, which constitutes 60 percent of the country's population. We stop only for a photo of it from an overlook. This capital city has all the bustle of a modern metropolis, along with gangs, pollution, and crowds. San Salvador is called "*la ciudad de las dos caras de la moneda*"—the city of two sides of the coin—because

DID YOU KNOW?

EL SALVADOR

El Salvador, the smallest and most densely populated Central American state, is the only one without a Caribbean coastline. On the north, it is bounded by Honduras and Guatemala, on the southeast by the Gulf of Fonseca and the Pacific Ocean.

Known as the Land of Volcanoes, El Salvador has experienced frequent and destructive earthquakes. We arrived within a few months after the disastrous February 2001 event.

The Pipil Indians, descendants of the Aztecs, likely migrated to the region in the 11th century. In 1525 Pedro de Alvarado, a lieutenant of Cortez, conquered El Salvador.

El Salvador was named "the Savior" when it achieved independence from Spain in 1821 and from the Central American Federation in 1839.

A 12-year civil war, which cost the lives of some 75,000 people, ceased in 1992 when the government and leftist rebels signed a treaty that provided for military and political reforms. The war was the result of gross inequality between a small, wealthy elite, which dominated the government and the economy, and the overwhelming majority of the population, many of whom lived—and continue to live—in abject squalor.

El Salvador's coastline, mostly undeveloped.

of the split between wealthy districts and poor areas downtown, where people make a living hawking whatever they can sell: DVDs, food, and hammocks. Though the city has many buildings destroyed by the civil war and by earthquakes over the years, it has been rebuilt several times. Many of the colonial buildings have been replaced; only a few are being restored.

We arrive at a quaint, colonial-style hacienda on the shores of Lake Suchitlán, the largest inland body of water in El Salvador. The proprietor shows us around. She is a charming woman with thick, dark brows and black hair pulled back in a clip, wearing bib overalls. We stop at a breakfast/dining area that features glass-fronted shelves on which is a display of primitive bowls and bags. She then leads us to a terrace, which overflows with lush plants trailing out of clay pots, and then past an old cart filled with flowers. Beyond the artistic display is a massive freshwater lake, stretching as far as the eye can see, surrounded by magnificent mountains and volcanoes, under huge puffs of sheep-clouds. After all this grandeur, our simple rooms—with woven cotton spreads, handmade lamps, and rough-hewn nightstands—seem merely an afterthought. Günter spreads open the paned-glass windows to the invigorating mountain air. Sleep will come to us easily this night. Even my back feels better here.

Tomorrow, sadly, we will head back.

The Cruising Seminar

We return from our inland tour to a yacht covered with coal-black flakes. The farmers in El Salvador burn the sugar cane fields after harvesting. When the wind comes up after the fires have died, the cinders blow away, and *this* is the result. We cannot simply wash down the cinders because they tend to smudge into a sticky, charcoal mess. We must sweep them off the deck, clean them from the scuppers, and pluck them from the window screens. It is a painstaking and miserable job.

Günter and I recover by heading to the marina to commiserate with other cruisers. A delegation of three cruiser women approaches us after our first beer. One sun-bronzed cruiser acts as the spokesperson: "We are putting on a seminar for those heading south to Panama. Since you've just come up from that way, could you head it up—recommend some ports, tell us where to get gas, and give us the lowdown on customs and immigration?" I think back to Bahia Elena in Costa Rica, the first time I was approached by such a delegation. This time, I won't be so quick to protest.

I reply without hesitation. "Sure."

The follow-up request is strange and unexpected: "Uh, could you please ask the young couple with the little baby whether they would talk? We understand you know them."

I freeze. I don't know how to answer.

By now, the story about a couple robbed at knife point in Banana Bay has spread throughout the cruising community. It had happened after we left there. Rumors abound. Yet, the cruisers are not talking directly to the victims, Jean-Marie and Maureen, because they don't know to deal with such a delicate subject.

"You must understand…," the woman continues to press her case, "of course, everyone is concerned about theft and personal safety in Golfito. Now, even more so. The cruisers here are wondering…do they even dare to stop there?"

Jean-Marie, a French yachtie, and his Dutch partner, Maureen, had been introduced to Günter and me by our new friends, Jean-Claude and Claudie. During a sundowner on their yacht, a monohull called *Finally*, they told us their frightening story. Maureen is still traumatized. Would she want to suffer more by repeating—reliving—her terrifying experience in front of a group of strangers?

Finally, I respond to the delegation. "She may not want to speak about it, but I will ask her."

⚓

Our part of the safety seminar goes well. About 20 to 30 cruisers are seated in folding chairs arranged in a snug semi-circle at the marina. After my brief talk, Günter and I field all the questions expertly. The applause afterwards tells us that the southbound cruisers appreciate the timely information.

Then Maureen—tall, blonde, and confident—walks to the front of the room holding two-month-old Laurent, accompanied by raven-haired Jean-Marie. The couple has decided, after all, that their story needs to be told.

"I want to tell you what happened to us, first-hand, and urge you to take precautions when you arrive in Golfito," Maureen begins. "*Never* go to an anchorage where you are the only boat, as we did. We moored in front of the old hotel—no longer open. It was a little way from the marina, which we thought would be okay. It wasn't."

"We had heard that dinghies and motors were being stolen if they weren't locked up," adds Jean-Marie, nervously riffling his black hair. "The people there are poor, so we always locked ours. We had been in Golfito about a week with no problems. We were on our boat, having dinner below, when it happened. I heard a noise. I went up the hatch to check it out. I looked over the stern, down to the water. It was dark, but I could see the form of a man who had swum to our boat. It was raining lightly, so we didn't even hear him. He had a knife… he was in the process of cutting loose our dinghy!

Church in Suchitlán, El Salvador.

By the time we left Barillas Marina, over twenty yachts had anchored in the Rio Lenipa, waiting for a weather window.

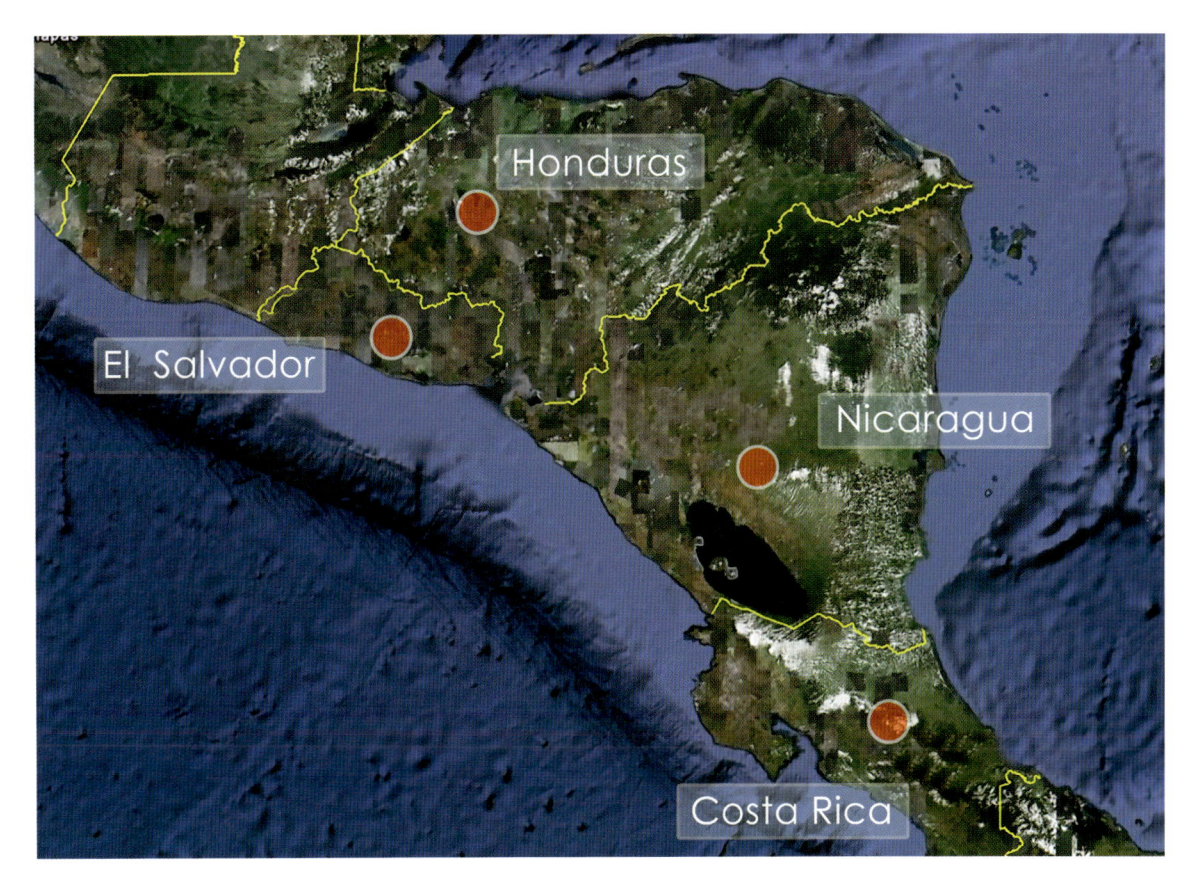

He would have taken it back to shore and we would have never known…I tried to stop him and somehow during the tussle he rushed right past me…and down the hatch. The next thing I saw, he was pointing the knife at Maureen, who was holding little Laurent. He was telling her to give him some money or he'd hurt the baby."

"I was never so scared in my entire life," Maureen cut in. "I still have nightmares…thinking about it. Jean offered him some money, only $20 or so that he could find quickly, and the man grabbed it, turned around, and left. That was it. Of course, I could not sleep all night. We left right away the next morning."

The room is silent as death. Then a few in the group begin to clap. Soon the room is filled with applause. The delegation comes up front to conclude the program. Afterwards, cruisers gather around to thank the couple. Jean-Marie and Maureen have made new friends this night.

Cruiser Charity

Cruisers take home a bounty of good will from the locals they meet as they sail around the world. This is a story about giving back. Canadian cruisers Malcolm and Jackie Holt arrived here on their Beneteau yacht, *Aeolus*, shortly after the devastating earthquake that occurred on January 13th in El Salvador. Their hearts went out to the families in the nearby mountain town of Usulután, who had lost almost everything they owned. The couple asked for donations from each new yacht that arrived at Barillas Marina. If the yacht crew could not donate money, they asked for a donation of labor.

By the time we arrived, the cruiser charity project was well underway. The Papagayos were raging along the coast of Nicaragua and on to Costa Rica. Fortunately for the project, that meant that many cruisers would be holed up here, waiting for an optimal weather window to continue south. Every day, a detachment of workers would leave their boats and head for trucks to be taken to the site of the devastation, 4000 feet up an extinct volcano. All converged on the little town, to teach and to assist poor coffee plantation workers in the construction of a new village.

Since Günter and I are well past the "strong young body" stage, we decide to donate money to the fund instead of offering our labor. We bid Malcolm and Jackie adieu, certain that we will keep in touch with such generous and loving sailors.

At the time of this publication, this cruiser charity project involved more than 100 boats, with cruisers from every continent donating time or money. Jackie and Malcolm stayed in El Salvador for most of the year. For more information about them and their ongoing effort, visit their website at http://lamerententerprises.com/index.html.

Two young men dressed in the garb of Roman soldiers.

Chapter 11
Semana Santa in Guatemala

Underway to Guatemala
13 º55.4" N, 90 º 47.9' W,
Puerto Quetzal, April 8, 2001

The El Salvador officials cross the river anchorage in their panga, board *Pacific Bliss,* and stamp our passports and the boat's exit papers. Shortly, we are underway, motoring back up the river toward the estuary, following *Makoko* and *Namanuk*, with little *Wind Gift* at our stern.

Pacific Bliss lurches and bucks over the shoals where I had fallen and hurt my back. We turn to sail up the coastline toward Guatemala.

Good riddance to this stretch of sea!

My back is improving gradually, but I worry about how my injury will fare during this overnight passage. The helm seats are quite high. To take the pressure off my sciatic nerve, Günter had purchased a child's step stool during our inland tour. Now, he places it right underneath my feet so that I can sit straight without dangling my legs. Since I had to return the kidney belt to its owner before leaving El Salvador, I am delighted that the gentle swaying with the sea seems to help the healing process.

We sail on into the night on a compliant sea, managing to keep up with *Makoko*. The smaller yachts fall behind.

The moon rises orange-yellow, and then brightens to white gold. All is well with the world. For now.

In the morning, Günter takes down the El Salvador flag and hoists the blue and white Guatemalan ensign. The sky-blue stripes depict Guatemala's location between the Pacific and Atlantic Oceans. The white stripe stands for the purity of the country's values—important after the 36-year civil war that ended in 1992. Crossed rifles in the center indicate Guatemala's willingness to defend itself by war if need be, while the olive branches symbolize the preferred peace.

By 1115, *Pacific Bliss* and *Makoko* have anchored successfully in the naval basin of Puerto Quetzal. This is the only port on the Guatemalan Pacific Ocean. We are deeper than we want to be, at 36 feet; at the shallower, recommended anchor coordinates, the allowance for swing room is not adequate. From the cockpit, we see men on a Guatemalan navy ship performing their duties. We conclude that we will be safe here and, we hope, not in the way of the navy.

We spend the next few days resting on board, and provisioning in San José, the small village nearby. During one visit there, we set up a private inland tour. A driver, who will also serve as our guide, will take the four of us to the Guatemalan highlands and then to Antigua in time for the legendary annual Good Friday procession.

Enjoying *Pana,* on Lake Atitlán

Our guide drops us off for our stay at the Del Lago Hotel and Spa in Panajachel. After checking in, we all unpack and enjoy a walk along the beaches of Lake Atitlán. Despite the hazy sky, the view is stunning: Lake Atitlán seems to float in the sky, a mile above sea level, the illusion created by the three majestic volcanoes that surround it. The mountains of Atitlán, Toliman, and San Pedro, all above 10,000 feet (over 3000 meters), hug the deep-blue lake. A giant volcanic eruption 85,000 years ago, which scattered volcanic ash from Panama to Florida, created this gorgeous lake. At about 5 miles

A young lady makes quesadillas in the Guatemalan highlands.

The lake town of Panajachel.

north to south and 11 miles east to west, Lake Atitlán covers almost 50 square miles and is 1000 feet deep.

Pana, as the locals call it, is the largest town on the lake and the jewel of the highlands. The four of us saunter from trading stall to trading stall, examining Mayan silver jewelry, multicolor-striped men's shirts, and women's colorful blouses and skirts. In another town, the beach town of San José, the men we met wore traditional western clothes. Here, at the lake, they wear the local *troje:* vertically striped shirts tucked into pants of swirling red, green, and silver—topped with woolen waist-belts. Some women wear colorful blouses in bright primary colors: marine blue, cherry red, and lemon yellow. Others wear white, lacy blouses with three-quarter sleeves and long, wrap skirts while they balance plaid bundles on their heads.

As usual, we sailors gravitate to the water. Sightseeing boats, some of them double-deckers, ply the shore, looking for *turistas* to take on scenic rides. Simpler motorboats ferry the residents back and forth between neighboring lakeside towns. We are tempted to go to other villages but opt for just taking it easy where we are. The day is pleasant for walking; we'll be spending plenty of time on the water in our own boats. Besides, we notice that many of the indigenous artisans and weavers are coming here, to Pana, to sell their products. We don't need to cross the lake to them.

We return to the main street, where the greasy scent of sizzling, hot oil in huge, metal vats of *pollos fritos* y *papas fritos*, fried chicken and fried potatoes, permeates the air. "Tacos! Quesadillas!" vendors shout as we pass. Rows of thatched roofs shade copious bunches of bananas hanging from the rough-hewn beams. Tables are piled high with oranges, pineapple, and other *frutas*. *Turistas* now crowd the stalls.

We retreat to a hotel balcony for sundowners, a pleasant departure from "the usual" in the cockpits of our sailboats. *Por la vida*. To life. Four beer bottles clink. As we sip ice-cold *Gallo,* doctored with salt and lemon, the flaming sun sends fiery tendrils across the vast lake, turning it blood red.

Amazing Chichicastenango

Chichicastenango means "place of the nettles." The local Mayan name is Siguan Tinamit, "town surrounded by canyons." The municipality of about 50,000 people is 95 percent Mayan. The primary language is Quiche, pronounced "kee-chay." This highland town has served as a crossroads and trade center since before the Spanish conquest in the 1500s. To this day, it remains a vibrant

197

A grandmother carries her grandson in the traditional fashion — in a sling.

marketplace.

And what a shopping mecca it is! Tarps cover booths that extend for blocks and blocks from all four sides of the whitewashed Church of Santo Thomas, in the center of town. We dodge locals and *turistas* as we weave from stall to stall, absorbing the breathtaking sights, sounds, and smells. Bright-eyed Mayan babies, in woven body-slings, peek over the shoulders of wiry children who seem too small to carry such a load… vendors haggle passionately while most of the crowd walks on…the aroma of incense mixes with that of food and treats.

Finally, we reach the church grounds.

The Catholic authorities built their famous church of Santo Tomas on the site of an existing Mayan altar. The "holy city" of Chichicastenango was settled in the late 1520s by indigenous Mayan nobility who were fleeing the Spanish city of Utitlan, the old provincial capital 12 miles away. The Indians were unable to escape conquest; however, for years they continued to worship their Mayan deities in secret while publicly observing Catholic rituals. Today, they are able to worship both openly.

A hubbub of activity still surrounds the church. During *Semana Santa*, Holy Week, festivals are held here every day. Clouds of incense envelop the worshippers and powerful religious elders. They have gathered from all over Guatemala to perform a mix of Mayan and Catholic ceremonies.

Elaborately dressed men of the *Cofradia*, spiritual leaders, perform their rituals outside the church doors. Then, while we stand at the side of the steps, as part of the crowd, the big wooden doors of the church begin to creak and groan. Soon they swing wide open. Out comes a group of 20-30 men and women shouldering a huge float complete with Jesus, angels, a red velvet-canopied bed, and an abundance of flowers. A path through the crowded streets opens magically as the procession moves on, away from the church.

Once the excitement has abated, we continue to walk through the marketplace. We finger tapestries and examine carvings and souvenirs. We pass by stalls of tomatoes of all sizes and shapes and chilies as big as plums and as small as kernels of corn. We stop dead at the rows of primitive masks, much like those that Günter has collected for most of his life. He selects a colorful jaguar mask to add to his collection. This will be a prize addition because the jaguar symbolizes the

Ruins of ancient Antigua.

superior strength and courage of the ancient Mayan warrior. Now he must negotiate the price, and this is difficult for him. The vendor, who happens to be a pretty young girl, would, like all Mayans, be offended if Günter paid the initial asking price. They must dicker. In the end, both parties smile as I take their photo. We move on to another stall to purchase lengths of Mayan fabric in geometric, saw-tooth patterns; we plan to use them in our home as table runners and sofa throws.

While walking through the market, I can't help but notice that all babies are carried in slings, on the backs or chests of mothers, fathers, and even children. I suppose they feel the soothing rhythm of life this way: walking, stooping, and performing daily chores. Some Mayan mothers even keep their breasts in babies' mouths, like pacifiers. I wonder if this "baby wearing and caring" keeps the babies here from crying.

Finally, we leave the colorful market to return to our car and driver. I ask our driver about the myth I've heard, that Mayan babies don't cry. "I never heard one cry in our walk through the market."

"Mayan babies do cry during the night," he answers. "Sometimes for several hours. No one worries about it. The Mayans say…when everyone gets quiet, it is the baby's turn to do the talking."

By dusk, we arrive in the historic city of Antigua. Our driver stops at the top of a hill that overlooks the city. "*El Cerro de la Cruz*, The Hill of the Cross," he announces. A huge stone cross on a bulbous platform dominates the foreground. The former Guatemalan capital spreads for miles below us, under the golden light of a setting sun. Beyond that lies the cloud-capped *Volcán Fuego,* Fire Volcano, one of Central America's most active volcanoes.

Good Friday in Antigua
April 13

The *Semana Santa*, Easter week, festivities here begin on Palm Sunday and continue through Easter Sunday. Although this is a huge event all around Central America, the largest celebration is right here in Antigua. Almost all of the city's 5000 inhabitants take part in some aspect of the huge processions, biblical re-enactments, and religious services.

During the evening prior to Good Friday, many residents lay out perishable carpets in front of their shops and homes. These are made of dyed sawdust, pine needles, seeds, and flowers. Many celebrants

Overlooking Antigua, Guatemala.

Indian lady weaves baskets for sale on the church steps, Antigua.

SEMANA SANTA

202

Procession through the streets of Antigua on the morning of Good Friday.

203

Antiguans make new carpets of flowers, cypress needles, and colored sawdust.

Good Friday's evening procession through Antigua.

Our friends Jean-Claude and Claudie, Antigua Plaza.

stay up all night. Marimba bands play all over town. Restaurants and bars stay open. The "Procession of Roman Soldiers" runs around the city's streets in the early morning hours, announcing the *sentencia*, the death sentence for Jesus. Others gallop on horseback. Hundreds of participants dress in deep purple robes as pseudo-Israelites to accompany the religious floats. The schedule and the order of the procession never vary from year to year.

Finding any public transportation at all in Antigua is rare during *Semana Santa*. Fortunately, the four of us had arranged for a taxi to pick us up at our hotel, Villa Antigua, at 5:00 a.m. The taxi drove us to the beginning of these blocked-off streets. Then we walked the procession route in the pre-dawn to view these delicate, meticulous carpets, which are such an integral part of the proceedings, before they would be trampled by the first procession.

This Good Friday morning, before dawn, Günter and I stand at a cordoned, cobblestone street watching the action. Beside us stand our friends Jean-Claude and Claudie. Tears cloud my eyes as we view one awesome production after another…participants costumed as Roman soldiers, with red helmets and gold shields, march alongside others clad as Jewish dignitaries …majestic floats slowly sway on marchers' broad shoulders…Mary, the mother of Jesus…and finally, the dramatic float of Jesus, himself, bearing His cross. This glorious procession ends just as the rising sun bursts over *Volcán Agua*, Water Volcano. This entire morning has blessed me with images that I will never forget.

After the morning's event, we join the street vendors, who never miss an opportunity to sell. They trailed the procession, hawking balloons, purple-robed baby rattles, and cotton candy. Repeatedly, we decline their insistent entreaties.

We stop at a coffee shop for cappuccinos, then wander to Parque Central, the heart of the city. The park is handsomely landscaped around a central fountain, making it a cozy square, with the grandiose cathedral on one side, the City Hall on another, the Palace of the Captains General on the third side, and a shopping arcade enclosing it on the fourth. All of us relax on a park bench for some time, watching the action: Guatemalan families stroll in the park; proud grandmothers show off their grandchildren, who wear round knit caps and colorful outfits. One girl across from us braids her sister's hair. A shoeshine boy spruces up Günter's topsiders.

At the entrance to the cathedral, three crosses have been raised, two already bearing statues of the condemned thieves. The third, in the middle, is empty, pending a re-enactment of the crucifixion at dusk. Contemporary Christian music wafts through the park from loudspeakers on the cathedral steps, adding joy to the ambience. We sit on the wooden park bench, taking it all in. Günter turns to me. "This is truly a Moment of Bliss."

After resting and enjoying the moment, we walk through the colorful shopping arcade, which overflows with hand-woven tapestries, handicrafts, and clothing.

Back at the hotel, Günter and I take a midday siesta. Later, we meet Jean-Claude and Claudie again at Parque Central. The park has changed dramatically. The mood is hushed, reverent, and expectant. Hundreds of spectators pack the square, sitting on every curb and even on the steps of the cathedral. Jean-Claude takes charge, directing us to a side street, away from the crowds. Earlier in the day he discovered a hotel where we could enjoy viewing everything in relaxed comfort.

Night falls. This time, the procession is muted. All the participants and most of the observers are clad entirely in black. A new carpet, made of cypress needles and flower petals, covers the entire length of the street. The advance guard walks on either side of the carpet, swinging bowls of incense. Mist swirls high into the night air, increasing the drama. Now a long line of heavy wooden platforms, 14 altogether, appears. They represent the Stations of the Cross. Underneath them, rows of participants, shouldering their burden, sway in sync to the slow, heavy beat of the funeral marching bands. We are mesmerized with the sounds of slowly beating drums, clapping cymbals, and deep-throated tubas. The thick incense creates a haunting, ghost-like fog. Crowds hush as the solemn procession passes by. The image of Christ is replaced by another of Christ being laid to rest, which will eventually stay at the church for the night.

When the entire ceremony is over, moved deeply by the performance, we drift silently to the hotel for dinner. We are seated at a heavy wooden table, surrounded by wall displays of swords and medieval armament. Somber and reflective, we discuss the suffering that Jesus endured to redeem mankind and how Peter had even asked to be crucified upside down. We focus on death and dying; we are not depressed, but in a fulfilled and contemplative mood.

Walking the ten blocks back to our own hotel, I consider the entire experience. *Powerful, majestic, and moving, this is another day in our journey that I will cherish for the rest of my life.*

The *Turista*

The celebrations in Antigua will continue throughout Easter weekend, but according to the locals, we have seen the best processions. We depart for Puerto Quetzal, the naval base, giving our driver time to leave us and celebrate with his family.

"Turista" is not always what you think. Here in

DID YOU KNOW?

GUATEMALA

Guatemala, the largest country of Central America, is divided into three main parts: the northern plain, the highlands in the middle, and the Pacific lowland. This country between the Caribbean Sea and the Pacific Ocean borders Mexico, El Salvador, Belize, and Honduras. It is smaller than the state of Tennessee, but has twice the number of people, with a population over 13 million. Yet Guatemala is home to the second largest rain forest in the world.

The main source of income is from agricultural products, especially coffee. Did you know that it was a Guatemalan who invented instant coffee? Guatemalans also invented blue jeans, chocolate, and the mathematical concept of zero.

Some 22 different languages are spoken in Guatemala; 21 of those are Mayan languages. Spanish is the official language. Reportedly, 85 percent of the Indians can't read or write because there are very few teachers who speak the Indian languages. All men and women over the age of 18 who can read and write are required by the law to vote. Others can vote if they wish.

Guatemalans are divided almost equally between Indians and Ladinos. They are distinguished from each other not by their ancestry, but by the language they speak, the clothes they wear, and where they live. An Indian can become a Ladino just by joining a Ladino community and leaving behind his Indian customs. The Ladinos are recognized more by their income and social class than their ancestry.

The Mayan civilization dominated the region for nearly 2000 years before the Spanish arrived in the early 16th century. Guatemala remained a Spanish colony for nearly 300 years before gaining its independence in 1821. It then remained a part of the Mexican Empire until it became fully independent in the 1840s. Since then, Guatemala's history has been divided into periods of democratic rule and periods of civil war and military juntas. Most recently, Guatemala emerged from a 36-year civil war, re-establishing a representative government in 1996.

Guatemalan fabrics

207

Buck on *WindGift* heading out from Barillas Marina.

Guatemala, it can mean "the trots," similar to Mexico's "Montezuma's Revenge." It is not a pleasant way to end our excursion, but this is one of the hazards of travel.

Two of us, Jean-Claude and I, had fish for dinner. Generally, ordering seafood inland in a developing country is not a great idea. Antigua was no exception. Close to the naval station, Jean-Claude and I can take no more. We manage to hold off the both-ends-elimination routine until we reach the gate to the naval base. We assume, wrongly, that the officials will let us use their facilities. They can't (or won't) let us in. We dash to the ditches, each to the opposite side of the road. I have slipped off my panties in the car and simply lift up my skirt. Afterwards, we are forced to hold it in again until we reach our boats by dinghy.

We both spend all of Easter Sunday sick on our respective boats. There is not a lot of "Praise the Risen Lord" going on!

From ecstasy to agony. What a way to end a perfect trip!

Buck, the Single-Handler

We left Buck back in the seas off the shoals of El Salvador, his little sailboat trailing far behind *Pacific Bliss* and *Makoko*. We didn't get to know Buck, even though we knew he had also anchored in the river next to Barillas Marina. The quiet, introverted sailor kept mostly to himself. When we began our highland tour, he had not yet arrived in Puerto Quetzal. Upon our return from Antigua, we were relieved to see *Wind Gift* anchored snugly in the basin, close to our larger yachts. At first, there was no sign of activity inside the small vessel.

"Most likely, he is sleeping it off after his single-handed passage from El Salvador. Let's leave him alone," said Günter.

On Monday, Claude invites us to sundowners and a light dinner on board *Makoko*. We plan to share our waypoints to Puerto Madero, our port of entry into Mexico.

"Claudie, can we invite Buck as well?" I ask over the VHF. "*Wind Gift* is the only other yacht in this harbor. I don't want him to feel left out."

"No problem. Of course, he is welcome on our boat."

Aware that Buck does not have a radio, Günter and I dinghy over to *Wind Gift*. From a distance, Buck appears small and frail. But up close, I can see that he is lean and wiry. His skin is as taut as leather, tanned by years under the blazing sun. He is stooped, perhaps from bending to enter the salon of such a small yacht. Its varnished wooden hull appears to be barely over 20

Masks for sale in Chichicastenango.

The navy anchorage at Puerto Quetzal, Guatemala.

feet long; I doubt that he can stand up straight inside.

"I don't usually like to leave my boat...well, especially after dark," he says.

"But it's only a stone's throw away," Günter argues. "You will be able to see *Wind Gift* from the cockpit of *Makoko*. We'll pick you up about 5:30."

Buck reluctantly agrees to the plan.

Later, we stop to pick him up. Then we tether *Petit Bliss* to the high transom of *Makoko,* and all three of us climb into their 53' Amel Super Maramu ketch. With its leaves spread, the table behind the steering wheel crowds the center cockpit. Claudie asks Buck to walk on the top of the seats to sit back in the corner, next to the mizzenmast. I also walk over the cushions and sit down next to Buck. Jean-Claude and Günter squeeze in beside us.

Claudie, stunning in a full-length sheath, her hair and make-up perfect, asks in her pert French accent, "And Buck, what would you like to drink?"

"Just water," Buck says.

"With gas or without?" She smiles graciously while setting out a tray of assorted cheeses, pâtés, and crackers.

"Just plain water," he mumbles as he looks down, embarrassed.

"Ice or no ice?"

Buck has no refrigeration. This will be a treat.

Claudie carries a bottle of a French red and a frosty chilled white up the hatchway from the galley.

"No ice, just a glass of water."

"Can't she understand me?" Buck whispers as he turns toward me. I can sense his frustration building.

"Would you like a little lime in it?" Claudie smiles disarmingly.

That does it. Overwhelmed and looking for all the world like a claustrophobic bantam rooster, Buck turns and gazes longingly at *Wind Gift*, lazily bobbing in the waves to our stern. "I don't know why people can't understand me. Don't I talk in plain English?" He stands abruptly. "I'm jumping. I will swim back to my vessel."

Buck begins to climb up out of his seat in the center cockpit and onto the stern deck. He hasn't bothered to squeeze past the crowded table.

"No, Buck. Don't jump!" Günter shouts.

Buck leaps toward the transom. Günter springs

from his seat and onto the deck, pleading. "Buck, let me take you back to your boat in my dinghy. You don't have to swim!"

Buck hesitates. Günter hops into our dinghy and pulls the starter cord. "Come on!" Buck climbs in and they speed off to *Wind Gift*. It is as close as our 9.9-horsepower outboard has come to leaving a roostertail wake.

"What did I do wrong?" Claudie has lost her usual composure.

"Nothing, Claudie," I console her. "I think that close quarters combined with social niceties are just too much for a simple single-handler."

She nods. "There is no doubt that Buck would have jumped in, clothes and all!"

"Single-handlers," I reply. "Why they sail alone… why they don't mix with other cruisers…I will never figure them out."

Early next morning, as dawn breaks, *Pacific Bliss* and *Makoko* prepare to pull anchor. Next stop: Mexico. I go to my station at the bow to pick up the windlass. As the anchor chain clunks over the roller, I scan the naval shipyard. *Wind Gift* is nowhere to be seen.

The strange, little man has disappeared.

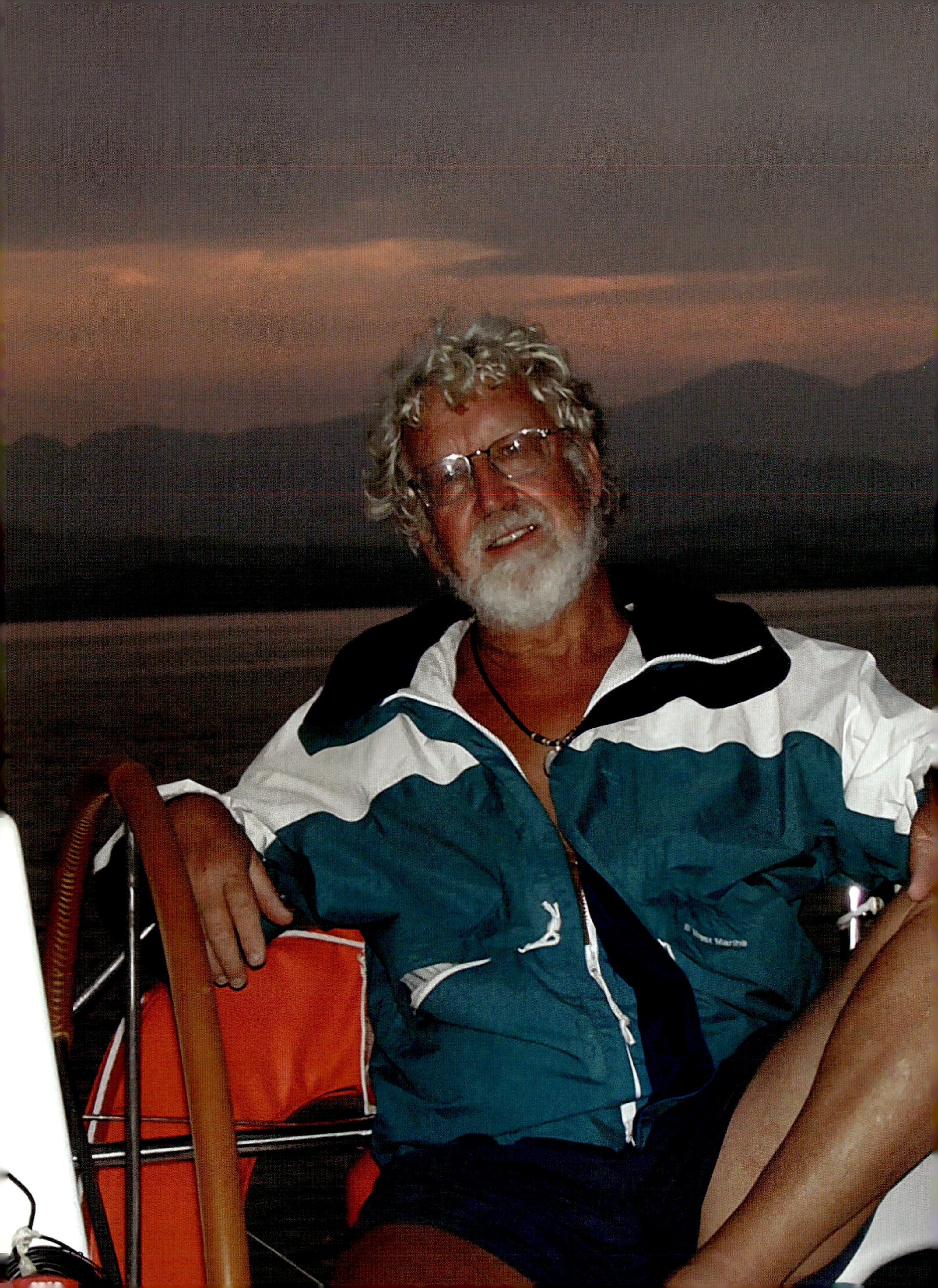

CHAPTER 12
MEXICO: MELTDOWN, MAGIC AND MAYHEM

**One Foot on the Shore:
Crossing the Gulf of Tehuantepec**
16° 01.37 N, 94°37.3 W
April 21, 2001

Thick haze envelops us, isolating our world of three. A lone frigate bird swoops toward *Pacific Bliss*. He checks out our bare rigging, snoops around the Mexican flag at the spreaders, and then glides away into the soup. On watch at the helm, I can barely make out the red port lights and green starboard lights of our buddy boats, *Finally* and *Makoko*. We have Force 4 winds, almost on the nose, but these are nothing to worry about. As I peer through the fog, my exterior demeanor is calm, I'm sure, but underneath, there is a nagging anxiety. We are crossing the notorious Gulf of Tehuantepec, where sailors are blown across the vast Pacific, sometimes, never to return.

The sun manages to break through, edging the clouds like a crown of jewels. The three vessels turn off their navigation lights in sync, as if communicating on some ethereal plane. The wind picks up to Force 6—to 18 knots.

Günter awakens and notes that the other two yachts have just hoisted their sails. Quickly, we follow suit. We sail close-hauled, hard on the wind, with waves crashing over the bow. "A little lumpy out here," Günter mumbles, as I set our breakfast on the cockpit table.

The three captains, Günter, Jean-Claude on *Makoko,* and Jean-Marie on *Finally*, communicate via the VHF while I continue to stand watch.

"I think we should sail directly to our waypoint #8 to give us a better point-of-sail," begins Jean-Claude. "Then we could be on a beam reach instead of enduring this misery…"

Jean-Marie interrupts. "You know what all the books and the other cruisers say: Keep one foot on the beach. Hug the shore because then there will be no fetch." Fetch is the distance that wind or waves can travel when there is nothing in the way to break their path.

"Yes," Jean-Claude counters sarcastically. "Hug the shore...with the wind on the nose. And then we motor uncomfortably all day long…making poor headway and burning up diesel."

This is a typical discussion between these two. And this is what it has been like, sailing between two Frenchmen.

"Don't take a chance with the Tehuantepecker." These words have been drilled into me by now. My guidebook says, "The berm along the western two-thirds of the Gulf is level and regular, and when you're close in, it makes a good radar image. You can get right in close because the bottom is level and regular, too. If you're overpowered by the wind, set a good storm anchor and ride it out. Onboard barometers and observations cannot predict the approach of a Tehuantepecker and the radio stations can only tell you that one is presently occurring. Running offshore could take you 500 miles away from the coast."

But the guys have all read the same warnings. I decide not to interrupt.

"You heard the cruiser stories back in Madero," says Jean-Marie. "One sailboat that tried to cut the Gulf ended up over 400 miles to sea and never was found."

"That boat must have had zip for an engine," Jean-

213

Claudie and Jean-Claude on board *Makoko*.

Little Laurent and Maureen in Huatulco.

Claude answers.

I can picture him, the alpha male of the three, straightening his tall frame, raising his chin like a Commander.

"Günter here has two engines and mine is big. Günter, you want to go across?"

As the navigator, I am well aware that cutting across the last half of the bay right now will put us about 12 miles from shore. The warnings about the fearsome Tehuantepeckers echo in my ears, but I resist the urge to grab the VHF. I also hate bucking against the wind, especially when it may not be necessary.

Günter takes the dare. "We'll go with you."

Jean-Marie backs off. "Well, I have a baby on board, still nursing, and his mother isn't standing night watches. I can't risk it."

"We understand," says Günter.

Leaving *Finally* behind, *Pacific Bliss* and *Makoko* change course, straight for waypoint #8, the Bahia Santa Cruz and the charming village of Hualtulco.

It's a fantastic sail, fast approaching 10 knots boat speed under a full main and jib. "This is where *Pacific Bliss* really shines!" I shout to Günter over the wind. "*Makoko* is now behind and to our port. She is heeled way over. I don't think she can go any faster."

On an adrenaline high, we trim the sails tighter.

I always thought of myself as just a cruiser. For the first time, I realize why competitive racing can be so much fun—not at 20-knot plus speeds, as in the Force 10 storm, but relatively safe, as we are now.

Seated together at the helm, Günter and I sail *Pacific Bliss* on the same course until early afternoon.

The VHF, inside at the nav station, crackles: "*Pacific Bliss…Pacific Bliss*, come on in."

Günter picks up the VHF.

"Jean-Claude here. I am pleased to be making such good time. Do you know that we may arrive at the bay and enter Hualtulco before dark? We could escape a second night at sea if we keep going like this."

"Let's go for it. Why slow down now?"

Günter joins me back at the helm seat. "Lois, you should go down for your nap now."

"I *love* this sail! Every nerve is on full alert. We're actually *racing* across the feared Gulf of Tehuantepec… and I'm supposed to sleep?"

"I'll keep the lead. Trust me. As the navigator, you must be alert tonight when we reach the entrance."

Reluctantly, I head for my bed and will myself to settle down.

Trying to nap, I think back on the past few weeks.

215

Mel (now deceased) and Nora talk with Günter in the golf club restaurant, Barra de Navidad.

We were the "good guys" crossing the feared Gulf of Papagayo. We hugged the shore all the way, just as we were told. We motored along faithfully on a glassy sea, this on a scorching day without the slightest hint of a breeze. Sunburned and dead tired, we arrived in El Coco to exit Costa Rica. That's where we first met Jean-Claude and Claudie. I remember Jean-Claude's retort during our first lunch together. "What? You actually hugged the shore? That takes hours! We cut."

Ah, those daring French! How I love their sense of adventure.

I drift off to sleep dreaming of Hualtulco, our next port of call... I'm sitting on the sandy beach with a piña colada as Günter slathers sun-tan lotion on my back...

The squawky sound of the VHF jolts me awake. Jean-Claude is calling, "Lead boat. Lead boat." I rush up the stairs to the nav station in the salon.

"*Pacific Bliss* here," Günter picks up the VHF, grinning as only a proud Captain can. "What's happening back there?"

"Do you know we are sailing over 12 knots boat speed? I cannot keep up. I am going to sell this bloody boat!"

Günter laughs. "Well, you know, Jean-Claude, catamarans are not confined to their hull speed...not like monohulls...not like your Super Maramu."

Jean-Claude huffs, "Maybe I buy a catamaran, next time...anyway, looks like we can make it into port before dark—barely. Let's hope. There's a lighthouse right at the entrance. That should help."

"Right," Günter replies. You can take back the lead when we get there." They break the connection.

"Why did you say that?" I ask him.

"When it comes to shallows or rocks, a catamaran should always let the monohull take the lead. They have the deeper keel."

Günter grins like a card shark who has just won the entire stash.

An anemic sun sets as the fog rolls in, enshrouding our boats. Up at the bow, I strain to find the entrance to the bay. The VHF squeals. I rush back to the nav station. "Jean-Claude, do you know where we are?"

"No. I called to ask you the same thing."

My stomach knots. "I checked the coordinates. We should have been there by now."

"The light at the entrance must have burned out. I heard that this is common in Mexico. Takes ages for the bureaucrats to repair anything."

"Drats! Should we turn back?"

Cruisers "hang out" on the beach at Isla Grande.

"Let's do that. Follow me."

Welcome words. I do not want to take the lead in the dark.

We have already doused our sails. *Pacific Bliss* creeps along, following *Makoko*. The new "lead boat" stops at what we assume is the entrance. We sit in the cockpit, motor idling, staring at their lights for a long time. We can hear the waves slapping against the dangerous rocks that guard the tricky entrance, but we cannot see a thing.

"Günter, their interior lights are on, so I know they are down in their cabin. Why are they just sitting there?"

"Maybe they're double-checking their charts…or the piloting instructions."

Minutes tick by interminably. Then slowly—very slowly—*Makoko* inches forward. We follow at a safe distance. She weaves through the entrance, toward one of the high rocks, then the other, blindly groping for the channel between them.

I hold my breath, expecting to hear "*C-R-U-N-C-H…!*" at any second.

Then, finally, *Makoko* is clear, heading toward the faint lights of town. As we follow her through the entrance, we spot the mast lights of other boats in the anchorage. But the lighthouse is dark. *Makoko* drops anchor first. I can hear their chain clunking through the silent night, stopping abruptly on the bottom. Soon our chain is clunking down, as well. The crashing of waves on the rocks is behind us now, the raw energy muted.

When we are settled, I reach for the VHF. "Jean-Claude, what took you so long out there?"

"Well, we had to get up our courage."

"What do you mean?"

"We were having a *pastis* on the rocks. We're French, after all."

Reunion in Hualtulco (Bahia Santa Cruz)
April 22

Finally arrives before dawn, guided in via VHF by Jean-Claude. Now, we have our buddy boats anchored on either side of us. Here, the water is so clear we can even swim in the anchorage, right alongside our boat. A gentle breeze keeps us cooler than we have been in a long time. After slogging up the long coast of Central America and crossing the Tehuantepec, we welcome this relief from the tropical heat.

Our little trio of northbound yachts bobs in the bay,

Günter calls our buddy boat *Makoko* on the VHF.

safe and content.

As expected, Hualtulco proves to be a delightful little tourist town, with a restaurant row and cute souvenir shops along the beach. All of us from the three yachts enjoy a delightful lunch ashore, listening to a string band. Little Laurent gets all the attention. He giggles and gurgles as his father lifts him onto his shoulders.

Later, as we dinghy back to our anchorage, Günter and I pass a tiny boat. "There's *Wind Gift*!" I yell. "Let's go back to our boat and return to welcome him here. I want to give Buck the photo of his boat I printed for him. I wondered whether we would ever see him again!"

I retrieve the photo from our boat, and we dinghy back to *Wind Gift*. Buck welcomes us on board as if the incident on *Makoko* never happened. He thanks me profusely for the photo. In return, he hands over a supply of well-used, mildewed books.

"Where are you going from here?" Günter asks.

"I'm leaving *Wind Gift* here and traveling inland for a while. I want to see some of Mexico's interior. I never have."

"Where will you keep your boat during the hurricane season? There's no shipyard here."

"I'll figure it out," he says.

A mere two days later, Buck manages to secure free storage for *Wind Gift* "on the hard," in a young man's yard that fronts the bay.

"I worked out a deal with the owner," Buck tells us. "In exchange for me giving him sailing lessons."

Two days later, he is gone.

Although we've e-mailed him, and left messages via his website: www.windgift.com, we have never heard from Buck since. I often wonder if he is alive or dead. His website is no longer operative.

Attitude Adjustment in Acapulco
April 24

Pacific Bliss and *Makoko* leave Huatulco the afternoon of April 24. We turn out of the bay, Bahia Santa Cruz, to find winds on the nose and bronco-busting waves—not a good omen for a safe passage. We will sail two overnights. Our passage is timed for a morning arrival at *Club de Yate*, Acapulco's premiere Yacht Club. *Finally* decides to stay another day to wash laundry and complete other chores.

The winds decrease during the evening, and hopes are high for a pleasant trip, after all. The next day, we experience about four hours of blissful sailing with 14 knots true wind, 19 apparent wind—ideal for our catamaran. We are thrilled to pass *Makoko*, leaving her in the seas behind our stern. When evening comes, we again take up our regular nighttime position, her red port light ahead to our starboard. The seas are lumpy again; however, though we must motor, with a NNW wind of only 12 knots, we can take it on the nose without too much discomfort.

By midnight of the second evening of our passage, with only 33 miles to Acapulco, the seas calm to long, easy swells. I take over the watch until 0400, realizing that Günter needs to be rested, sharp, and alert at the helm for docking maneuvers. This will be the first time we will be alongside a dock since the Balboa Yacht Club in Panama. I grab two hours' sleep before Günter awakens me.

"Look at those spectacular cliffs!" he says. "We are entering Acapulco Bay. I didn't want you to miss this!"

"Wow! This is like being in the middle of a huge bowl—like the center of an amphitheater."

The rising sun casts a warming glow over the heights as we motor through the circular bay. On three sides, high-rise condos and massive hotels perch on every cliff. This is one crowded piece of real estate. How different from the remote, scarcely populated Central American coast!

We had made reservations, weeks in advance. We had fantasized a "real marina" such as this…with electricity, water, and yacht services. And this one even has a pool!

We side-tie to *Makoko* at the marina's fuel dock, waiting for it to open. I fill out the logbook: another 256 miles added to Voyage One. Then I collapse into a deep sleep. When I awaken, *Makoko* has left for their permanent slip, and Günter is busy fueling *Pacific Bliss*. We have been assigned a convenient slip close to the office and pool, with a dock on two sides. We back in, pick up the Med-mooring ball at our bow, and settle in.

What luxury!

"After the mud flats of Panama …the cesspools of Puerto Quetzal and Madero," Günter says, "I am so ready for this…"

"Me, too. I'm tired of commercial ports where *Pacific Bliss* grows a filthy mustache on her hull. I read that this was Mexico's first private yacht club. Decadence is coming..."

We hook up to dock electricity and attach the fresh water hose. Jorge, an energetic young Mexican, stops to introduce himself. He is looking for work. I tear the sheets off our bed and stuff them into the laundry bag, along with our clothes. He slings the bag over his shoulder and returns promptly with a receipt. "*Manana.* Tomorrow." He points to our dirty boat. "*Trabajo?* Work?" We negotiate for the cleaning. Dollars will be just fine. $20 for the hulls and the deck, another $20 for the inside, and an extra $10 for removing the rust from the stainless steel fittings. We are in business. And fast!

This evening, we fall into that wonderful, carefree sleep that only security at a dock can bring. Sudden storms? Anchor dragging? No worries. Nothing can wake us up. We are safely tied to a dock.

In the morning, we worry about *Finally,* the vessel we've come to call "the baby boat." They should be here by now. We take a walk around the marina and check the fuel dock. *Finally* is nowhere to be found.

"If they are not in the harbor, they must be out there. Most likely, in the bay by now," says Günter. We return to our boat. "They must be within VHF range." He picks up the VHF. They do not answer our call.

At 0800, it is *Amigo Net* time. I turn the SSB to frequency 8122. When the program comes to the "vessels underway" section Maureen reports: "The water intake pump for our engine has given out. We don't have a spare. Without an engine, we were forced to sail all night. Then the wind died. *Finally* was drifting dangerously close to the cliffs. We're okay now, but barely moving in a light breeze."

The captain of *Nanamuk*, with whom we sailed before, comes on the Net: "Tell Jean-Marie to try substituting the galley pump." Detailed instructions ensue, and *Finally* is finally on the road to recovery. Günter keeps in touch with *Finally* during the day. Jean-Marie is careful not to push the boat's jury-rigged engine, sailing whenever he can.

While *Finally* struggles to reach port, we are having our own problems with Mexican bureaucracy. The entire morning is taken up with Mexican customs—again. We had already checked into the country in Madero, a designated point of entry. We did it the day before sailing across the Tehuantepec to Hualtulco; now, the local officials want us to check into Acapulco as well.

Mexican law requires checking in and out of the country only once. However, most towns in Mexico ignore the law and force cruisers to check in at every port they visit. They want the "extra" revenue it brings. Consequently, many cruisers decide to sail past most of these towns. Why spend half-a-day checking in and many hours checking out if the plan is to stay only a few days? I had arrived in Mexico by plane many times, as a tourist. Back then, I could never have imagined the complicated procedure required when entering and leaving the country by boat.

Take Madero, for example, the first Mexican port we entered. Günter was sick underway there from Guatemala. Along with a fever and sore throat, he had heaved, sporadically, over the side, spilling his gut. I had taken most of the watches. When we arrived, we were both exhausted. But we had little chance to rest in that dirty, industrial, backwater port.

First, navy personnel boarded and searched our boat. They informed us that the captains, Günter and Jean-Claude, had to check into Harbor Administration, the Capitania, and Immigration, all miles away. As navigator, I was not permitted to take Günter's place. When they say they want the "captain," they mean it.

Harbor Administration and Capitania is located behind a high wall that restricts access. To reach the building, one must walk miles before finding an entrance. Günter was weak and had not eaten.

Nevertheless, he dinghied to the wall, climbed over it, then walked around a fence, through a shipyard, around a building, and into the offices. This shortcut saved him miles and hours of walking. Looking back, I marveled at how he managed to do it in his weakened condition. Furthermore, he had to check into immigration as well, which entailed hitching a ride to the airport eight miles away. The entire process took four, hot-and-humid hours. Today, in Acapulco, it takes as much time, and is as frustrating as it had been in Madero. What a waste of time!

The next day, Günter and I awaken to find *Finally* anchored in the harbor, near our berth. She had limped into port during the night.

After breakfast, Günter and Jean-Marie comb Acapulco for engine parts. Günter—walking fast, as usual—slips off a curb and takes a bad spill, spraining his ankle. He limps back to *Pacific Bliss*. I treat the swelling with ice cubes in a zip-lock bag, wrapped in a towel. It doesn't look good. This injury, I fear, will plague Günter for some time to come.

My back and hip still cause me trouble and pain. What a sorry pair we have become!

Here we are, halfway into Day 3 in Acapulco, and we have not even been to the pool! I take a seat at the salon table alongside Günter as he presses ice to his ankle. I open the laptop and begin to draft a "feel-sorry-for-me-here-in-Paradise" e-mail to my family that I'll send out later. The hard drive crashes. It is our only computer.

"We *must* have that computer working before we leave here," Günter says, scowling at his ankle. "We need it for navigation."

I reach the meltdown stage. "I've had it!" I slam shut the cover of the dead laptop and slump over it. I can taste the salt of tears running down my face. "When we reach San Diego, that's the end of cruising...*I wanna go home.*"

"And I don't blame you. I feel miserable, too. But, first things first. We have to fix that computer."

"I'll have to take it into town." I pack the laptop into its heavy, waterproof case, then trudge through the midday heat to the marina entrance. I wait at the curb to catch a yellow VW taxi into town. The vinyl-covered seats are torn. The hot, woolly stuffing bursts through the tears. The rusty windows are rolled down. Of course, the cab has no air conditioning.

The driver drops me off at the nearest computer repair shop. But that shop doesn't troubleshoot; they can only sell me new parts—or a new computer. The vendors direct me to another shop a few, hot blocks away. But they cannot help me, either. I trudge most of the length of the main street, dripping sweat.

Finally, I reach a shop where a young man—who looks about 14 but must be older—relieves me of my increasingly heavy load. My hip is screaming in pain, shooting arrows down my thigh. I slump into a chair.

The computer geek replaces the hard drive and transfers our files.

By the time I shamble back into the street, the sun is setting over the bay.

I return to Sundowner Time. Jean-Claude and Claudie are on board our boat, sitting next to Günter in the salon. Well into his second *Cuba Libra*, Günter has found a wonderful way to deal with his pain. I'm furious with envy.

"They fixed it?" he asks.

"Yeah. What's next?"

He hands me a drink. "What's next is that *Makoko* wants to leave tomorrow."

"Yes, we need to 'aul ass," says Claudie.

"I taught her that phrase," says Günter, grinning. "But, Claudie, it's 'haul ass.'"

"H-h-haul ass," she laughs. "We need to be in the Sea of Cortez soon so that we can fly back to France from there."

"We...we just can't leave here *tomorrow* already." I struggle to hold back the tears. *My drink isn't strong enough for this news.* "We haven't done anything here but work. We haven't even been to the pool yet. And what about sightseeing? I wanted to see the Acapulco divers."

"I can barely hobble around, let alone sail..." Günter adds.

"My back is killing me..."

Now I know what is meant by a "pregnant pause." No one says a word.

Finally, Jean-Claude explains, "You don't have to come with us. It's just that we've made commitments to family."

"I understand," Günter says, relief flooding his face. "*Our* only goal is to get north of Cabo San Lucas by June 1. That's the beginning of the hurricane season in Mexico. If we don't, our insurance won't cover us."

"It's settled then. You two need to stay back and rest. I can see that."

"Hey, buddy-boat," Günter says. "Let's toast to a safe passage for you and some much-needed R&R for us."

⚓

"I'm *not* leaving this slip!" Günter hops around the cockpit on his good leg. It is Day 4 in Acapulco and our luck hasn't improved. "They want us to move. When he comes back, I'll tell him we have engine trouble."

"What? *Who* wants us to move?" I fume.

"The dock master just came by. He is sending his boat boys to help us move to another slip...way, way toward the far end of the marina."

"But we have reservations. They assigned us *this* berth."

"Not anymore. He said that another boat has to come in here."

"Why here? Let 'em send the new arrivals to other the end!"

"They're probably VIPs."

Two speedboats arrive to pull us out from the dock. Günter uses his engine trouble ploy, but it doesn't work. "Mister, no need to start your engine," one driver says.

Günter is livid. "You better not damage anything, or you'll pay for it," he shouts to the boys as they rev their outboards.

I look with longing back at the pool that was so close and will now be so far away. "Well, we'll just have to hobble to that pool and make the best of it," I mutter in exasperation.

We re-settle in our new space, adjusting dock lines and fenders until Günter is satisfied. After lunch, I offer him my cane from El Salvador. We hop like two lame kangaroos to the palm-lined swimming pool. Ahhh…! The cool water salves our bodies and our souls.

Many of the cruisers we know or have met over the Amigo Net have congregated here. As the afternoon comes to an end, the talk turns to how to celebrate sundowners, the best part of a sailor's day. The cruisers decide to have a Roman party. Since our boat has the most space, the entire group comes on board. Most have not bothered to come in character wearing togas. A cruiser event, we discover, is a snap to organize, and spontaneous parties like this often turn out to be the best.

Each family brings its own wine or beer and a dish that is easy to serve. With the sun setting over the bow, we all gravitate there. Soon drinks and plates are scattered all over the trampoline and on the deck next to the mast. Little Laurent sits in his infant seat cooing and laughing. A dozen or so cruisers lie about munching on finger food, imitating gluttonous Romans. Günter is in his element: "Life is looking up!" He loves hosting a bunch of cruisers and discussing destinations, weather forecasts, and the latest challenges "*messing with boats*."

⚓

Several days later, Günter and I sit on benches hewed into a natural amphitheater, overlooking the *La Quebrada* cliffs. I sip my frozen pina colada while Günter swigs a cold Corona. The early evening air bristles with anticipation. The assembled tourists turn en masse to watch the five *clavadistas*, young men, file one by one across the lower platform.

Yes, this is a tourist trap, but it is also a spectacular must-see event if one is already in Acapulco. Since the

Lois shows off her new necklace purchased in Acapulco.

1930s, generations of brave *clavadistas* have hurled themselves from jagged cliffs 136 feet high into the churning water below. They dive into a narrow, rocky channel only nine and one-half feet deep; they must time it perfectly with the tidal waves to avoid hitting the bottom and being crushed.

The crowd hushes. The divers climb hand-over-hand up to a jutting rock over 90 feet high. Every eye watches them as they grasp the ledge and pull themselves up. They straighten like young gods and walk tall, to the shrine of the Virgin of Guadalupe set into the cliff. There, they offer a prayer

I toy nervously with my new silver necklace. The crowd's anticipation builds…

The first diver walks slowly to the edge of the highest cliff. The audience watches in dead silence. Then it gasps in unison, as he dives, swooping gracefully like an eagle, to knife into the churning sea far below. We erupt in cheers, then hold our collective breath as the next diver comes forward. With each dive, I worry that the boy might break his neck. Divers' necks have suffered damage, I learn later from a web search. But so far today, thank God, there are no fatalities. The fifth and final diver is a boy, barely a teenager. Because he is so young, the audience roars with special appreciation as he makes his dive.

Later, the divers walk through the crowd, like heroes, to collect well-deserved tips.

The venue empties gradually, but Günter and I sit in silence as the twilight turns to night.

I reach for Günter's hand and squeeze it tight. "Well, have you adjusted your attitude yet?"

"Yes. I feel so much better. You're talking about the saying on our *Lats and Atts* jackets, right?"

"Aha. You know it well."

Together, we chant it like a mantra: "The difference between adventure and ordeal is…attitude!" Our kiss is as deep and dangerous as the cliffs below.

"Think we can we manage it tonight?" Günter asks. "With all the injuries?"

"Yes, we can," I answer, and I give him my biggest smile.

Cruiser Camaraderie: Z-Town, Isla Grande, and Barra de Navidad
May 5

A mammoth cruise ship pulls into the only dock in Zihuatanejo as we sailors watch from the decks of our yachts. Sailing vessels are not allowed to use the dock, even when the cruise ship is not here.

I count 12 yachts anchored in the bay, taking refuge from the *Pineapple Express*, a storm that typically brings high winds, low visibility, and lots of rain. This storm has brought no rain so far, but it has produced swells that would drive surfers crazy with joy.

Later, Günter and I decide to meet other yachties on shore for *Cinco de Mayo* celebrations. We are the first to set out in our dinghy. Near the shore, Günter turns off the outboard motor. He pulls it up to keep the propeller from dragging. A huge wave turns the dinghy sideways, and, now, we have no steerage. We leap into the water to pull the dinghy through the surf. Despite our injuries, Günter and I strain to pull *Petit Bliss* up on the beach. A group of young male tourists, laughing and speaking German, are sitting on the breakwater wall, watching us struggle. But they offer no help at all.

We meet our friends and loiter in the town for a few hours. Bands play on street corners. White paper streamers, hanging over the streets, flap in the wind. We stop for *pulpas* (appetizers) and fresh red snapper at one of the many beachside cafés.

"My shorts are still wet and full of salt and probably won't dry all day," Günter complains.

"Just part of cruising," I answer him. "I'm getting used to walking around these Mexican towns in wet clothes."

"Even though we are in 'civilization' now," Günter grumbles. "Somehow I thought it would be different further up the coast. Why don't these towns think of cruisers when they plan their facilities?"

"Why should they? Cruisers don't spend much money." I point to the cruise ship dominating the harbor. "Not compared to the hundreds of customers in that ship over there."

When we return to our dinghies, they are filled with sand, plastic bags, and trash. Children have been using them as playhouses, while their parents, standing by and watching, are indifferent to our annoyance. Disgusted, we empty *Petit Bliss* of the trash (there *are* trash cans nearby!) and launch her into the breaking surf. I push as far as I can, holding onto one side, while Günter pushes on the other. The next wave breaks hip-high. Günter tries to hold the dinghy steady. "Jump in! Now. Before the next wave hits," he orders.

As I lean to lift my leg over the side of the dinghy, my backpack loses equilibrium and slides toward the surf. It has my camera inside! I swing it around just in time and heave it into the dinghy. And then fall back into the surf.

G-r-r-#*+@^##!!!! I seldom swear, but the words fly out of my mouth in an angry jumble. I climb on board, sopping wet.

Günter teases me: "Your mother, Sigrid, would have washed out your mouth with soap."

I ignore the wisecrack. "Well, I've learned my lesson. From now on, I need to fasten my backpack tight in front, instead of just slinging it over my shoulders."

Inside, I'm fuming. *Why do cruisers have to work so darn hard and endure so much? It seems we always*

DID YOU KNOW?

MEXICO

The three colors of Mexico's flag hold deep significance for the country and its citizens: Green represents hope and victory, white stands for the purity of Mexican ideals, and red brings to mind the blood shed by the nation's heroes.

The flag's dramatic emblem is based on the legend of how the Aztecs traveled from Aztlán to find the place where they could establish their empire. The god Huitzilopochtli advised them that a sign—an eagle devouring a serpent atop a Nopal cactus—would appear to them at the exact spot where they should begin construction. On a small island in the middle of a lake, the Mexicans came upon the scene exactly as Huitzilopochtli had described it. They immediately settled there and founded the city of Tenochtitlán, which is now Mexico City, the country's capital.

At the beginning of the 21st century, Mexico's population surpassed 100 million. Over 25 million live in Mexico City. It is the fourteenth largest country in the world and the fifth largest in the Americas. Mexico is the most populated Spanish speaking country in the world.

The Mexican people descended from the Aztecs and the Mayas; 89 percent of the Mexican population identifies itself as Roman Catholic.

Hernando Cortez conquered Mexico during the period 1519-21 and founded a Spanish colony that lasted nearly 300 years. Independence from Spain was proclaimed by Father Miguel Hidalgo in September 1810, initiating a decade-long struggle. An 1821 treaty recognized Mexican independence from Spain and called for a constitutional monarchy. The planned monarchy failed, and a republic was established in 1824. Mexico's severe social and economic problems erupted in a revolution that lasted from 1910-20 and gave rise to their 1917 constitution.

Mexico is the world's leading producer of silver.

Emblem on Mexico's Flag

Paper streamers are hung for the *Cinco de Mayo* celebrations in Zihuatenejo.

have to suffer to enjoy the good times. Only another cruiser could understand how I feel!

The next day, we cruisers commiserate with each other and decide we've had enough of Z-town. The unanimous decision is reached; we will motor over to nearby Isla Grande, where we can simply wear our swim suits while dinghying to the beach. The small island serves as a day-trip destination for the cruise ship passengers. But by late afternoon, the tourists will have departed…and we will have the beach all to ourselves. And we deserve it!

When we arrive, we discover a beach with thatched-roof huts and cabanas. It even has a restaurant. Once ashore, we relax inside the cabanas and gaze out at the bay. We see our vessels lining the horizon: *Quest*, a newcomer, replaces *Makoko*; *Finally* is there; and, of course, *Pacific Bliss*. A new trio has been formed.

By dusk, everyone else has left, and our little group has the island all to itself—just as we had planned. We get to know the sailors on *Quest,* Judy and John and their pre-teen son, JJ, who introduces us to their cat. The huge, fluffy pet sits contentedly in the bow of their colorfully painted wooden dinghy, taking it all in. The family has sailed almost around the world from Vancouver, Canada, where they live and where JJ will return to school after a few years of "boat-schooling."

Jean-Marie and Maureen sip drinks as they swing little Laurent in a hammock hung between cabana poles.

The evening is glorious: purple twilight makes silhouettes of statuesque lava rocks. They stand like sentinels, guarding the entrance to the bay. Back on our three vessels for the night, we sailors are happy and content, bobbing on the calm seas.

But this tranquility is shattered. A sudden storm awakens Günter and me at 0230. The furious wind gusts to Force 4, Force 5, Force 6, and then Force 7. Lightning flashes through the opal sky. Thunder booms and bounces off the lava rocks. Soon, sheets of rain flood the deck. The wind gradually winds down and, by 0625, the *Pineapple Express* has roared on past. The three boats' anchors have held fast. In the east, the mountains of Ixtapa glow with the fiery light of dawn.

⚓

Sometimes, the best cruising delights come from unexpected places. The resort at Barra de Navidad was never on our itinerary. But when one of our cruising friends lets us in on their little secret, cheap rates because they want yachts in their new marina, so that guests at their five-star resort can view them from their

Marina at Barra de Navidad.

windows….the race is on to get there.

The next day, the trio of yachts departs for beautiful Barra. Of course, *Pacific Bliss* arrives first; she is a catamaran, after all.

Once there, we are told that it will be $25 a night for yacht berthing. We're overjoyed. That's peanuts, compared to $200-plus we would have to pay for a hotel room, which would give us nothing more than a view of the marina and the 27-hole, championship golf course. And we have our choice of berths along the newly-installed, nearly-empty docks.

We leave our yachts in the marina as a convenient "home base" each day, while we explore the surrounding bay, Bahia de Navidad, with our dinghies. The town itself is a small farming and fishing village of fewer than 4,000 souls. It has recently "discovered" tourism as a source of revenue. New shops and restaurants are opening, and the buzz of construction is everywhere. The mostly secluded beaches are kept pristine, and the food that is served is wonderful and inexpensive.

We spend several blessedly uneventful days relaxing in this resort environment. They evidently thought our yachts were wonderful "window dressing" for the Grand Opening of their new restaurant, which overlooks the marina.

This Cove Is Magic
Bahia Tenacatita
19° 18' N, 104° 50' W
May 14

Pacific Bliss wends her way through the bay, Bahia Tenacatita, avoiding Roca Central, a 12-foot-high rock in the middle of the bay. Then our vessel changes course to tuck in behind Punta Chubasco, a high cliff that will protect us from the prevailing northwest wind. Three vessels—two sail boats and one power boat—are already anchored in the cove.

Günter and I find it difficult to focus on anchoring because wildlife surrounds us. Giant pelicans swoop and dive to catch jumping fish. Twin sets of dolphins trail us as we cut the engines. They swim playfully from one vessel to another, leaping in pairs to get attention.

After we anchor, we spend the remainder of the afternoon and early evening on deck, admiring the teeming life in this cozy cove. At the stern, a brown-and-white pelican catches a large fish for her evening meal. Other birds swoop down to pluck their dinners from a swirling school of silvery baitfish. Günter dives into the water to check the knot meter, which has quit working again. He discovers that this bay, much like those in Costa Rica, is packed with algae, which he scrapes from the meter to make it work properly.

Lois and Günter touring Puerto Vallarta.

Problem solved.

After Günter dries off, we watch the surf crash against the shoreline, massive breaking waves churning up white froth like a giant mix-master. The sound is majestic…overwhelming. I turn to Günter. "Impressive. But there will be no dinghy landing this day!"

"How about tomorrow? Günter asks. "Let's check the guidebooks."

Our anchoring spot is near the reefs at the entrance to Boca de Rio Las Iguanas. This spot is where an extraordinary Jungle River Trip begins. All three of our guidebooks insist that this is an adventure one *must* experience. This tantalizes us.

We wonder whether the surf will die down sufficiently for us to undertake this exciting trip. Rumors of those who have attempted—and failed—the Jungle Trip have been circulating. A cruiser couple we met in El Salvador succeeded, but two couples we met in Barra Navidad said that they "turtled," cruiser talk for overturning one's dinghy completely.

At this stage of our cruising life, Günter and I have become skeptics: Yes, if you do not overturn your dinghy it might be interesting. But, safety is paramount for us now. Halfway along the Mexican coast, we are taking no chances. We can taste California and home. With our injuries healing, we want to make sure we get back to San Diego healthy and in good shape. Still, we are pensive. Shall we take the Jungle Trip or not?

Sitting in this cove, amongst God's creatures, we have become centered again. Our R&R in Mexico, especially those days surrounded by the luxury of the five-star resort in Barra de Navidad, has been good for us. We are ready for another adventure, if it comes naturally, but we are no longer inclined to push our luck. We are content here on *Pacific Bliss*, contemplating the magic of this cove, enveloped in this Moment of Bliss. The setting sun turns the sea into a river of gold and shrouds the hills on shore with a mystical purple haze. We are in no hurry; tomorrow, we'll decide what we want to do.

The surf pounds us to sleep this night, eventually dulling our senses with its deafening regularity. Music from the hotel across the bay drifts in, muffled by nature's decibels.

The next day, Tuesday, the surf rolls in higher than before. The weather forecast on the 0800 Amigo Net predicts up to 15-knot variable winds, increasing Thursday through Saturday to 25 to 30 knots, Force 6, NNW at Cabo Corriente. NNW is the direction we must head, and this is the cape we must round on the way into Banderas Bay, Puerto Vallarta, our next destination. Cabo Corriente is another one of those dangerous capes of the world that mariners dread. The cape brings confused seas and winds that typically gust

Pacific Bliss docked in Nuevo Vallarta.

an additional 10 to 15 knots *above forecast*.

I turn to Günter after the Net. "If we wait one more day in this magic cove, we may face strong headwinds. Assuming we could make 5 knots motoring, the apparent wind speed could be up to 35 knots or more. That's gale strength!"

"It's obvious," he replies. "Our decision has been made for us. We will not take that Jungle Trip after all."

Immediately after the Net, we say our good-byes via VHF. We have a two-day weather window, and we plan to take advantage of it.

Later in the voyage, we hear about two tourists who were killed when their jet skis overturned during this perilous Jungle Trip.

Struggling toward Paradise

Leaving the cove immediately gives us the option of anchoring in Bahia Chamela, 35 miles away, before dark—or, if the weather permits, continuing to Vallarta. We prefer to be in Vallarta *ahead* of the weather, rather than being stuck in a storm anchorage, waiting for it to change.

Quest decides to leave with us. But *Finally* is not prepared to go. "We want to finish our breakfast," Jean-Marie informs us, "then I have some work to do on the boat, and after that, we want to check out the possibility of going to shore. It looks so beautiful over there."

Never mind the pounding surf.

We haul anchor and motor throughout the morning. In the afternoon, a breeze comes up; we experience a nice sail alongside *Quest*. It appears as if we will have a charmed passage. If the wind is going to change, it will usually do so by 1130, or 1300 at the latest. By 1400, the buddy boats contact each other via the VHF, and we congratulate ourselves on our decision. We reach our waypoint #4, Bahia Chamela, with perfect weather. Both vessels decide to continue on, even though we know full well that from this bay there will be no storm anchorage for another 55 miles. In addition, the guidebook advises sailors not to pull into *that* anchorage at night because of its rocky, dangerous approach. Knowing the risks, we hope to avoid it.

Our plan is to round Cabo Corriente by early tomorrow morning, before the usual wind kicks up, and to reach Vallarta by noon.

By 1700, the wind has clocked to the prevailing NW, with headwinds of 20 knots. John, *Quest's* captain, calls to tell us of his decision to turn back to Chamela: "We have only one motor and only a twin-blade prop. We're only making 2 1/2 knots in this stuff."

"That's too bad," Günter says.

"Yeah, if this weather gets worse," John answers, "we'll make no progress at all. We've been there, done that with our boat. Wish we had yours…with two engines…What will you do?"

Cactus used to make Tequila.

It is a difficult question. Günter and I discuss our options: *Pacific Bliss* can easily make 5 knots with its twin Volvo Pentas, even with 25 knots of wind on the nose. It will be uncomfortable, of this we are certain. But we should be at our destination before the weather worsens. The other choice is to return to Chamela with Quest.

Günter calls back. "We've decided to push on, John…see you in Vallarta."

We press on through the chop. By 2100, the sun has set through a murky haze. Clouds move in to cover what's left of the moon; the sky turns pitch-black. The wind that was expected to die after sunset *increases* to 25 knots. The waves heighten accordingly.

So much for weather forecasts!

"There is nothing we can do about it now." Günter has reached the stoic stage. "We might as well hunker down and tough it out."

Pacific Bliss braves the churning sea like a bucking bronco. She heaves and creaks and groans. "We've spent half a year and over 8500 miles with her. We have trusted her to carry us through. She won't let us down now," Günter rationalizes.

There is no way we can eat dinner. We slobber peanut butter over crackers to give us some energy for the battle ahead. After this quick snack, Günter sits on the settee close by, while I "man" the nav station, backing up Ray, our autopilot. Two long hours later, Günter takes over, and I rest beside him. We dare not go down below when off watch. No sails are raised, but both of us need to be alert. The headwinds vary from 25 to 30 knots as the hours drag on. With our radar, we can make out the outline of the cape ahead, but every so often, one of us goes outside to peer through the night. We see nothing—not even the shore. By 0200, we have a reprieve: The winds lessen to a manageable 16 knots. This allows us to resume our watch schedules.

Finally, we round the dreaded cape. We are relieved and exhausted, yet proud of our success. On the other side lies the vast Banderas Bay. At the bay's end are the two cities of Nuevo Vallarta and Puerto Vallarta. I continue on watch until 0600, then collapse into my bunk. Günter takes over, motoring on for miles into the calmer waters of the bay. By 1130, we cut our engines and tie up to Slip B15, reserved for us in the Paradise Village Marina.

At last, we have reached Paradise!

We tour a Tequila factory near Puerta Vallarta; some bottles hold the infamous worm.

This Is Paradise
Paradise Village Marina, Beach Resort and Spa
Nuevo Vallarta, Mexico
May 17

But for the grace of God (and some wise navigational planning, I might add), we could be waiting in some miserable anchorage, hoping for a "weather window" that does not materialize. In a bizarre way, the worsening weather outside makes our being here, safe and snug, even more of a pleasure. We envision pampering ourselves for a long time.

This truly *is* Paradise. Similar to Barra, we yachties pay only $25 per day (plus tax) for a slip, yet enjoy all the privileges of a premiere resort destination. Many of the cruisers plan to spend the summer here, waiting out the hurricane season.

Although we are not staying here, we are permitted to use the amenities. The hotel is massive, designed to imitate a Mayan pyramid. It is surrounded by three swimming pools, two Jacuzzis, a full service spa and exercise facility, tennis courts, a jogging trail, a travel agency—and even a mini-zoo.

A modern shopping plaza rises next to it, with two floors full of every shop and convenience one could imagine, plus two internet cafés with computer-hosting that actually doesn't crash. But before we send even one *Hola!* message announcing our arrival, we swagger around this marvelous decadence, licking maple nut ice cream cones and sipping iced cappuccinos.

We lounge on the white sand beach in the afternoon, paging through brochures we picked up at the hotel. We ponder whether we should take a touted one-day "cultural tour" inland.

I slather suntan oil on Günter's back. "Maybe we'll do that—one of these days."

"But then, maybe not." He stretches on a beach towel like a languid, jungle cat.

Pacific Bliss was the first of our group to arrive. During the early morning of our second day in port, we search the docks in vain for others. We listen to the 0800 Amigo Net and discover that our buddy boats are safe in various anchorages along the way. Having missed the weather window, they are creeping along, from bay to bay. At last, we hear from *Finally*, the baby boat. We have worried about Maureen and Jean-Marie and little Laurent as if they were our own family; in fact, we call them "the kids." This night, we wait up for them until

Lois and Günter toast to their wedding anniversary.

we are certain they are safe.

"It's like having teenagers again," I tell Günter, "waiting for them to come home at night."

Eventually, "the kids" arrive, and we conceal from them how truly worried we were.

The Escape Adolph Tour
Puerto Vallarta and Tepic, Mexico
May 24

We enjoy a wonderful week, partying with our cruiser friends. We discover food that is magnificent and Puerto Vallarta shopping that is equally superb. On the weekend, the hotel hosts special events, such as Western Night. We attend one such event featuring a mechanical bull rodeo contest—kitschy, yet cool. It's something to watch, but I wouldn't dare get on the "animal."

We have acquired a new crew: Sharon and Stu, a middle-aged couple from Utah, arrive during our second week here. We have known Stu since last November. He sailed as crew on our sister boat, *Enduring Echoes,* from France to St. Lucia. In fact, Stu was the one who removed Günter's stitches back in Gibraltar. But we meet Sharon for the very first time, and her eagerness to get underway impresses us. Both of them can't wait to cross the Sea of Cortez and unfortunately, as with most crew, they are limited on time. This will be their three-week vacation.

There is nothing to delay our departure—except Hurricane Adolph. I have been tracking Adolph, the first hurricane of the 2001 season, every day at the internet café. Adolph surprised meteorologists by turning toward land instead of dying at sea; early storms rarely make it ashore. For a few days, he appeared to be turning toward Banderas Bay. But then he snaked back toward Cabo, the tip of Baja California.

And that's the direction *we* must go.

Until I e-mailed them, our family and friends in the States did not even know that Adolph had been born and was causing mayhem at sea. That's the U.S. media for you. If a hurricane is not causing tremendous coastal damage or loss of life, it is hardly worth a mention, no matter how ferocious that hurricane might be. But the yacht insurance companies do care. Ours refuses to cover *Pacific Bliss* after June 1 for damage due to a "named or numbered" tropical storm. With only a week to spare until that date, Günter and I are as eager as Sharon and Stu to get underway.

I check the internet again for the weather forecast. By now, I have learned what websites to check and have become somewhat of an expert on tracking storms. The weather forecast brightens our hopes. Hurricane Adolph has changed his path again. We are free to go.

Departure day has arrived. We are all are on board. As we leave our berth, we wave farewell, play *Amazing Grace* on the stereo, and head for the fuel dock. We are on our way. While the crew is fueling, I head for the office for one final check on the weather. To my despair, the news is not good. Adolph has turned yet again. I return to our boat to inform our crew.

Everyone is sorely disappointed, but I'm worried about the deadline on our insurance. Should we sail or shouldn't we?

"You're the navigator, Lois," Günter says firmly, his jaw set. "What should we do?

The final decision is yours."

I am torn, but I come to my senses: The safety of the boat and crew is my first priority. "We'll have to turn back and re-dock. I hope the marina still has our berth open."

⚓

Two days later, the entire motley clan climbs into our rented van: Judy and John of *Quest*, with their 10-year-old son, JJ; Maureen and Jean-Marie of *Finally*, with baby Laurent; and Sharon, Stu, Günter, and me of *Pacific Bliss*. We are all packed in, with little room to spare. To our surprise, JJ has brought along his cat and caged parrot. The van is beginning to look like a Guatemalan chicken bus!

We had decided to leave Puerto Vallarta behind by taking an inland tour while Adolph made up his mind. Why sit around and wait when we can experience the excitement of Mayan culture? The Nuevo Vallarta travel agency had set us up with hotel reservations in the ancient town of Tepic.

We find that the hotel is in a dusty and down-to-earth location, which we like. It's off the beaten path, and that suits us fine. After we check into the hotel, JJ goes into the underground parking garage and surreptitiously retrieves the cat and the caged parrot from the van. He covers them with his jacket and, like a thief avoiding the police, he sneaks them into his room, praying all the while that they'll keep quiet and undiscovered for the next three days.

Tepic lies about 225 kilometers northwest of Guadalajara, the capital and largest city of the Mexican state of Nayarit. It sits on the banks of the Rio Mololoa and the Rio Tepic. Founded in 1542, it is now a city of 300,000.

The first day here, we walk to the square plaza at Tepic's center. Centuries old, it is filled with Mexican farmers in for the weekend. Tepic is the major urban center for a rich farming area growing sugar cane, tobacco, and citrus fruits. Tepic is also home to many Huichol Indians. Clad in plumed sombreros and colorful embroidered clothing, these Indians are world famous for their peyote-inspired arts, yarn paintings, and funky, fluorescent textiles. Most travelers pass by this little gem of a colonial city, unknowingly missing out on its Spanish cathedrals, museums, and vibrant art boutiques. Not a single tourist can be seen anywhere. The town is ours.

Though its private claim to fame doesn't mean anything to tourists, the city is proud of its great heroes: Juan Escutia, though only a boy, fought to prevent invading U.S. forces from capturing Chapultepec Castle in Mexico City; Luis Miramontes, a chemist, co-invented the first contraceptive pill; Alexander Forbes became the British consul to Mexico at Tepic and authored the first English language book on California; and actress María Antonieta won national fame as *La Chilindrina* in the Spanish-language television show, El Chavo del Ocho.

It's interesting how small towns, even in Mexico, proudly boast when their local boys or girls make good.

The next day, we drive to the extinct Sangangüey volcano and its crater lake. While we picnic, the parrot squawks insistently, demanding to be let loose to chase the lone white heron prancing along the shoreline. JJ is determined to keep his pet. I avoid the ruckus by walking off to photograph a stand of magnificent flame trees. Their fiery red flowers are reflected in the lake's navy blue depth.

At the next stop, we climb over unkempt Mayan ruins, co-opting the entire place for ourselves. The experience is a welcome departure from that of the well-known frenzy of Cancun, on the Gulf of Mexico, where buses transport hordes of tourists to the nearby Mayan structures.

In the evenings, we sample traditional Mexican food at various restaurants framing the square and sip on margaritas every night at sunset while listening to local string bands.

At one restaurant, our final night here, the entire ceiling glows with candle-lit, gold-star chandeliers. They also grace the tables as centerpieces. Günter signals the swarthy waiter with the bushy mustache: "Where can I buy one of these?"

"We purchased them in Guadalajara."

"That's too far away for us. Can we buy one of yours to take back as a souvenir?"

"*Si.*" He hooks one down and hands it to Günter with a gracious grin.

Before we leave Tepic the next morning, Günter proudly packs his treasured star candle into the crowded van. Now there's hardly room to breathe. "We will use it as mood lighting on the boat when we don't want to waste electricity," he explains.

The crews return from the "Escape Adolph Tour" to Paradise Marina. We are annoyed to find a party already in progress at our docks. It is the weekly Cruiser Networking Party at docks B and C. We had arrived in Paradise on a Wednesday afternoon and, within hours, had been invited to all the weekly parties. Now, we realize that it is another Wednesday, and it's party time again. As we trudge past the partiers with our luggage, Günter turns to me with a sour look, and says "This means we are beginning our third week here."

A Tour of *Tepic* Mexico

1. John and Judy of *Quest* near the crater lake of the Sangangüey Volcano; 2. The Flame Tree blooms in May;

232

3. Tepic's market square; 4. Lois stands atop Mayan Ruins; 5. Local children at the lake.

233

A lone egret reflected in the inland lake near Tepic.

I'm aghast. "We can't let this happen. I refuse to attend yet another party."

How I've changed!

I drag my luggage into the cockpit and pick up my briefcase. "I am heading *directly* to the internet café before it closes at 9:00 p.m. I want to check the weather."

"Good idea," Günter replies, climbing on board. "Looks like the boats here are not battened down… they don't expect a blow. Obviously, there's no wind or rain…yet."

"Exactly. Instead, it's humid and still. We need to find out what is going on. Perhaps Adolph is not arriving after all."

"Yes, life has been too good here," Günter says. "We're becoming soft and lazy. If the weather is okay, it's time to go out to meet the elements!"

While surfing the web, I find that Hurricane Adolph has become famous. He is the only May hurricane to reach Category 4 strength since record keeping began in the East Pacific. One website provides the history: On May 7, a tropical wave left Africa. It moved unnoticed across the Atlantic Ocean until May 18, when low pressure began to organize along that wave in Costa Rica and Panama. By May 25, about 250 miles south-southwest of Acapulco, the disturbance developed into a Tropical Depression. Adolph took an atypical east-northeast track, so prediction models varied greatly; one *did* predict an eventual Mexican landfall, here in Banderas Bay. Adolph, upgraded to a hurricane, turned northward on May 27, and on May 28, it passed within 165 miles of the Mexican coast. Now he is turning westward out to sea, where he is expected to die. Good!

Farewell, Paradise! It's time for us to go back to sea.

Crossing Cortez
May 31

It is Thursday, the day after the dock party. We rush to begin our passage from Nuevo Vallarta by mid-morning. We bid fond farewells to our cruising buddies and newfound friends.

This day appears ideal for our departure. Some cruisers predict that we might even be able to *sail*, a novel thought, since we are following the coastline *north* to California, and the prevailing NNW wind tends to follow the coastline *south*. But Adolph just might do us a favor: Typically, in the aftermath of a hurricane, *south* winds begin to blow, which would push us *north*.

However, there's another reason why we must rush out of port: We couldn't possibly wait until Friday! The longer one remains in port, the more one becomes bound by the rules and superstitions of sailors. Leaving on a Friday would be tempting fate. We dare not break the sailors' cardinal rule: "Never, *ever*, leave port for a major passage on a Friday!"

By Friday noon, we reach the halfway point in our crossing of the Sea of Cortez. We have traveled 138 nautical miles during this passage, with another 138 to go. We actually sailed for a few hours! According to my logbook, this rare event occurred on Thursday, during a light, 11-knot breeze from the SSW. Amazing! This has been the *only* sailing Stu and Sharon have experienced so far on *Pacific Bliss*. Otherwise, we've been motoring all the way. Whatever direction our waypoints took us, that is the way the wind turned. Right on the nose…or a slight bit off the nose…that has been Stu and Sharon's fate, hour by hour, watch after watch.

As for Sharon, she has been sad and seasick most of the time. She languishes in her pajamas, day and night, curled up on the settee. Her previous sailing experience had been on the Great Salt Lake. She has never encountered the confused ocean waves and long rollers that are lingering after Adolph.

Stu, however, is no neophyte. He remembers well the Force 9 storm that delayed our sailing out of Canet, France, after the catamarans had been built. He experienced the aftermath of that storm as a crewmember of *Enduring Echoes* and helped to hand-steer the craft across the Atlantic. Stu has no trouble standing watch.

Günter and I are delighted to have him on board. His seamanship allows the three of us to settle into a three-hours-on, six-hours-off watch routine. And better than that, this permits Günter and me to sleep with each other! In the same bed, at the same time, while at sea!

22° 43' N, 109° 35.6' W. I enter these coordinates into the logbook as we approach Cabo San Lucas. It is already June 2, past the date when our insurance requires us to be out of the hurricane zone. However, I'm not worried about coverage at this point, because Hurricane Adolph was downgraded yesterday to a tropical storm. He is far out to the western sea, beyond Baja California, and no longer a menace to us.

Now, strong winds have arrived from the west and northwest.

Could this be the beginning of the notorious northwest winds of the Baja Bash?

At 0400, I am on watch, and the situation does not look good. White-crested waves race toward *Pacific Bliss* as she resolutely heads on her northwest course to Cabo. The wind speed is between 20 and 25 knots; the seas are confused.

Almost on the nose again. Just our luck.

I grimace as I don my foul weather jacket, harness, and life vest. I cat-walk to my usual watch position at the starboard helm. Günter and Stu are off watch, both in their berths below; chalky-faced Sharon remains curled up on the settee.

Pacific Bliss lurches and sways like a drunken

235

Baja Bash

1. Bix and Günter raise the storm jib in Cabo San Lucas; 2. John Marie climbs the mast; 3. Stu and Sharon our Cortez crossing crew; 4. Bix enjoys the "Baja Bash"; 5. Fueling from barrels in Turtle Bay; 6. Fixing the dinghy; 7. Jean-Marie climbing higher up the mast;

236

8. Bix and John are the "spotters" for Jean-Marie; 9. Jean-Marie and Laurent.

sailor as she plows into sharp waves that crash over the twin hulls and onto the trampoline. Behind the helm seat, other waves race beneath the hull, spraying rooster tails. After assessing the situation outside, I grope along, toward the nav station, clutching handholds. There, I fill out the logbook again: *Force 6, 22 knots W, motoring.* I stir up a mug full of hot Nescafé, adding powdered chocolate and cream. I bring the crude concoction to the starboard helm and sit there.

I will my body to relax to the rock-and-roll of *Pacific Bliss*. Eventually, I become one with the elements.

Fueled by my drink, I warm to the stark beauty of the night, letting it seep into my soul. The moon flames three-quarters full and golden, well on its westward dive into the sea. The brighter stars refuse to dim, defiantly twinkling high over my head, as if to cheer me onward. The foam and froth of the waves over the dark sea remind me of the Starbucks cappuccino that I will definitely have when we reach San Diego later this month. The wind does not reach gale force. This is not a severe storm but simply waves and sea reacting to wind change. Dawn breaks, and I begin to see the welcoming lights of Cabo San Lucas, straight ahead.

This morning, I am at one with Pacific Bliss, and the whole, wide world seems wonderful.

Cabo San Lucas: Papagayos, Tehuantepeckers, and Now the Baja Bash
Marina Cabo San Lucas, Baja
June 3

Pacific Bliss is docked at slip G91 in the new Marina Cabo. Here we face the "hurry-up-and-wait" routine again: We rush to provision, and then we wait. This time, though, we are exceptionally eager. Before us lies the 800-mile passage up the coast of Baja California to San Diego and home.

The beat north, from Cabo to San Diego, is called "The Baja Bash," because the route goes directly against the prevailing NW winds. The Bash begins with a successful rounding of the Cape, one of the most exposed in the world. The seas that slam into this cape get a good run all the way from Japan. It will be scary and challenging, but we can't wait to start.

The marina is sparkling new, positioned within a square, dominated by the deep-pink Plaza las Glorias Hotel. It is surrounded by shops and restaurants on three sides and open to the sea on the fourth. The good news is the marina's convenience to amenities; the bad news is the marina's location—right in the center of all the action. This marina—it turns out—is an extension of Southern California. Most people speak English here, and the North American tourist is king. A majority of the 335 slips hold huge sports fishing boats and pleasure yachts. The few sailboats in the harbor belong to cruisers-in-transit, like us, sailors who are anxious to get north and out of the hurricane belt. They are well aware that the storm season has come early this year.

The pleasure yachts are party boats, the kinds that rarely leave the dock. Partying on shore and on these boats goes on well into the night—accompanied by blaring, obnoxious rap music that jars our sea-calmed senses.

Günter and I provision with U.S. brands for the first time. How boring! The cultural challenge is gone. When we venture beyond the secure marina gates, salespeople accost us, pretending to man "information" booths, while actually attempting to sell timeshare units. The grating of civilization on such a grand scale is offensive to our cruisers' tender ears. We want to leave as soon as we can.

Our good-bye to Sharon and Stuart takes place at a corner café. While enjoying a huge Mexican breakfast, we reminisce, laughing about JJ, the cat, and the parrot. Our new crew, Bix, a judge from Las Vegas, arrives from the airport and joins us here. Bix is bald-headed and jolly, yet he is serious, because he is on a mission. He has been referred to us by our yacht broker, David. He is considering the purchase of a Catana 431. There is no better way to find out what a boat is made of than doing the Baja Bash!

We return to *Pacific Bliss* with Bix in tow, to plan our passage.

Cruising in this part of the world is quite the paradox: The month of November brings an annual migration of cruising boats, heading south from California; it is the beginning of the annual Mexican cruising season. Though yachties would prefer to sail to Mexico, the prevailing northwesterlies are at their lightest, and cruisers are forced, instead, to motor. Conversely, the month of May brings a migration north, toward the U.S. border, to avoid the hurricane season. Unfortunately for sailors, the prevailing winds then are at their strongest, and once again, the cruisers are forced to motor. Migrating sailors, during the annual Mexican cruising season, just can't seem to win.

Going south from San Diego during this time of the year would be a sleigh ride, especially in our catamaran. One could make 200-mile days, just as we did crossing the Atlantic. Who would even want to stop? Heading north in May is another matter. Planning potential stops is essential. Only two ports in Baja California provide refuge during strong northwesterlies: Magdalena Bay and Turtle Bay. Since we will be motoring, we plan to fuel at Turtle Bay anyway. If we don't need to take refuge, "Turtle" might well be our only stop. Our provisions must last until we reach San Diego.

Hope springs eternal among sailors. And Günter is always thinking ahead…

"Our only hope against this trip turning into a typical Baja Bash," he says, "is that *another* tropical

1. Churning sea off Cabo Falso; 2. Cabo on a calmer day.

San Diego seas.

depression will develop on Mexico's mid-coast.

"What would that do?" Bix asks.

"It could follow Adolph's example and turn into a second early hurricane…That would generate winds from the south to push us forward.

"Fat chance!" I shake my head. "You dream!"

"Yeah. We have to prepare for the worst," Günter concedes.

While tourists revel into the night, the cruisers here retire early. We spend our days worrying and getting our yachts ready to meet the inevitable Bash. Preparing for the worst means replacing our jib with the North® storm sail that we have on board, but have never used.

Fortunately, the cruising community helps each other. Our buddy boats, *Quest* and *Finally,* arrived a few days after us. John and Jean-Marie come on board to assist Günter and Bix. They take down the jib and replace it with the new sail. That tough job takes an entire morning.

In my role as navigator and weather-woman, I have been monitoring patterns for the local weather and for rounding the Cape and heading north. I receive daily faxes on the computer. I also check weather sites at the internet café twice a day and listen to various SSB nets each morning.

When we are provisioned and ready to leave, Günter and I stop at the Port Captain's office. We ask Tim Schaaf, the captain, for additional advice. "Check the wind speed and direction here in the harbor, then add 10 to 15 knots to determine what you'll find at the Cape," he cautions. "Get up at midnight. If you DO NOT have significant wind then, go back to bed and set your alarm for 3:00 a.m. If it is still calm, take off at 4:00 a.m., or if you prefer, wait until dawn. That gives you plenty of time to round the Cape."

We thank him and turn around to leave. He calls us back. "If you DO have wind in the early morning, sleep in…because you won't be going out that day."

Back on *Pacific Bliss*, I enter the forecasts into the logbook: *6/4 0300 Wind 20K to 25K, WNW F6; 6/5 0530, Wind gusting up to 20K, WNW.* It's obvious that we will not be going out this day.

I feel like a runner, poised at the starting block, heart pumping, full of adrenalin, ready to race at any time—and the gun won't go off!

Bashing the Baja Capes
June 6

At 2200, it is dead calm at the dock. So far, so good! Günter sets the alarm for 0230. When the alarm goes off, he checks the weather again. The wind is rising, but it is only 6.2 knots, so far. He wakes me, then goes to the other hull to wake Bix. "We have the weather window we need. We're off."

Günter starts the engine, while Bix and I cast off from the pier. By 0300, we are out of the marina and into the sea. It is pitch black. We motor along, past the first cape, and on toward Cabo Falso. The wind picks up to Force 6 from the west, pushing us toward the dangerous cape, toward those angry waters where the two seas meet. Once we are there, the waves attack us like the demented sea monster we encountered off the coast of Baranquilla; he is still waiting for us, eager for his final revenge. Günter guns the engines. He is determined not to slack off. *Pacific Bliss* could crash into the sharp, ragged cliffs off the cape.

"The dinghy is loose!" I shout over the wind. *Petit Bliss* hangs on for dear life, its side with the heavy outboard dropping dangerously close to the seas below.

Günter and Bix rush to the stern, while I take the wheel.

"The eye-bolt broke!" yells Günter. "The other side could come loose any second. We'll never pick her up in *this*."

The two men lean precariously over the wildly bouncing dinghy.

"Bix, we will have to put a sling around the dinghy. Lois, slow 'er down, but don't lose forward motion! And stay clear of those rocks!"

The men could lose their balance! But the dinghy must be secured. And I must focus on my steering.

Pacific Bliss lunges, barely moving forward. She begins to turn sideways.

"Give her more power!" Günter yells.

I gun the engine some more, but she barely straightens out. The rocky cliffs are coming up fast—too fast.

I glance back at the men. Their bodies are stretched dangerously far over the dinghy—too far. They have fashioned two slings, one for each side; now they struggle to tie her down. Finally, they succeed.

Günter rushes back to the helm. He yanks the wheel from me. "Now, we can really gun it—full bore."

Pacific Bliss jolts and swerves back on course.

Gabrielle, a 30-foot monohull ahead of us, calls on the VHF. "We're facing headwinds over 25 knots out here; we've got to turn back."

I try to convince them to brave it out. "It will be better once you round the cape."

"No can do."

We know they've turned because we see their lights coming toward us. Two ships passing in the night. But we push on.

By 0445, the headwinds have not diminished. They are still at 22 knots; however, the seas are less confused. And by 0630, as dawn breaks, the wind drops to 13 knots. Briefly, it sneaks back up to 16 with one final blow. But, by mid-morning, it finally lessens to a reasonable 8 knots.

Yea! We made it! We have cleared the notorious cape.

Bliss in Baja

Writing this story of our maiden voyage has been a joy. It has been a way of reliving all the wonderful experiences we had and beautiful people we met. Günter's feelings are no less passionate than my own. Having rounded the cape, heading into our last leg of this journey, he is as moved as I to express those feelings in words. So, here are Günter's thoughts:

Mag Bay, a Blessed Landfall
(By Günter)

Once past Cabo and Cabo Falso, wind and seas improve, and it becomes a good trip throughout the day. The following day, a marine layer of dense fog forms; it brings with it high humidity and limited visibility. But that does not slow our progress or hinder our plan to make landfall in a large bay called *Bahia Santa Magdalena* or, for gringo sailors who don't understand Spanish, *Mag Bay*.

My morning watch starts at 0600. As we near the wide entrance of the bay, the marine layer of fog starts to lift, and I can discern the outline of the entrance. There are high cliffs on both sides and a wide expanse of calm sea, all of which promise a safe and pleasant anchorage. The fog lifts completely; the view of cliffs and bay is magnificent, and I am enchanted. Putting on my tape of old sailors' songs, I sail in, singing with the music, filled with the joy and magic of this moment.

Hundreds of years ago, this bay was a refuge for Spanish galleons that sailed from Acapulco to the Philippines loaded with copper, silver, and other trading goods after having returned from the Orient with gold, silk, and spices. This morning, I feel a sense of kinship with those ancient mariners who plied these same waters bravely, in ships that could barely go to weather. They were the rugged ones. They had none of the means on board that make life underway so easy: water maker, GPS, VHF, Single Side Band Radio, telephone, freezer, refrigerator, and, what the modern sailor would be lost without—the indispensable autopilot. However, the mountains, wind, and ocean have always remained the same throughout the centuries, and they can be enjoyed today, just as they were by those ancient mariners.

We can all share these same Moments of Bliss.

Magic in the Night
(By Günter)
June 9

I have the first night watch from 2100 to midnight. When I start my watch, the night is pitch black—there is no moon, and only a few stars can be seen. Suddenly, green streaks rush across the sea and flash close to our boat. I hear snorting noises. For a moment, I'm startled. But I quickly realize that a pod of dolphins has surrounded us! They create an eerie phosphorescence as they flash through the water. For quite a while, they keep up with *Pacific Bliss*, surging back and forth, leaping from the water, suddenly accelerating, dodging very close to the stern, and then racing away. I have been feeling quite lonely during this watch, but this display of nature's life around me makes me feel like I am part of the larger world—and this is very comforting.

Later, around 2300, as I sit in the cockpit facing the stern, I watch a huge, golden moon rise slowly from the horizon. Nearly full, it illuminates the sea and, in the light, I see *Emerald Star* close to us, visible until now only by her navigation lights. The moonlight gives me the shape of the boat; I recognize her hull and mast as she glides northbound with us through the calm water. This moon paints the surface of the sea with ever-changing silvery patterns. But its magic must give way to the rising sun. For a brief period of time, I am the benefactor of the beauty of both moon and sun.

Such are the Moments of Bliss that make a sailor forget the discomfort of stormy seas.

Night Watch in Baja
At Sea, 29° 14' N, 115° 48.4' W
June 14

Before taking over the watch from Günter this night, I don my navy fleece-lined jacket and fasten my red fleece cap under my chin. It will be cold, and I'll need this extra protection on top of the sweat pants and fleece top I am already wearing. The heavy clothes remind me of our departure from France last November, when it was so cold I thought I'd never be warm again. We are now well north of the tropics, at Latitude 29. The cold California Current, sweeping down from Alaska, not only cools the water but also chills the air. But the good thing about this frigidness is that it means we are only 340 miles from San Diego—*we are almost home, and we can make this distance in three days and two nights!*

I climb to the starboard helm seat. My eyes strain to see something, *anything,* in the nothingness of the night. There is no moon. There are no stars. There is no horizon. Just an inky void. But I am comforted by our Furuno® radar system. If any freighter comes my way, and I can't see it in this darkness, Friendly Furuno will keep me safe, as it reveals the ship's distance and direction.

I settle into the gentle rocking of *Pacific Bliss*. My mind wanders to friends and family. *What will it be like to see them again? I have missed them dearly. Our grandchildren will be nine months older—a "sea change" at their ages. But what about the adults? We have changed; have they?*

I try to picture our condo. It has been so long. What will it be like living there, with all its modern conveniences? Will I automatically conserve water when I fill the sink or take a shower? Will I never again leave on an unnecessary light? Will the bombardment of news—radio, TV, and newspapers—grate on my cruise-mellowed senses? Will I long to be "out there" again, or will I relish the benefits of civilization? Will I continue the dichotomy of living in one place and longing for the other?

Coming Home
At Sea, 31° 58' N, 117° W
June 15

I enter into the Ship's Log: *Bearing of 328°, 8 nm off Ensenada, 26 nm to our waypoint between the Coronados and the mainland, 40 nm to our waypoint off Point Loma, San Diego.* We have reached Ensenada but have no intention of stopping there. At an average cruising speed of 6 knots SOG (speed over ground), our ETA (estimated time of arrival) at the customs dock will be 1830 (6:30 p.m.)

I perform my last duties as Net Control for our informal Northbound Net. Twelve vessels have become part of our Net from Cabo to San Diego: *Finally, Quest, Emerald Star, Reaching Deep, Loon, Unencumbered, Basta, Liberty Call, La Capriole, Scrimshaw,* and *Sundowner*. Their owners and crews are part of our circle of cruising friends. Because *Pacific Bliss* will be the first of our fleet to arrive, someone else in the Northbound Net will have to take over my job as controller. My final obligation completed, I can now consider the many details that will face us when we reach port: things like emptying the refrigerator, stripping the beds, gathering up the laundry, and packing the clothes we will need immediately.

Finally, we motor through the familiar Pt. Loma entrance and into the vast San Diego Bay. Tears cloud my vision. We're home! We pull into the customs dock. Although Günter and I have no problems, because we are U.S. citizens, *Pacific Bliss* must suffer through immigration as if she were a foreigner. This beautiful ship, which has become another member of our family, was "born" in Canet, France. Nevertheless, the immigration process goes smoothly.

That done, we make a few essential calls and then crash, relieved that we discouraged a welcoming party upon our arrival. We can celebrate later.

Early the next morning, Markus and Sabine, our son and daughter-in-law, arrive at the dock in a flurry of excitement and love. After kisses and hugs, I notice the familiar package that Sabine holds in her hand. She is an angel. She remembered. *Starbucks!* My first cappuccino, my nine-month dream, has arrived!

California poppies.

Chapter 13: Re-entry

San Diego, California

1. Lemon trees front San Jacinto mountains; 2. La Jolla Shores; 3. Sail Bay; 4. Saguaro cactus.

245

"There is nothing like returning to a place that remains unchanged to find the way in which you yourself have altered."
Nelson Mandela

Yucca Valley.

Chapter 13
RE-ENTERING AND RE-EVALUATING OUR LIVES

Re-entry
San Diego, California
Re-entry is both exhilarating and overwhelming, not at all what I expected. Günter and I are proud of what we have accomplished on our maiden voyage: sailing *Pacific Bliss* from France to California. But there is no time to rest on our laurels during this intense and bewildering adjustment to life on land.

Through the first few days, we adjust *physically* to life on land. I grope my way to the bathroom while the entire nine-unit condo building sways on ocean waves. I dare not close my eyes during my morning shower for fear of losing my balance. Günter continues to do the cat-walk, grabbing furniture for handholds.

After nine months at sea, our home seems like a deluxe suite in a five-star hotel. I walk around it like a queen, appreciating the sitting room and balcony with their bay view; the king-sized bed that I can walk around on three sides; and modern kitchen with its double oven, double dish drawers, and five-burner cook-top.

"Didn't we leave some wine here for our return?" I open the fridge door wide, letting all that precious cold air escape.

"Did you forget that we have a wine cooler?" Günter teases. "We added it when we remodeled, remember that?"

"Well, at least I didn't forget we have a bathtub." I pour myself a glass of wine. "I'm going to take my wine there…like we did in France…and add lots of bubble bath. France was the last time I had a tub bath, before we moved onto that $$XX## boat!"

"Watch your language. You know in your heart you love her still…"

However, the *social* adjustment to land life is much more difficult than the *physical*: During our first get-together with friends, one person asks a question, then another interrupts before Günter or I can finish our reply. Often the questioner interrupts my reply to her own question with the next question! No conversations come to a conclusion. And we cannot complete the telling of even one of our adventure stories. Our experiences must be condensed into sound bites; in fact, we are forced to mimic those TV talking heads who now grate on our nerves.

Social life on land is quite complex and disjointed. Everyone appears to be rushing about doing nothing, but puffed with importance because of how "busy" they are. During phone conversations, our friends tell us they can't talk very long, and then go on endlessly about how busy they have been in the last 24 hours and how busy they will be in the next 24.

No one is living in the present.

The concept of time is different on land from that at sea. Here, much time is spent planning the next day, the next week, the next month, the next year. Reluctantly, we take our Day Timers out again. We cannot keep all the minutiae in our heads anymore. To adjust, we begin to partition our lives into "time bites" once more. On *Pacific Bliss*, only the time of the day was important; the date or the day of the week didn't really matter. We had a decorative wall calendar that provided the dates for all of 2001; it was not the type you could write on; it was made of bamboo. What mattered on *Pacific Bliss* was the state of the winds and the sea, the distance to the next safe port or anchorage, and how we planned to get there. Our brass ship's clock was always set on

247

local time. The clock at the nav station was set on Zulu (Universal) time. An alarm reminded us of our morning SSB nets or that we needed to set up the computer to receive the weather fax.

Life at sea was simple.

Driving on land is another bummer compared to the ease of moving along at sea. My first day behind the wheel of our Nissan, I pull out of our underground parking garage tentatively to face the traffic on Riviera Drive. I know better than to attempt a left turn into the busy street, although that is the direction I need to go. I wait patiently for the traffic to ease so that I can make a right turn followed by a U. Eventually, I realize that I will need to be very aggressive if I do not want to sit here forever. I hit the gas, and off I go. At the shopping center, the driver behind me gives me the finger when I slow down for one of those concrete speed bumps. On *Pacific Bliss,* as helmsman, I would have twenty minutes, after spotting an oncoming vessel, to decide whether or not to change course.

Life was slow.

Life on land, in a large metropolitan center such as San Diego, brings with it congestion, traffic, and rage. Our first week home, we encountered road rage twice. A sense of entrapment or futility seems to erupt at the least provocation. In contrast, cruisers have the whole wide world to live in, with the seven seas as our highway!

Life was mellow.

At sea, Günter and I find it easy to "be still and know that I am God." On land, we discover that we will need to *seek out* stillness and peace. Tranquility will not come to us as it did on the ocean, carried on the wings of glorious dawns and majestic night skies.

Life was serene.

As the months pass, we decide to build "corners of joy" into our everyday lives. We vow to look for "islands of peace." We might not be basking in Moments of Bliss as we did on *Pacific Bliss,* but we're living. We set up specific times and places for prayer and meditation. We pull our chairs before our large picture window and consider the ever-changing beauty of the bay. However, it takes more effort on land to achieve a spiritual equilibrium.

Life is good here. Yes, I could remain on land and settle into an easy retirement.

Now that we have had time to think about it, Günter and I realize that our Voyage One was all about control. We left San Diego to escape the corporate world where we were no longer in control of our fate. Lured by the tantalizing freedom and independence offered to us by the sea, we abandoned the restraint and disappointment of business.

Being out of control is usually an undesirable condition. Right at the outset, in Canet, Günter and I lost control being forced to change schedules and delay crews from arriving until our yacht was ready. Another moment when control was not in our hands was when a Force 10 storm compelled us to take refuge in Estartit, Spain. And this was only a warning shot across our bow! The Force 10 storm off the coast of Colombia was even worse: It was our giant wake-up call about losing control, "letting go, and letting God." And finally Hurricane Adolph delayed our crossing of the Sea of Cortez. Voyage One began and ended like bookends—we were out of control at the beginning and out of control at the end, months behind our original plans—as we beat our way up the Baja Bash. But it was a lesson, that everyone must learn sometime before he or she departs this earth.

There is a certain peace in being out of control. It reminds one of how much there is to lose and how fast one can lose it.

Re-evaluation and on with the Quest

To stay on land or to go back to sea…that is the question. The answer does not come easily. One day, I fret about the dangers we will face "out there," and Günter chides me for even thinking such things. "Hey, there's danger everywhere. I walked a few blocks to the dry cleaners to find the clerk still shaking…she'd been stretched out on the floor behind the counter while a robber took the cash from the register. If I'd showed up only a few minutes earlier, who knows what could've happened to me?"

Some days, seeing the wind churning whitecaps on Sail Bay, Günter is the one who hesitates. "Lois, to think we'll be 'out there' again, in worse than this… sailing through a long, stormy overnight…or sweating it out in a windy anchorage, worrying that the anchor might drag."

On other days, I hunger to be where cruisers meet and become instant friends. During a typical sundowner, women talk about things that matter—where to get provisions, how to cook local food, and how the weather is shaping up for the next passage, while the guys talk about essential repairs and " just messing with boats." I confess my frustrations to Günter: "I can barely keep my big mouth shut when the most critical concerns around our condo community are about someone's taking another's parking spot, what plants should be where, or when and why another homeowner did…or didn't…say the appropriate—or P.C.—thing."

After many such discussions, pro and con, we make our decision: We will go on.

During our sojourn on land, we have come to understand the words of Pat Conroy: "Once you have traveled, the voyage never ends, but is played out over and over again in the quietest chambers…the mind can never break off from the journey." Our own journey has

Northbound Net cruisers' party.

become a part of us, and *Pacific Bliss* has become our trusted friend and family member. Günter and I brought back with us a vision of a wider world, a world where values matter and differences don't. With it came a new understanding and appreciation of cruising's highs and lows, and indelible memories of the characters we met along the way.

Cruising is an altered state of consciousness, one which I struggle for words to describe. I know, though, it makes me long to be transported out of myself again, to be placed into another dimension of time and space, to be back in our cocoon underneath the stars, back where the past merges with the present and time grows to insignificance. "Wander-thirst" takes over again. New people are everywhere to be met, new cultures to be explored, and new adventures to be undertaken.

Landlubbers since June, Günter and I begin to formulate our plans: Voyages Two and Three will take us to the South Pacific Islands and all the way to Australia. They will be voyages of risk—of that we are sure—but they will also be rich in renewal and reward. We must upgrade *Pacific Bliss* for the long passages ahead. Because we will be far from any marine services and yacht clubs, we will have to be more self-sufficient than ever. But ah, such freedom!

God isn't finished with us yet.

Captain Jack steering *Pacifc Bliss* on San Diego Bay. May he rest in peace.

Epilogue

The cruisers of the Northbound Net enjoyed a homecoming party in San Diego, then continued on their ways.

Günter and I did sail on, of course, to the remote Marquesas and far beyond, during Voyage Two. It took us eight years and 34,000 nautical miles to circumnavigate the globe, and to return to our starting place, the same dock at the marina in Canet, France. After this remarkable accomplishment, we returned to our home in San Diego, where I am enjoying my new careers of writing and photography. Günter has found his satisfaction and fulfillment in tutoring inner city children; he brings science, physics, and math to them in the "Kids at Heart" program of UPLIFT, a local charity.

We sold *Pacific Bliss* to a U.K. family, who continue to care for her well. She enjoys sailing with children on board. She has repeated our passages through the Med, on to Gibraltar, to the Canary Islands, across the Atlantic to the Caribbean, and, at the date of this printing, she is in Cartagena, Colombia. But being family, she also suffers from "wander-thirst." I feel certain that she will continue to follow the path of her first circumnavigation.

Enduring Echoes sailed the Caribbean Sea for a few years before being sold. Brenda and Pratt still reside in Utah.

Finally sailed up the west coast of the United States to Canada, where little Laurent was enrolled in daycare. He improved his English and, with his father speaking French and his mother speaking Dutch to him, he became the first tri-lingual four-year-old I've ever known.

Makoko continued on to the South Pacific as a buddy boat with *Pacific Bliss* during Voyage Two, sharing our challenges and successes.

If you've enjoyed reading about our circumnavigation so far, you will want to follow us through the next phase of our grand adventure. More excitement awaits you in the next book of this series: *In Search of Adventure and Moments of Bliss: SAILING THE SOUTH PACIFIC*. And be sure to join us on our website: www.PacificBliss.com.

Appendix A: Glossary

Aft towards the stern or after part of a boat
Anti-fouling paint bottom paint that defers the growth of algae, barnacles, etc.
Apparent wind the velocity of air as measured from a moving object, as a ship
ARC *Atlantic Rally for Cruisers*, first organized by Jimmy Cornell, a sailing legend
ASA navigation exam a test given by the American Sailing Association to certify navigators for sailing or cruising
Autopilot electro/mechanical steering device for automatic course keeping
B&G a manufacturer of marine instruments and displays; we used the term to refer to our display at the nav station
Amidships toward the center
Anchor Light a white light always displayed at night when the boat is at anchor, six feet off the deck of the bow
Back winding; aback when the wind catches a sail in the opposite side of its working purpose
Beating sailing a boat to windward by tacking or zig-zagging at an angle to the wind, since a boat cannot sail directly into the wind
Beam the breadth of a ship at its widest part
Berm a land barrier separating two areas of water
Big Ditch cruising slang for the Panama Canal
Big Pond cruising slang for the Atlantic Ocean
Bilge the space underneath the floorboards of a yacht
Bilge pump a pump placed in the bilge set to pump out water when it reaches a pre- determined level
Bitter end the tail end of a line
Bimini a protective cover of cloth, wood, or fiberglass
Bimini shades on *Pacific Bliss*, canvas sides that are zippered to attach to the central, hardtop bimini and can be unrolled and attached to the lifelines
Boat Speed There are two types of boat speed: speed relative to the surrounding water and speed over ground (SOG). If the water is completely still then they are the same.
Bollard a short post on a quay or boat used to secure a rope
Boom a spar to which the bottom edge of a sail is attached which pivots at its forward end to allow the angle of the sail to be changed
bosun's chair a board or canvas seat with a rope attached used to haul a person up the main mast using a halyard
Boulangerie French bakery
Bow the front part of a boat
Bowsprit a pointy projection from the bow from which the lower end of the jib is connected as well as the bobstay underneath; (this does not apply to *Pacific Bliss*)
Broach or death roll This can happen when a boat is out of control when going downwind. The boat can swing sideways and gets rolled over by the waves.
Buddy boat a companion boat to keep one safe when underway, like a buddy swimmer or diver
Brightwork wooden parts on a boat which are varnished
Bulkheads load-bearing walls that keep the boat together structurally
CAD (computer-aided design) the use of a computer with sophisticated software graphics to design products or systems
Careen to place a boat on her side so that work may be carried out on her underwater parts. This term applies to a monohull, not a catamaran.
Catamaran two-hulled sailing vessel
Chandlery a marine store that sells all kinds of boat-related products—needed and unneeded—to make a hole in your wallet when cruising
Ciguatera a toxin accumulated in reef fish that is poisonous to man
Cleat a T-shaped piece of wood or metal to which a rope can be secured by taking two or three turns over and under the arms (ears) but only *after* making one complete turn around the base
Cleat off to secure a line or rope to the boat and to a stationary fixture on shore
Close-hauled all sails pulled in tightly when sailing into the wind; the same as beating (see Points of Sail in Appendix C)
Cutter a sailing vessel with one mast rigged with two foresails
Cockpit a recessed part of the deck containing seats and the steering station
Crest of a wave the top of a wave
Dagger board an adjustable centerboard that acts like a keel when lowered. When raised, it allows a catamaran to surf.

Pacific Bliss has two dagger boards, one at each hull.

Davits Spars that extend over the stern of a boat to raise or lower the dinghy

Day sailing sailing only for the day, with the intention return to port before dark

Depthsounder an instrument that measures how deep the water is

Dinghy a small boat that is towed behind or carried on a larger boat; also called a *tender*

Dogwatch the typical mariner's day is divided into six watches, each four hours long, except that the 4:00 to 8:00 pm watch may be "dogged"; that is, divided into the first and second dogwatches, each two hours long, to allow men on duty to have their evening meal. In pleasure sailing, dogwatch has come to mean whatever the crew decides it to be. On *Pacific Bliss*, we called the 12:00 to 3:00 a.m. watch our "dogwatch."

Downhaul a line that pulls something down to the deck, e.g. the spinnaker had *downhaul* and *outhaul* lines on each side

Doldrums an area with no wind or light variable winds just north of the equator in the Atlantic and Pacific oceans, situated between the trade winds

Double-reefing the main putting two reefs into the mainsail

Draft the depth of water below the keel (in the case of *Pacific Bliss*, the draft was the depth below the hulls, or the bottom of the dagger boards when down)

Dry dock the storing of the boat out of the water

EPIRB Emergency Position Indicating Radio Beacon. A dictionary-size device that communicates directly with a satellite in the event of an emergency, relaying the position of the ship in distress. Ours identified *Pacific Bliss* and whom to contact (our sons).

Fathom six feet

Fetch the distance wind or waves can travel without obstruction

Fender a bumper slung over the side of a vessel to prevent damage to the hull when moored on a dock or rafted (side-tied) to other boats

Foot the bottom edge of a sail

Freeboard the height of a boat from the surface of the water to the deck

Furling the method of stowing a sail on a spar

Force 10 (F10) Force 10 on the Beaufort wind scale, see Appendix B; Force 12 is a hurricane

Forces 1-12. wind states on the Beaufort wind scales, see Appendix B

Genoa (jenny) the large triangular front sail on a boat; we used the term alternately with jib; when partially furled, it served as a smaller foresail

GMT Greenwich Mean Time. Can also be called UTC (Universal Time Zone) or Zulu Time

Go to weather to go toward the direction of the oncoming wind (see no-go zones, Appendix C)

Halyard rope or line used to raise (haul) or lower (douse) sails

Hand steer steering by hand instead of the autopilot

Hank to attach a sail to a stay

Hatch a square opening on a deck that has a hinged cover or lid

Harness Think of a dog or horse in a harness. Sailors wear these to attach themselves to jacklines that run the entire length of the boat to protect them from falling overboard.

Head the toilet and/or bathroom on a boat, or the top of a sail

Helm the means by which the rudder and hence the direction of the vessel are controlled. *Pacific Bliss* has two helms (which we call the steering wheels). A tiller can be used instead of a wheel and called the helm.

In irons The boat is pointed too close to the wind for the sails to generate any power (unless they are backed, see above). The sails will be luffing (flapping) in the breeze and making noise, like a flag.

ITCZ Intertropical Convergence Zone (the doldrums) the area encircling the earth near the equator where winds originating in the northern and southern hemispheres come together. The location of the intertropical convergence zone varies over time. Over land, it moves back and forth across the equator following the sun's zenith point. Over the oceans, where the convergence zone is better defined, the seasonal cycle is more subtle, as the convection is constrained by the distribution of ocean temperatures. Sometimes, a double ITCZ forms, with one located north and another south of the equator. When this occurs, a narrow ridge of high pressure forms between the two convergence zones, one of which is usually stronger than the other.

Jib a small triangular sail in front of the main sail

Jibe (gybe) a maneuver that changes the mainsail from one side of the boat to the other when the wind is blowing from behind

Keel the lowest part of the boat, weighted in a monohull to provide stability

Ketch a two-masted sailing ship with the steering station located astern of the aft mast (mizzen)

Kevlar a trademark for a reinforcing material used in tires and bulletproof vests
Knot meter Indicates how fast the boat is moving in the water, in nautical miles. The actual progress influenced by factors such as current and leeway (as opposed to the absolute geographic movement determined by a GPS).
Lanyard a piece of rope attached to something for easy retrieval
Lee the side that does *not* have the wind blowing on it, as in "the lee of the wind"
Lee shore a coastline on which the wind blows
Lee cloth; lee board a board or canvas rigged to prevent a person from rolling off the bunk in high seas, not necessary on a large catamaran since it does not heel more than a few degrees
Leech the aft edge of the sail
Lifelines safety cables stretched along the entire deck *Pacific Bliss*
Lines ropes on a boat
Lying a hull sails down and just drifting at the mercy of the seas
Luff 1. The part of a sail closest to the mast; 2. Allowing the sails to flap in the wind
Mahi-Mahi a delicious fish, also called dorado or dolphin fish
Mast foot a structure that supports the mast on the deck of a sailing boat; multihulls are always deck-stepped and well supported via the heaviest component of the boat's structure, which is the central crossbeam. The compression at the mast foot can be huge; this tension is reduced by the tension of the forestay which in turn pulls up from the forward crossbeam.
Mole a massive wall, usually made of stone, that extends into the sea and encloses or protects a harbor
Motu a Polynesian reef islet
Monkey fist a weighted ball secured to the end of a casting line
Monohull single-hulled vessel
Multi-meter any instrument that reads out multiple parameters
Nav (navigation) station the brain area of a boat occupied by charts, radios, laptops, and navigation instruments and aids
Navteq® a weather forecasting system
Old Salt a sailor who has years of experience at sea
Overfalls a turbulent surface of the sea caused by conflicting currents or the wind moving against a current
On the hard when a boat is put up on land, usually for storage or repair in a shipyard
On the hook at anchor
On the nose wind in your face; heading into the wind
Painter a rope attached to a dinghy for towing or mooring
Points of sail direction of a vessel in relation to the wind (see Appendix C)
Port left side (think "port wine" and "port," each word equals 4 letters; the longer word for right is *starboard)*
Port bow front of the boat on your left as you face forward from the stern
Puddle Jump Cruiser slang for crossing the Pacific Ocean
Reach sailing ninety degrees to the wind; the most comfortable point of sail
Reinforced trades strong trade winds
Reef to reduce the area of sail (see Appendix C)
Rhumb line In navigation, a rhumb line (or *loxodrome*) is a line crossing all meridians of longitude at the same angle, i.e. a path derived from a defined *initial* bearing. That is, upon taking an initial bearing, one proceeds along the same bearing, without changing the direction as measured relative to true north. A rhumb line appears as a straight line on a Mercator projection map. On a plane surface this would be the shortest distance between two points but over longer distances and/or at higher latitudes great circle routes provide the shortest distances.
Rig to fit out a boat or its mast with sails and rigging
Rode a rope or chain, especially one attached to an anchor
Rogue wave an unpredictable, abnormally large wave that occurs on a seemingly random basis in the oceans
Roller furling rolling up the sail into the headstay like a window shade
run, broad reach, and beam reach these define points of sail. Refer to Appendix C
Salon the living room area of a yacht (also called saloon)
Scuppers The narrow space between the bulwarks and the deck through which seawater or any other water on deck may run-off
Seacocks valves which open and close pipes going through the hull of a boat
Seamounts underwater mountains
Settee a seat or sofa on a boat
Sevu Sevu a formal Fijian ceremony where kava is usually drunk
Sheet A line (rope, cable or chain) used to control the movable corner(s) (clews) of a sail. The *Mainsheet* is attached to

the boom, and is used to control the mainsail. The *Jib Sheet* attaches to the clew of the jib, and controls it. The *Spinnaker Sheet* attaches to the clew(s) of the spinnaker.

Side-tie to fasten alongside another yacht or a dock

Shackle A u-shaped metal connecting link with a straight pin closing the u. The pin has an eye at one end and a short screw at another.

Shoal a shallow area with banks of sand, mud, or rock; a bubbling and swirling sea in this area warns one of rocks below the surface.

Shrouds the main lateral supports of the mast standing rigging consisting of strong wires that attach to the deck

Spar any stout piece of wood or metal used as a pole to support sails and rigging on a ship, thus the boom, main mast and jib pole can all be called spars

SOG (speed over ground) the movement of the boat relative to the bottom of the ocean

Step the mast erect a mast and attach the standing rigging

Spindrift spray that blows from the surface of the sea; spindrift begins with a Force 7 sea state (see Appendix B)

Spinnaker a large triangular sail set at the front of a yacht for running before the wind

Spreader support that holds the shrouds away from the mast

Spring line a line used when the boat is docked to keep her from moving forward and aft

Standing rigging cable securing the upper part of a mast (shrouds and stays)

SSB (single side-band) radio a method of long-range radio communication

Starboard right side

Starboard bow front of the boat to your right as you face forward from the stern

Stays wire supports for fixed spars. The headstay also serves as an attachment for the jib

Stern back end of a boat

Stink potter a derogatory term that sailors use to describe a motor yacht

Supermarche a French market

Surf to ride the waves on a catamaran

Tack to change a yacht's course by turning through the wind, so that the wind then blows on the opposite side of the yacht

Tachometer a gauge that shows the RPM (revolutions per minute) of an engine, thus indicating its speed

Toerail a small wooden edge which surrounds the deck of a boat to keep your foot from sliding off

Topping lift the rope which controls the height of the outer end of the boom

Topsides the act of being on the outside deck of a boat relative to a person "down below"

Trampoline, net a fabric deck stretched on the braces connecting the hulls of a catamaran, resembling a gymnastic trampoline

Transom the horizontal portion of the stern of a boat

Traveler a sliding fitting to which the mainsheet is attached, keeping the boom in the same place as it is moved in and out

Triangular main sheet system type of sail rigging used on a Catana catamaran

Trimaran sailing vessel with three hulls

Trough of a wave the lowest part of the wave between crests

True wind speed and direction of the actual wind as if the vessel is not moving

Warp a line attached to the stern of a boat to slow down the speed

Watermaker a machine which through reverse osmosis creates potable water from seawater. Ours is a Spectra® brand

Windlass a device which hauls up the anchor; on *Pacific Bliss*, ours was electric

Wind states (Beaufort Force states) see Appendix B

Wing on wing opening the foresail and mainsail to maximum amount of surface of capture all of the wind available

World Cruising Routes "The Bible for Cruisers" by Jimmy Cornell

Yaw To erratically deviate from a steered course as when struck by a heavy sea

Yawl a two-masted sailboat with the steering station forward of the aft mast (mizzen)

Zulu Time Greenwich Mean Time. Zulu is used in the military and aviation.

Appendix B: Beaufort Scale of Sea States

Admiral Francis Beaufort was a 19th century British tar in the days of the old wooden tall ships. The scale he developed has been ridiculed by mariners for being patternless because there is no apparent uniform progression in the scale. Force 2, for example, describes winds from 4 to 6 knots, Force 3 from 7 to 10, and Force 4 from 11-16. Then Force 5 covers only from 17-21. The wind differences vary from 2 knots to 3, then 5, and back to 4.

Our *Pacific Bliss* Ship's Library contains a book called Mariner's Weather by William P. Crawford. He claims that the lack of symmetry was not part of Beaufort's plan, and defends his damaged reputation by saying that the Admiral was not referring to wind speed at all! He says that what the esteemed Admiral had in mind was the number of sails that should be furled as the wind strengthened. In light airs, just one would be taken in, whereas in a gentle breeze might require three. In a near gale, seven would come down, and in a violent storm, eleven.

There is now a tendency to express wind value in knots instead of Beaufort scale. The *Pacific Bliss* multi units mounted throughout the boat allow the user to choose whichever he or she wishes as a display. We tend to use the Force scales in the cockpit display. A read-out in knots suggests a misleading exactness whereas a Force reading allows for some slack. Force readings make it easier to give instructions to the crew; for example, during the Atlantic crossing, the instructions were to take down the spinnaker at Force 7 so that we wouldn't blow it out.

The following chart will help you understand the forces and sea conditions we encountered during our Night of Sheer Terror during Voyage One:

Beaufort Scale: Comparing Wind Speed and Sea Conditions

Force	Knots	Probable Wave Height (in feet)	Description	Sea Conditions
0	0-1	--	Calm	Sea smooth and mirror like.
1	1-3	1/4	Light Air	Scale-like ripples without foam crests.
2	4-6	1/2	Light Breeze	Small, short wavelets; some crests begin to break; foam of glassy appearance. Occasional white foam crests.
3	7-10	2	Gentle Breeze	Large wavelets; some crests begin to break; foam of glassy appearance. Occasional white foam crests.
4	11-16	4	Moderate Breeze	Small waves, becoming longer; fairly frequent white foam crests.
5	17-21	6	Fresh Breeze	Moderate waves, taking a more pronounced long form, many white foam crests; there may be some spray.
6	22.27	10	Strong Breeze	Large waves begin to form; white foam crests are more extensive everywhere; there may be some spray.
7	28-33	14	Near Gale	Sea heaps up and white foam from breaking waves begins to be blown in =streaks along the direction of the wind; spindrift begins.
8	34-40	18	Gale	Moderately high waves of greater length; edges of crests break into spindrift; foam is blown in well-marked streaks along the direction of the wind.
9	41-47	23	Strong Gale	High waves; dense streaks of foam along the direction of the wind; crests of waves begin to topple, tumble, and roll over; spray may reduce visibility/
10	48-55	29	Storm	Very long waves with overhanging crests. The resulting foam in great patches is blown in dense white streaks along the direction of the wind. On the whole, the surface of the sea is white in appearance. The tumbling of the sea becomes heavy and shock-like. Visibility is reduced.
11	56-63	37	Violent	Exceptionally high waves that may obscure small and medium size ships. The sea is completely covered with long white patches of foam lying along the direction of the wind. Everywhere the edges of the wave crests are blown into froth. Visibility reduced.
12	64-71	45	Hurricane	The air is filled with foam and spray. Sea completely white with driving spray; visibility much reduced.

Source: From the Weather Bureau Observing Handbook No. 1, Marine Surface Observations (Wash. D.C. National Weather Service, 1969)

Appendix C: Points of Sail

The points of sail for a monohull are the same for a catamaran.
A. In Irons (into the wind) B. Close Hauled C. Beam Reach D. Broad Reach E. Running

The points of sail are the most important parts of sail theory to remember. The no-go zone (shaded) is about 45° either side of the true wind for a racing hull and sail plan optimized for upwind work. On some cruising yachts, the best course achievable upwind is 50° to 55° to the true wind. On *Pacific Bliss,* we were able to achieve a 45-degree course to the apparent wind. No sailboat can sail directly into the wind; attempting to do so leads to the sails luffing (flapping uncontrollably).

There are 5 main points of sail. In order from the edge of the no-go zone to directly downwind they are:

- close haul (often about 45° to the apparent wind - the least angle that the boat and its rig can manage).

- close reach (between close hauled and a beam reach).

- beam reach (90° to the apparent wind); this was the fastest point of sail for *Pacific Bliss.*

- broad reach (between a beam reach and running).

- running (close to directly downwind), this is the most pleasant point of sail. "May you have fair winds and following seas," is the mariner's blessing, because those conditions allow a boat "to run."

Sail trim relative to the point of sail

On a beam reach sails are mostly let out; on a run sails are all the way out; and close hauled sails are pulled in very tightly. Two main skills of sailing are trimming the sails correctly for the direction and strength of the wind, and maintaining a course relative to the wind that suits the sails once trimmed. With a gentle following wind, the captain might order the sails set wing-on-wing (one sail on each side) or the spinnaker hoisted. The wind pushing the boat from the stern allows the spinnaker to open up, called "ballooning." If the wind is too strong, or the boat suddenly changes course with this light sail up, it can tear; this is called "blowing out the spinnaker."

Reducing and increasing sail

An important safety aspect of sailing is to adjust the amount of sail to suit the wind conditions. As the wind speed increases the crew should progressively reduce the amount of sail. On a boat with only jib (or genoa) and mainsail this is done by furling the jib and by partially lowering the mainsail, a process called "reefing the main."

Reefing means reducing the area of a sail without actually changing it for a smaller sail, such as the storm jib that *Pacific Bliss* had on board. Ideally reefing does not only result in a reduced sail area but also in a lower center of effort from the sails, reducing the heeling and keeping the boat more upright.

We often repeated on board the standard Old Salts' advice: "The first time you even *think* of reducing sail you should go ahead and just do it." As for increasing sail, the English say it best: "When you *think* you are ready to take out a reef, have a cup of tea instead."

Points of Sail

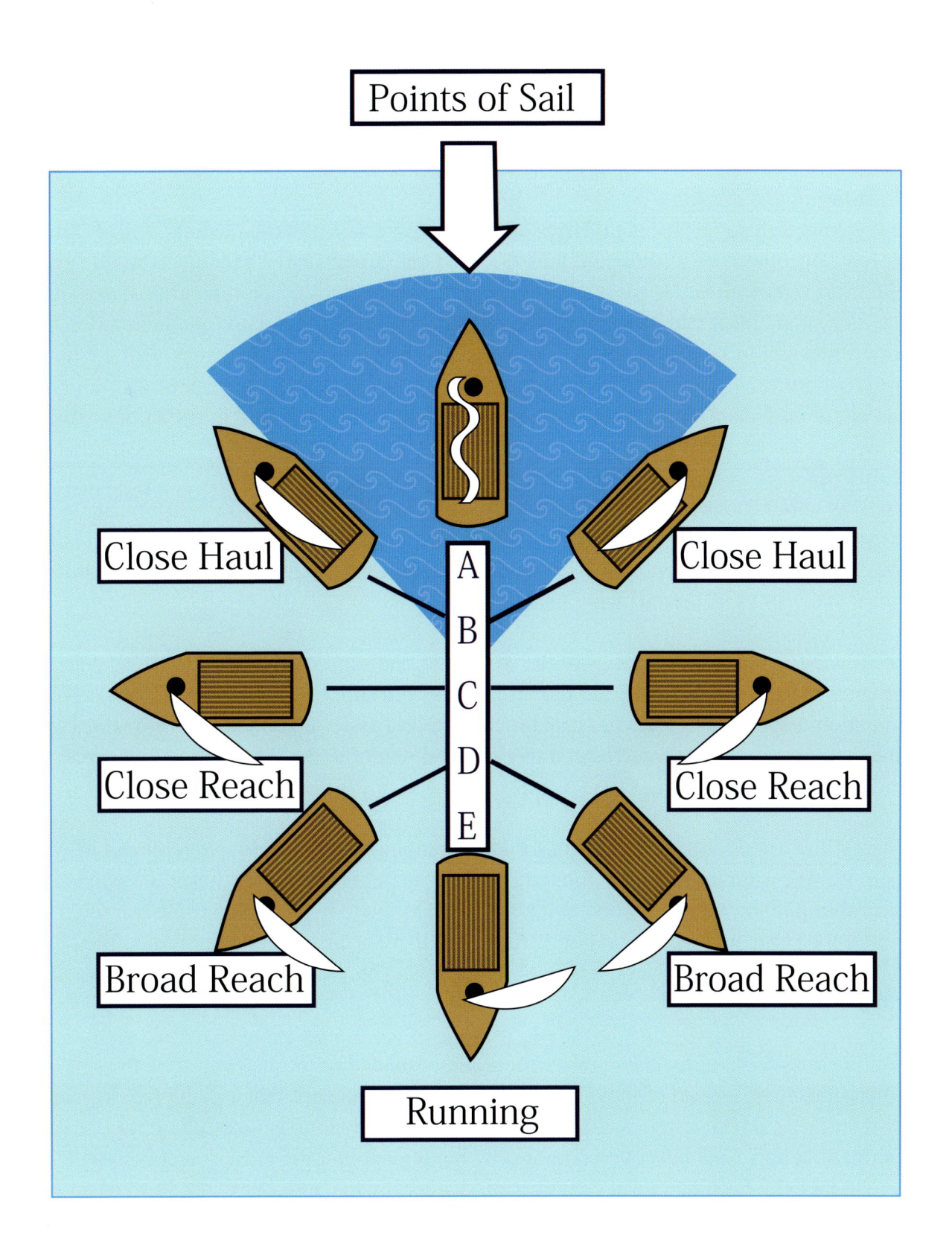

- A
- B
- C
- D
- E

Close Haul
Close Haul
Close Reach
Close Reach
Broad Reach
Broad Reach
Running

Appendix D: The Physics of Sailing

Sailing is the art of controlling a boat with large (usually fabric) foils called sails. By changing the rigging, rudder, and sometimes the keel or centre board, (or the dagger board in the case of Pacific Bliss) a sailor manages the force of the wind on the sails in order to change the direction and speed of a boat. Mastery of the skill requires experience in varying wind and sea conditions, as well as knowledge concerning sailboats themselves.

Types of Sailing
While there are still some places in Africa and Asia where sail-powered fishing vessels are used, these craft have become rarer as outboard and modified car engines have become available even in the poorest and most remote areas. In most countries people enjoy sailing as a recreational activity. Recreational sailing or yachting can be divided into racing and cruising. Cruising includes extended trips, short trips within sight of land, and daysailing. Most sailors on extended voyages who are not racing call themselves "cruisers." When a cruiser completes an entire circumnavigation of the globe, he or she is called a "circumnavigator," a rare breed of individual with a title coveted in the sailing world.

Energy capture
Sailing is all about capturing energy. Sails are airfoils that work by using an airflow set up by the wind and the motion of the boat. The combination of the two is the apparent wind, which is the relative velocity of the wind relative to the boat's motion. Sails generate lift using the air that flows around them, in the same way as an aircraft wing generates lift.

The air flowing at the sail surface is not the true wind. Sailing into the wind causes the apparent wind to be greater than the true wind and the direction of the apparent wind will be forward of the true wind. Some high-performance boats are capable of traveling faster than the true wind speed on some points of sail; for example, Hydroptère set a world speed record in 2009 by sailing 1.71 times the speed of the wind. Iceboats can typically sail at 5 times the speed of the wind.

The energy that drives a sailboat is harnessed by manipulating the relative movement of wind and water speed: if there is no difference in movement, such as on a calm day or when the wind and water current are moving in the same direction at the same speed, there is no energy to be extracted and the sailboat will not be able to do anything but drift. Where there is a difference in motion, then there is energy to be extracted at the interface. The sailboat does this by placing the sail(s) in the air and the hull(s) in the water.

The sailing vessel is not maneuverable with the sail alone. The torque caused by the sail lift would cause the vessel to twist instead of move forward. In the same manner that a plane requires an elevator with control surfaces, a boat requires a keel and rudder. The sail alone is not sufficient to drive the boat in any desired direction. Sailboats overcome this by having another physical object below the water line. This may take the form of a keel, centerboard, dagger boards, or some other form of underwater foil, or even the hull itself (as in the case of catamarans without centerboard or in a traditional proa). Thus, the physical portion of the boat that is below water can be regarded as functioning as a "second sail." Having two surfaces against the wind and water enables the sailor to travel in almost any direction and to generate an additional source of lift from the water. The flow of water over the underwater hull portions creates a hydrodynamic force. The combination of the aerodynamic force from the sails and the hydrodynamic force from the underwater hull section allows motion in almost any direction except straight into the wind. (Imagine that you are squeezing a wet bar of soap with two hands, causing it to shoot out in a direction perpendicular to both opposing forces.) Depending on the efficiency of the rig, the angle of travel relative to the true wind can be as little as 35° or greater than 80°. This angle is called the "tacking angle."

Tacking is essential when sailing upwind. The sails, when correctly adjusted, will generate aerodynamic lift. When sailing downwind, the sails no longer generate aerodynamic lift and airflow is stalled, with the wind push on the sails giving drag only. As the boat is going downwind, the apparent wind is less than the true wind and this, allied to the fact that the sails are not producing aerodynamic lift, serves to limit the downwind speed.

Effects of wind shear

Wind shear affects sailboats in motion by presenting a different wind speed and direction at different heights along the mast. Wind shear occurs because of friction above a water surface slowing the flow of air. Thus, a difference in true wind creates a different apparent wind at different heights. Sailmakers may introduce sail twist in the design of the sail, where the head of the sail is set at a different angle of attack from the foot of the sail in order to change the lift distribution with height. The effect of wind shear can be factored into the selection of twist in the sail design, but this can be difficult to predict since wind shear may vary widely in different weather conditions.

APPENDIX E: BIBLIOGRAPHY

Bitchin, Bob. *Letters from the Lost Soul, Five-Year Voyage of Discovery and Adventure.* New York: Sheridan House, 2000.

Casson, Lionel. *The Ancient Mariners: Seafarers and Sea Fighters of the Mediterranean in Ancient Times.* 2nd ed. Princeton: Princeton University Press, 1991.

Coe, Michael D. *The Maya: Ancient People and Places.* 6th ed. New York: Thames and Hudson, 1999.

Copeland, Lisa. *Just Cruising.* Vancouver: Romany Publishing, 1993.

Copeland, Liza. *Still Cruising.* Vancouver: Romany Publishing, 1995.

Cornell, Jimmy. *World Cruising Routes.* Camden, Maine: International Marine Publishing Company, 1995.

Dana, Richard Henry Jr. 1st ed. *Two Years Before the Mast and Other Voyages.* Library of America, 2005.

Dor-Ner, Zvi. *Columbus and the Age of Discovery.* New York: William Morrow and Company, Inc., 1991.

Dunmore, John. *Who's Who in Pacific Navigation.* Melbourne: Melbourne University Press, 1992.

Eastern Caribbean. Melbourne: Lonely Planet Publ., 2001.

France: Catalan. Watford, Hertfordshire: Michelin Travel Publications, 2000.

Hayden, Sterling. *Wanderer.* New York: Sheridan House, Inc., 1963.

Hiscock, Eric. *Around the World in Wanderer III.* London: Adlard Coles, 1956; New York: Sheridan House, 1997.

Hiscock, Eric. *Cruising Adventures, a 3-book series: Wandering Under Sail, Come Aboard, Sou'west in Wanderer IV.* New York: Sheridan House, 1977.

Hoefer, Hans, David Schwab, and Mitch Epstein. *Caribbean: the Lesser Antilles.* Singapore: APA Publications, 1990.

Irwin, Aisling, and Colum Wilson. *Cape Verde Islands: the Bradt Travel Guide.* Chalfont St. Peter, Bucks, England: Bradt Publications, 1998.

Johnson, Donald S. *Phantom Islands of the Atlantic: The Legends of Seven Lands That Never Were.* New York: Walker and Company, 1994.

Jones, Tristan. *The Incredible Voyage: A Personal Odyssey.* 1st paperback ed. New York: Sheridan House, 1996.

LaBrut, Michele. *Getting to Know Panama.* Republic of Panama: Focus Publications, 1977.

Leonard, Beth. *Following Seas: Sailing the Globe, Sounding a Life.* Windsor, Connecticut: Tide-Mark Press, 1999.

McCollough, David. *The Path Between the Seas: The Creation of the Panama Canal, 1870-1914.* New York: Simon and Schuster, 1977.

Miller-Rains, Pat and John E. Rains. *Cruising Ports: Florida to California via Panama.* San Diego: Point Loma Publishing, 1999.

Miller, Pat and John E. Rains. *Mexican Boating Guide.* San Diego: Point Loma Publishing, 2001.

Miranda, Carolina A., and Paige R. Penland. *Lonely Planet Costa Rica.* Oakland, CA: Lonely Planet Publications, 2004.

Miranda, Rosalind. *Best of Multihulls: The Book of Cruising (Volume 2 Cruising Around the World West to East)*. Boston: Chiodi Advertising and Publishing, Inc., 1991.

Monsarrat, Nicholas. *The Cruel Sea: Classics of War*. Short Hills, New Jersey: Burford Books, 2000.

Moore, Denton Richey. *Gentlemen Never Sail to Weather*. 2nd ed. Prospector PR, 1993.

O'Brien, Sally, and Sarah Andrews. *Canary Islands*. Footscray, Vic.: Lonely Planet Publications, 2004.

Porter, Darwin, and Danforth Prince. *Frommer's Caribbean*. Hoboken NJ: Wiley, 2004

Roth, Hal. *After 50,000 Miles*. London: Stanford Maritime, 1978.

Roth, Hal. *Always a Distant Anchorage*. 1st ed. New York: W.W. Norton & Co., Inc., 1989.

Roth, Hal. *The Hal Roth Seafaring Trilogy: Three True Stories of Adventure Under Sail*. Camden, Maine: International Marine/McGraw Hill, 2006.

Sale, Kirkpatrick. *The Conquest of Paradise: Christopher Columbus and the Columbian Legacy*. New York: Alfred A. Knopf, 1990.

Silverberg, Robert. *The Longest Voyage: Circumnavigators in the Age of Discovery*. Athens, Ohio: Ohio University Press, 1972.

Slocum, Joshua. *Sailing Alone Around the World*. New York: Sheridan House, 1954.

Spain: Balearic and Canary Islands. Watford, Hertsfordshire, England: Michelin Tyre PLC, 1998.

Theroux, Paul. *The Mosquito Coast: a Novel*. Boston: Houghton Mifflin, 1982.

Theroux, Paul. *Pillars of Hercules: A Grand Tour of the Mediterranean*. New York: Random House, 1995.

Thomas, Stephen D. *The Last Navigator*. New York: Henry Holt and Company, 1987.

Wilson, Derek. *The Circumnavigators, a History*. New York: Carroll & Graf, 2003.

Wood, Charles E., and Janet Steele. *Charlie's Charts of the Western Coast of Mexico (including Baja)*. Surrey, BC, Canada: Charlie's Charts, 1999.

Wood, Margo. *A Prairie Chicken Goes to Sea*. Surrey, BC: Charlie's Charts, 2002.